P

CLASSIC
ROCK

keyboard

PRESENTS

CLASSIC ROCK

EDITED BY ERNIE RIDEOUT

Backbeat Books

AN IMPRINT OF HAL LEONARD CORPORATION
NEW YORK

Portions of this book are adapted from articles that originally appeared in *Keyboard* magazine.

Published in cooperation with Music Player Network, New Bay Media, LLC, and Keyboard magazines. *Keyboard* magazine is a registered trademark of New Bay Media, LLC.

Published in 2010 by Backbeat Books
An Imprint of Hal Leonard Corporation
7777 West Bluemound Road
Milwaukee, WI 53213

Trade Book Division Editorial Offices
19 West 21st Street, New York, NY 10010

Printed in the United States of America

Book design by Damien Castaneda

Library of Congress Cataloging-in-Publication Data

Keyboard presents classic rock / edited by Ernie Rideout.
    p. cm.
  ISBN 978-0-87930-952-7 (pbk.)
   1. Rock musicians--Interviews. 2. Keyboard players--Interviews. I. Rideout, Ernie. II. Keyboard (Cupertino, Calif.)
III. Title: Classic rock.
  ML399K49 2010
  786'.1660922--dc22
                                2010004186

ISBN 978-0-87930-952-7

www.backbeatbooks.com

To *Keyboard* magazine—the talented individuals who created it and who continue to do so—and especially the readers, whose musicianship and creativity never cease to amaze me. Thanks for the ride of a lifetime.

CONTENTS

CLASSIC ROCK. WHAT QUALIFIES A SONG OR AN ARTIST TO BE CLASSIC?

Popularity and radio airplay are factors. If a song was everywhere, it was a part of life for a lot of people. Just a glimpse of a familiar album cover is sometimes enough to evoke an era; the songs themselves can transport a listener back in time—emotionally, at least.

Identification with the artists is another big reason for letting them into the classic rock club. Some songwriters personified an entire generation; they articulated the hopes and disappointments of everyone of a certain age. These artists are in many cases still the spokespeople for whole demographic segments of the population.

When it comes to music that involves keyboards, though, the criteria get a little more involved. Those who themselves were inspired to take up the piano, organ, or synthesizer as a result of listening to these classic artists have deeper ties to the music than casual listeners rocking out to the radio during their commute home. As a result, the artists in this book have an even deeper story to tell you.

For one thing, "classic" implies "static." But in the case of the keyboard instruments of rock, there's nothing static at all. Sure, the artists whose stories you're about to read faced more than one challenge that are timeless and unchanging. Songwriting is a primary theme. Performance is another.

Interpersonal dynamics are huge, too.

But equally significant is the constant evolution of keyboards—nothing has ever remained static as far as electronic instruments are concerned. This was just as much an issue for Keith Emerson in the late '60s as it was for Tony Banks in the early '90s.

Unlike those made by many musicians, though, the gear decisions the artists in this volume made weren't typical consumer choices. As you'll see in the following chapters, it certainly wasn't about the price. Portability was rarely a factor. Convenience didn't enter into it either. It was always about sound, and how it felt to play the instrument.

To be clear, acoustic pianos weren't undergoing radical modifications during this time. The heavy development of the modern piano all went down in the 19th century. The Hammond organ was also rather stable in its design—though you'll read about some surprising modifications to pianos and organs alike in the chapters ahead! The rapid development was with synthesizers, electric pianos, and electronic keyboards. In the '70s, dozens of synthesizers were introduced, each offering unique new sounds and, in many cases, new performance controls. In the '80s, synthesizers and keyboards alike had MIDI capabilities, which enabled artists to create entire systems of interconnected instruments. The '80s also saw the advent of sampling, which let artists record the sounds around them and almost immediately use them in their songs and performances. The '90s brought the virtualization of synths and keyboards as instruments with all the performance capabilities of physical instruments were created entirely in software.

To a keyboardist, all of this is fascinating, to be sure. Most serious players today go through the same decision-making processes that these classic artists did. But the most interesting thing about the interaction between the artists in this book and the technological upheavals they faced is how their choices about how they made sound affected the music that we still love to hear today. You'll read about songs that were made instantly recognizable and emotionally compelling by the way a particular synthesizer could be phrased. Often, a choice of gear distinguished the artist from the competition. In some cases, the new technology enabled a renaissance of creativity for particular bands. Heck, everyone in the Grateful Dead was using a MIDI rig during their live shows in the '90s—including Jerry Garcia himself, who played entire solos by triggering synth sounds from his guitar!

Just as fascinating are the stories of artists who tried new technology, fought with it, and then abandoned it. How their music survived and improved in spite of the modern gizmos they used provides lessons we can all apply. In every case, the common theme is that the song is the most important thing of all. The keyboard sounds were integral to the song, but the music itself was king.

Which is why we still hear the work of all of the artists in this book on drive-time radio. These players made music that everybody still loves to listen to—because it's great music, not just because it has some cool synth sounds, or some screaming organ, or some pounding piano. That's all definitely part of it, but the point is that every artist in this book has given the world a bunch of great tunes to groove along with. That's what makes them classic rock artists.

Keyboard magazine was in a perfect position to chronicle this revolution in composition and performance as it occurred. Dominic Milano and Robert L. Doerschuk—who did the bulk of the interviews in this book—were just like the people they interviewed: interested in great keyboard performances, curious about new technology, and excited about great music in general. They were anything but unbiased journalists, but that's what makes these interviews so compelling. The artists themselves recognized kindred spirits in Dominic and Bob, and they opened up for *Keyboard* magazine as a result. You can almost feel in these articles how the artists wrestled with and adapted to the new technology, and most importantly, how it affected their music.

If you were with us when *Keyboard* originally published these interviews, you'll enjoy the juxtaposition of these particular artists. In many cases, they not only knew each other but drew inspiration from each other's music—and they told us so. The styles covered are diverse, from piano rock to prog, and from synth-heavy pop to freestyle rock and roll; it's bound to bring a smile to the face of anyone familiar with this world.

If you missed out on these particular chapters of rock history, you're in luck. The lessons on songwriting, practicing, orchestrating, synth programming, and the business of music in the following pages can help you to improve your own music. We've also provided current discographies and website information so you can discover new worlds of music and find out what these artists are up to today.

Then you can go out and make your own classic rock!

ERNIE RIDEOUT
Former editor in chief, *Keyboard* magazine
Menlo Park, California
November 2009

FROM
BLUES
TO
PSYCHEDELIA

AL KOOPER

BY ROBERT L. DOERSCHUK

MAYBE YOU REMEMBER him from the Blues Project, or from the *Super Session* album with Mike Bloomfield, or from the immortal organ doodles on Bob Dylan's "Like a Rolling Stone." Or from one of hundreds of other songs you've heard. If you don't, get ready for a big slice of rock history, courtesy of Al Kooper.

You've been involved with synthesizers since their earliest days in rock. Did you get deeply into programming?

I went through that, very much so. Downstairs, in the graveyard [the basement of Al Kooper's house], I have the first synthesizer you could buy in America: the Putney VCS3. The whole focus of the thing was the patchbay, connecting this to that. I didn't understand it at all. Then it had a few knobs and its own keyboard. So I'd just smoke a joint, stick the pins in the patchbay, and see what happened. I got the greatest space sounds out of it that way, better than anything you could imagine. I used it on an album I was making at the time called *A Possible Projection of the Future*. The title track, which is about me projecting what my life was going to be like at age

80, starts off with this VCS3 making all these ridiculous sounds! It's great! This was back in '65 or '66; these were the first synthesizers that you could play live. So I got in very early.

Has more modern music technology affected your method of songwriting?

Definitely. It's much easier to write songs now, because I'm very adept at [Mark of the Unicorn] Performer. I can go that fast [*snaps fingers*] because of doing the music for the TV series *Crime Story*. So I have a finished record at the same time that I've finished the song. It's very rewarding to finish the song and have the whole band done at the same time. As a writer, it's inspiring, so you write better songs.

Is there a typical way that a song is born? Is it ever inspired by a particular sound?

Never. Never, ever. Usually what inspires me is listening to somebody else's music. If something is beautiful, it makes me want to write a song. Kings X does that. I got very inspired by that last night, so I went over and I started writing a song. It's in progress; it's still on there now.

How do you feel about techno and other sequence-driven dance music styles?

Can't relate. I did one song like that on my album *Rekooperation* called "Looking for Clues," because I've always loved the song. I made demos of the whole album on my songwriting gear, and this demo came out so good that I didn't want to re-record it. In fact, I was able to replicate the exact sounds on the original Robert Palmer record, which was a very techno-oriented album. This was his Gary Numan period. I've always loved the song, and I've always wanted to do it in some way, shape, or form. So this was perfect, to play it as an instrumental on keyboards. It's the only track on the album that's done on machines, and the only track on the album where I'm not playing a B-3; I'm playing a Korg organ. But the drums, the bass, the horns, the groove, and everything else sounds exactly like the Robert Palmer record. I also liked the solo that I played. I was intimidated by it; I didn't want to try and play it again. So I said, "Fuck it, it's my record. I'm keeping it." And I did, so I got shit from everybody. Maybe I'm wrong for doing it, but it feels good to me.

How does the Korg organ sound to you, especially on an album that's got so much real Hammond?

Here's the deal. I don't have the energy to do this, but somebody is going to come along someday and figure out how to sample a fucking organ. Nobody has done it yet, because they don't take the time to do it right. The B-3 has peculiarities compared to other keyboard sounds, in that the higher you get, the louder it gets. It's never been sampled that way. The high *C* on a B-3 is the loudest thing on the organ. It's screaming! That's what's great about the Rascals, about "Like a Rolling Stone," and all the Hammond organ records—that high *C*. It's never been sampled loudest on any sample I've heard. That's one of the things that are wrong. Then, of course, the harmonic frequencies are very peculiar because of the drawbars. They go to a certain point, then they jump down an octave in the third and fourth harmonics. Nobody's sampling that, so it's not gonna sound like a Hammond organ. Many people have gotten very close in the middle register. But even they admit they can't get the top yet.

What about the XB-2?

I don't know yet; I haven't spent that much time with it. When that came out, I went over to Hammond and introduced myself. They offered to give me one. I said, "No, I'd like to wait for the two-manual model, because I don't really play a one-manual organ. I'm very much a two-manual guy. It would be like having a great chick and having to have safe sex. I want to wait until I can fuck your two-manual organ." I called this guy for a year, waiting for it to get UL-approved and shipped into the country. Finally, after hanging me up for over a year, he told me, "I can't give you one. They're too expensive." So he fucked me!

When you play with your band in New York, do you have a Hammond onstage along with all the other stuff?

No, no: Along with the Hammond, I have my other stuff. Please! See, I carry a card in my wallet; it has my Korg Ml sounds on it. So wherever I go, I can plug that in and have my personal Ml sounds. There's this thing I do here in Nashville; I will do it in New York too, but it's not as much fun. I have a great pedal steel sound. I use the whammy bar, and I've become very adept at playing that pedal steel. When I play with this great local band in Nashville, it used to piss off [guitarist and leader] Michael Henderson tremendously, because he's a purist. He just wants me to play piano, and I would play vibes and pedal steel and all this stuff. Which is why I didn't stay in his band very long. We're still friends, but it's this purist thing. Also, I really approached the gig with a sense of humor, and he did not. It was fun while it lasted.

Is your New York band very different from your Nashville band?

Very much so. My Nashville band is not my band; it belongs to Sam Bush. It's called Duckbutter, and we never rehearse; we just call songs out and play them. It's a bar band with famous people. My New York band is a very serious, killer band. It's pretty well represented on the record. It's Jimmy Vivino on guitar. He's fantastic; he plays on the *Conan O'Brien* show. I've got my old buddy Harvey Brooks on bass. The drummer chair revolves, but I've pretty much been using Anton Fig. He's played my music better than anybody I've played with in a really long time. We used to have an additional keyboard player, Ed Alstrom, but now Jimmy doubles keyboard, so sometimes when I play guitar, he sits down and plays keyboards. His guitar playing is a little better than his keyboard playing. I've achieved parity: I'm about the same on both.

What kind of an impact have home studios had on an industry that was formerly based on live performance?

Well, I'm into that myself. I do both. I make demos at home, so that I don't have to go and spend all this money at the studio; I spend it at the music store. And I still go out and play gigs with an un-MIDIed Hammond organ that I rent from SIR.

FROM BLUES TO PSYCHEDELIA

Are you saying that you're uninterested in MIDIing a Hammond?

That would be interesting, but I don't have a million dollars. I don't even have a Hammond organ, so what does that tell you?

I just stick an Ml on top of the organ and play pedal steel a little bit. I love to play "Sleepwalk" on a gig, especially on an M1! [*Laughs.*] But playing pedal steel on an Ml is really a slap in the face in this town. They're so horrified that they love it. They can't believe that I have the balls to do that here in Nashville.

Of course, you'd better not try it unless you really can pull it off.

Well, I can't play as well as a pedal steel player can. I'll never be able to; it's not set up like that, because he can play two Middle *C*s at one time and I only have one. You can't duplicate that kind of stuff. The bass is another really difficult one. My approximations are so-so, but the sounds are right on.

What is the secret to approximating a bass guitar part on keys?

You have to think like a bass player. You have to listen to bass players, then transpose what they do onto the keyboard. I call that Zenning on an instrument. You play it like the guy would play it. For scoring music, it's great to take that to another place, where you can't do that on an instrument. Then you get into that great thing of transcending the instrument. I had a bell tree sound on one of my synths. [Producer] Michael Mann was very fond of using slow motion in *Crime Story* for certain violent sequences. Every time there was slow motion, I'd put up the bell tree sound, then put my entire hand down on the low- to midsection of the keyboard and hold it there. It was very nonmusical, but in fact a very musical thing would happen. It really was slow motion—a bell tree in slow motion. Every time he used slow motion, I would do that sound.

That, in turn, made it part of the show's identity.

Exactly. You could never do that with a bell tree. And yet, what a great sound. So you could transcend the instrument in a very nonmusical/musical way.

Is there any particular keyboard part that for you, stands out in your catalog?

I like what I did on "You Can't Always Get What You Want." I hear it a lot. I laugh at "Like a Rolling Stone" because that was my baptism as an organ player. I didn't really know what I was doing, but I did know what I was doing. It's cool, but "You Can't Always Get What You Want" was nice playing for what the song was. I like the Wurlitzer that I played on George Harrison's "All Those Years Ago": It starts the record off, and it's very me.

How did someone as inexperienced as you were at the time get to play the organ part on "Like a Rolling Stone"?

I was invited to watch. I was friendly with Tom Wilson, the producer. He had cut some of my songs with other people. At that time, I was a songwriter/session musician. I was also a big fan of Bob Dylan, so I came with my guitar, sat down, and plugged in. I was gonna say, "Oh, I thought you hired me to play!" I was young, you know—big stones [*indicates testicle size*]. Before Tom got there, Dylan came in with Mike Bloomfield, who I had never met. Mike was carrying a

Telecaster with no case. It was snowing outside, so the thing was wet and everything. He took a towel from the studio, wiped it off, plugged it in, and started warming up. I had never heard anyone play like that before, in any context. So I said, "Fuck this," put my guitar in the case, and went into the control room like I was supposed to. Young as I was, I wasn't about to make a fool out of myself. Then Tom Wilson came in; he hadn't seen me sitting out there, which was very good. It was, "Hey, how ya doin'?" "Good. Hey, thanks for letting me come." So the session goes on. Halfway through the session, they say to Paul Griffin, the organist, "The organ's not making it. Why don't you try playing piano?" I go over to Tom and I say, "Why don't you let me play the organ? I've got a great part for this." I'm full of shit, right? I was just ambitious. He says, "Oh, man. You're not an organ player. Come on, now." But he didn't say no! Then somebody says, "There's a phone call for you, Tom." And I'm thinking, "He did not say no. He just said I wasn't an organ player." So I went out there. The organ was buried behind all kinds of shit; you couldn't even see it. So I don't think he even knew I was gonna play organ on the next take. In fact, I couldn't even hear the organ.

So you couldn't tell how the drawbar registration sounded.

Registration? If he had turned the fucking thing off, I wouldn't have known how to turn it on! It's complicated to turn on a Hammond organ. Thank God he didn't fuckin' switch it off! So, anyway, they start playing. I can hear the band in the headphones, but I can't hear the organ. It's been turned off in the mix. I'm enough of a musician to know what each note sounds like, even though I'm not actually hearing it. I played the whole take without even hearing the organ.

Did you know the song through hearing previous takes?

Not really. If you listen to the first few verses, I play on the upbeat of one. It goes, "The chord . . . me . . . the chord . . . me. . . ." because I was waiting to hear what the chord was.

You did come up with a nice organ figure to lead into the vocal at the top of the song.

Well, that was based on listening to a lot of gospel music, which had a lot of organ stuff. But that record was very sloppy.

Still, once you've heard it, you remember it.

Well, I prefer the next album, *Blonde on Blonde.* The musician in me is almost offended by *Highway 61.* I'm amused by all the mistakes on it. But, yeah, it's very real. Now, *Blonde on Blonde* was all that Dylan had brought to the table, plus we made it sound like a record. He was still doing what he was doing, and everyone else made it into an actual album. It's the most like a record of any record he ever did. The musicianship was so high on that record; those guys did amazing things.

With that sort of perspective, describe what distinguishes your new album, *Rekooperation.*

It's very fulfilling this time because it defines me as a player. I've never been able to do that before. If you listen to this album from start to finish, you could then recognize me playing somewhere else in some other context.

Al Kooper: "Usually what inspires me is listening to somebody else's music. If something is beautiful, it makes me want to write a song." Photo by Neil Zlozower

You hadn't done that prior to this album?

I don't think so. Maybe over the course of a body of work, but who is gonna sit down and listen to all of that? Here, it's self-contained for the first time, in one situation. I mean, on the records I did before, I had other things to do.

As on *I Stand Alone*?

Yeah. I had to put sound effects between each song, didn't I? [Laughs.]

On *Rekooperation*, the emphasis seems to be more on locking into a groove than on composition.

Well, you may laugh at this, but the thing that holds this record together is sex. There's a lot of music sex on this record. It's not a concept where I went in and said, "I'm gonna make this kind of a record." But there are some very sexy moments here.

What are some of the sexier parts of *Rekooperation*?

There's a new song that I wrote; it's the only kind of '40s song I've ever written in my life. It's called "How 'My Ever Gonna Get Over You?" My key role on it is as the songwriter, because all I do is hold chords on the organ and play a couple of glisses on the piano. But Hank Crawford plays the lead on it, and he is one of the sexiest sax players who ever put a reed in his mouth. He changed my life. On his first solo album, he does "Misty," with five horns, bass, and drums—no comping instruments, no piano, no guitar. The horn writing had to be so astute to pull that out. The five other horns had to become the piano or the guitar. It takes very sensitive writing to do that, because you depend on a guitar or a piano to help you through a song. Also, the horns were able to lay out a lot, because the bass player,

Edgar Willis, was so brilliant. It's just one of the greatest records I've ever heard in my life: "Misty" by Hank Crawford, on an album called *More Soul*. It's not on CD, which is the bane of my existence. From that point on, I didn't even want to know about tenor sax. In fact, Blood, Sweat & Tears, which had four horns, had no tenor sax. That was unheard of: To not have a tenor sax in that lineup of four horns is nuts! We had two trumpets, an alto, and a trombone, only because I'm fuckin' sick and a Hank Crawford maniac. Compared to a great alto player—which we did have in Blood, Sweat & Tears, with Fred Lipsius—a tenor sax cannot cry. I'm not demeaning any tenor players, because they also do things that alto players can't do. But I love saxophones to cry, and no one cries like Hank Crawford.

Had you ever worked with Crawford before these sessions?

I had never met the guy before. But he played so incredibly on my song. That was one of the most thrilling things about making this album—just to be in a room with this guy I've idolized for 30 years.

Two outstanding pianists—Dick Hyman and Johnnie Johnson—played on your album as well.

I hired a lot of piano players because there's a big difference between an organ player and a piano player. I like playing with great piano players, because I'm better on organ than on piano. There's a very big distinction between the two. Yet it's great when you have both on a track. "Like a Rolling Stone" is a great example of that.

Who was the piano player on that date?

Paul Griffin, a wonderful musician. So in "How 'My Ever Gonna Get Over You?", I wanted these little piano tinkles. Dick was there; he had done "I Want a Little Girl." He is considered the best piano player in New York; he does all the Gershwin stuff in the Woody Allen movies. He was in my big band back in 1969. After Blood, Sweat & Tears, I went out on the road with a 15-piece band, and Dick was the piano player. I hadn't worked with him since then, due to geography more than anything else. So I called him up, and it was great to be back with him again. I got him specifically for "I Want a Little Girl," but then I thought he could play good on this, too. He did a take, and I said, "You know, Dick, what it needs is that kind of thing that the piano played on those Johnny Mathis records." He looked at me and said [*archly*], "I played on those records." So without missing a beat, I said, "Then you know exactly what I mean, don't you?" Was I embarrassed that I didn't know that! [*Laughs.*] But, of course, who could do it better? That's some fuckin' piano playing: "Chances Are," "It's Not for Me to Say." That's really sensitive, beautiful shit, and he gave me the same shit on my thing. So here's Dick Hyman doing his thing, and Hank Crawford doing his thing. And I'm gonna get royalties for this? Is this a beautiful country or what?

What about Johnnie Johnson?

Jimmy plays in his band. And who isn't a fan of Johnnie Johnson? Of course, we did "Johnny B. Goode."

Where did you get the idea of slowing it down as much as you did?

I like taking songs that have been done a million times and coming up with a fresh way to do 'em. That way, when somebody sees you're doing the song, they go, "How can you do 'Johnny B. Goode'? Everybody in the world has done that song! What idiot would do 'Johnny B. Goode' and 'Don't Be Cruel' on his fuckin' album?" But you fuck with the arrangements and you get something new. Dylan used to say to me, "Why do you bother coming up with these great arrangements? Why don't you just write new songs over the arrangements? Then you'd be the writer!" But I wish I could do a whole album like that sometime. If this one is successful, which I don't seriously count on, it would be great to do that.

Do you get these sorts of arrangement ideas pretty spontaneously? If someone assigned you to specifically come up with a new concept for "Johnny B. Goode" the results would probably be less inspired.

That's correct. They're very spur-of-the-moment. One of the things I do well is that I'm a really good arranger. Technically, I'm not a great player. I'm the first to admit it. But what got me through all of this is that I play nice notes to make up for the fact that I can't be all over the place. Instead, I play with a certain amount of taste. That gets me through, because I can't do the Keith Emerson thing.

Is *Rekooperation* a sign of your return to recording after 12 years out of the picture?

That's really up to the public. If the public accepts this in some way, shape, or form, then I certainly wouldn't mind continuing to do it. There was this great moment when we were cutting "How 'My Gonna Get Over You?" It was just the four of us. Hank and Dick didn't play, so it was me, Harvey, Jimmy, and Anton. Like I said, this thing was very '40s, and I wanted it to be authentic, so we had this organ trio happening, with Jimmy doing a Thom Bell kind of guitar thing. But it had to be like a '40s thing. It was a great take, so when we finished I put my arms around everybody and said, "We just played like men. I don't know if you've ever done that before, but this is the first time in a studio that I've sat down and played like a man." And on a few other things too. It's a much more mature record than any one I've ever made. It's not a pop record. It's not a jazz record either. It's just a music record.

Are you hoping that some single release, possibly of "How 'My Gonna Get Over You?", will give the album some lift into the charts?

I never conjecture things like that. I've learned, as John Prine would say, what a great big goofy world this is. My motto has always been, "If you don't expect anything, you are never disappointed." So I made the record, I'm deliriously happy with it, and they promised to give me enough copies for me to hand out to my friends. Above and beyond that, who knows?

So the music business hasn't quite nurtured your sense of idealism?

Well, when I was in Blues Project, we were put on the bill with many of these people we were imitating: Muddy Waters, Howlin' Wolf, Jimmy Reed, people like that. As a matter of fact, during two weeks that we were sharing the bill with

Muddy Waters at the Cafe au Go-Go, Otis Spann used to give me lessons every afternoon. He showed me positions for scales, like playing the VI minor for the major scale, and his licks, his timing approach, and so forth. I had just become a keyboard player; I was a guitar player before that. It was relatively new for me to be a keyboard player. I had really just gotten into blues super-heavy too.

Those lessons must have had a big impact on you.

That was a very unusual thing. I mean, what was I? Twenty-two or 23. But I'd ask him, "Do you think tomorrow afternoon, maybe you could show me some stuff? I mean, you're the best there is." And he'd say, "Why, sure!" So after the first day, I said, "Come on, let's go across the street. I'll buy you dinner. In fact, I'll make a deal with you: You do this with me every day you can do it, and I'll buy dinner after every lesson. And drinks." He'd laugh and say, "Well, that sounds like a good deal to me!" I got two weeks' worth of lessons that way.

Later on, after Otis died, I would sometimes go sit in with Muddy. I would always call "Long Distance Call," which was one of Otis' great things. Now, Muddy would forget that Otis taught me. We'd start playing, and I'd do exactly what Otis played. Muddy would turn around and smile at me, and I knew that he remembered. Otis was a great guy. There's a picture of Otis and me in this album.

Since you were such a novice, why were you playing keyboards in the Blues Project at all?

Because I was Bob Dylan's keyboard player. That's why I was asked to join the band. It was a very embryonic band; they weren't successful or anything. They didn't even have a record deal. But I accepted their invitation because I thought, "What a great way to get my keyboard chops up, now that I'm gonna be a keyboard player," which happened just in the space of one afternoon. "Won't it be great to be in this band? I can constantly practice, and there's no pressure. I guess we'll just play in clubs."

Then—wham, bam—we're cutting an album, we're on the radio, we're travelling across the country. But still I thought of it mainly as a great way to improve my playing. It was a good choice, but I gave up a very lucrative session career to Paul Harris; he got all my dates.

These were keyboard sessions?

Yeah. At the time I joined the Blues Project, right after "Like a Rolling Stone," I was getting two or three sessions a day. Then we had to go out on the road, so I had to turn my back on that.

Didn't you consider yourself stronger on guitar than on keyboards at that time?

Well, at that point I wasn't very good at either, if the truth be told. I had a lot to learn on both instruments. But I digress. The point I was going to make was that, we used to work with all these blues acts. We'd look at them and say, "Geez, poor guys. They got ripped off so bad by the record companies. What a fuckin' shame." Listen: These guys did great compared to me! I'm the one who got fucked! Now, when I see this body of work that I did and what I received for it,

FROM BLUES TO PSYCHEDELIA

it's unbelievable.

Unbelievable, but not unknown in this business.

The difference is that in those days, in the '50s and '60s, I got into it because I loved music. I didn't want to do anything else. All I wanted to do was to play music. If I could make a living doing that, it would be the greatest thing in the world. I knew early on that I was going to make my living in music. I didn't know how. I certainly didn't know I was going to be a keyboard player, or even a recording artist. But I knew that I would be devoted to being involved in music in some way, shape, or form. If I could pay the rent, and buy clothes and records and food, that was enough for me. I didn't look at the big picture. I was just delighted to be doing these things. Now, when you don't chase the money, the other people can smell it instantly, and they take it because you don't give a shit. It's true: I didn't give a shit, because I was so wrapped up in the music thing. Nowadays, people get into it for the money. They dye their hair fuckin' purple, and go get $400,000 because there's no other band where everybody's hair is purple. That's the bane of my existence. I could live very comfortably if I got what was coming to me right now.

Was it just a question of making bad business decisions?

It's a question of everything. I dreamed up Blood, Sweat & Tears myself, in my own little head. It was my concept. I never got a penny for it. *Super Session*? Never got a penny for it. Lynyrd Skynyrd? The manager has all the checks sent to him. It's indefensible. All this money is gone. It should come to me. That's very sad.

Who can you blame other than yourself?

Well, it would have been great if I was sharper. But I did all this stuff, and now I can't go back and rectify it. That, I feel, is wrong.

What's the lesson here, as far as younger readers are concerned?

If you're in this for your life, if you're consumed with music like I was and not really concerned with anything else, then you should track these things. The demographic has shifted. Now there are more people sitting in houses across the world who would rather see Eddie Vedder than me. That's what happens. It always happens. It's gonna happen to Eddie Vedder; he's gonna be in my situation. He should get his Pearl Jam money to take care of him when people are going to see Joe Shmoe and don't give a shit about Eddie Vedder.

You're really saying that a love of music in this business is a weakness that others can exploit. If you get into music to make money, you stand less of a chance of getting screwed than if you get in because you love doing the thing for which the business theoretically exists.

And that's called "ironic." Now, I get songwriting money. That's very nice. I should have had publishing too. I don't want to be a pig, okay? But I didn't get it. A lot of people don't. It's very funny: I have publishing now, because nobody is interested in my songs. As a result, I am now the publisher of my songs. I'd be very happy to make a 50-50 publishing deal, so I don't have to chase this shit down all the time. Things happen.

For instance—this is very funny—I'm in a part-time band called the Rock-Bottom Remainders, that consists of Stephen King, Dave Barry, Matt Groening, Dave Marsh, Amy Tan, Ridley Pearson, Barbara Kingsolver, Tad Bartemus, Roy Blount, Jr.—a million of these famous authors. We do all '50s and '60s songs, and play for charity. I'm the music director: I'm supposed to make these guys sound good. As a result of this band, I've become very friendly with Stephen King. So next February they're doing a miniseries of *The Stand*, which was my favorite Stephen King book. In the book, there's a character who has the number one record at the time the story is taking place. The lyrics are in the book. So Stephen calls me one day and says, "Would you be interested in writing the music to 'Can You Dig Your Man?'?" I said, "Do we have to use the same words?" He said, "Well, yes, we do." "Well! This is a challenge, Steve! Let me see what I can do."

So I wrote something to his lyrics, and I wrote some additional lyrics as well. I had this great singer from here, John Cowan, who was in the New Grass Revival—best singer in town—sing the demo. I did it on machines here in the living room. I mixed the track, minus guitars and vocals, down to a cassette—not a DAT, a cassette. Then I went into a recording studio and bounced the cassette onto two tracks of a 24-track. Then I put acoustic and electric guitars on, and John sang and did background vocals. I mixed it, and I sent it into *The Stand*. Everybody loved it—and they used it as the master in the movie. We're talking high-tech here, but the things I can do on here sound like records. So there it was, from my living room to millions of living rooms, from a fuckin' cassette! I love the low-tech-ness of it, but no one will know that when they see the show.

You've got a DAT machine here. Why didn't you use it?

I just didn't want to bother with it. I happened to have the cassette player patched up at the time.

What else is on the table in the months to come?

Well, I'm executive-producing a Harry Nilsson tribute album; he's in ill health nowadays and his accountant embezzled all his money, so it's the humane thing to do, this kind of record. I'm also playing my 50th birthday gig. It's gonna be Feb. 4, 5, and 6 at the Bottom Line in New York. It'll be, like, my whole life laid out before me, divided into three sections: the Blues Project, *Child Is Father to the Man*—which is the Blood, Sweat & Tears of my ilk—and then all of the people from this current album. We're gonna do two shows a night. Then I'm gonna die there, in the dressing room of the Bottom Line. [*Laughs.*] Somehow we're gonna video and audio it.

Sounds like a homecoming.

Well, I played at the Bottom Line with the Blues Project on our reunion tour, and in March I played there with this Blood, Sweat & Tears thing. But to have them both on the same bill and this new album is a once-in-a-lifetime thing.

Who will be in the BS&T lineup?

Jim Fielder, who has moved here to Nashville. Anton on drums. Steve Katz. . . .

He'll also be doing the Blues Project set?

Yeah. And so will Freddie Lipsius, Randy Brecker, Tom "Bones" Malone on trombone, and Lew Soloff.

Why isn't the original drummer, Bobby Colomby, in on this?

Bobby doesn't play drums anymore. His license plate used to say EX DRUMS. He also copyrighted the name that I made up—Blood, Sweat & Tears—and neglected to pay any of us royalties, so he was not the most popular choice in this lineup, as you can imagine. I'll tell you, in my resume, I'm very embarrassed by Blood, Sweat & Tears. The band that most people know by that name is not what I wanted to do. I wanted to do that album, *Child Is Father to the Man*, and what I would have done next, which is really different from what they did. When I left, they went into that other place where they really wanted to go but I was trying to hold down. So I never play that up. If someone says, "What have you done with your life?," I'll say, "I was in the Blues Project, I did the *Super Session* album, I played with Bob Dylan and the Rolling Stones and the Who and Cream and all those guys."

I never want to mention Blood, Sweat & Tears because I don't want people to think I had anything to do with those "Spinning Wheels" or any of that other stuff. So when it came time to do this reunion thing, it was obvious what to call the band. And it works.

What did you do with the group last March?

We did this amazing show. We played that first album, in sequence, from start to finish, with a string quartet doing the parts live. It was the most incredible show I've ever been involved with. If you love that album, it was the greatest thing you could see. Some of that stuff we had never played live, like "House in the Country" and "My Days Are Numbered." I rearranged "My Days Are Numbered" so at the end there's a ten-minute fuckin' trumpet battle between Lew and Randy, with a great groove behind them. They start out trading bars: 16-16, then it's 8-8, 4- 4, 2-2. It's just the greatest. Then I did that song that I sing with just the strings playing; I'd never done that before. We just played the whole album in sequence, just the way it was. That was the weekend of that giant blizzard in New York.

What kind of turnout did you get?

We did good. We made money. [*Waves fist in air and smiles*.] New Yorkers!

Portions of this article originally were published in the January 1994 issue of Keyboard *magazine.*

FOR MORE ON AL KOOPER

As it happens, Al Kooper didn't die in the dressing room of the Bottom Line on his birthday back in 1994. In fact, Dr. Kooper is still rockin' and talkin'. You can connect with him at his official website, www.alkooper.com.

A SELECTED AL KOOPER BIBLIOGRAPHY AND DISCOGRAPHY

There's nothing quite like listening to Al Kooper talk about his life in music. If you want more, pick up a copy of his latest book, *Backstage Passes and Backstabbing Bastards* (2008, Hal Leonard).

The list of great artists Al Kooper has performed and recorded with is huge. This is a very small selection of a few of the greatest examples of his playing and presence.

AS A LEADER
2008 *White Chocolate*
2005 *Black Coffee*
1995 *Soul of a Man: Al Kooper Live*
1994 *Rekooperation*

WITH BOB DYLAN
1986 *Knocked Out Loaded*
1978 *Masterpieces*
1970 *Self Portrait*
1966 *Blonde on Blonde*
1965 *Highway 61 Revisited*

WITH THE BLUES PROJECT
1967 *The Blues Project Live at Town Hall*
1966 *Projections*

WITH THE WHO
1967 *The Who Sell Out*

WITH BLOOD, SWEAT & TEARS
1968 *Child Is Father to the Man*

WITH JIMI HENDRIX
1968 *Electric Ladyland*

WITH MOBY GRAPE
1968 *Grape Jam*

WITH THE BUTTERFIELD BLUES BAND
1968 *In My Own Dream*

WITH TAJ MAHAL
1968 *Natch'l Blues*

WITH MICHAEL BLOOMFIELD
1968 *Super Session*

WITH THE ROLLING STONES
1969 *Let It Bleed*

WITH ALVIN LEE
1980 *Free Fall*

Shown here in 1977, Ray Manzarek is surrounded by a collection of classic keys, including, clockwise from lower left: Hammond C-3, ARP Odyssey, ARP String Ensemble, Hohner Clavinet, and Rhodes electric piano.

Photo by Glen La Ferman

RAY
MANZAREK

BETWEEN NIGHT AND DAY ARE THE DOORS

BY ROBERT L. DOERSCHUK

LOS ANGELES HASN'T changed much since the '60s. As always, days drift by like smog banks in a starless sky. Nights are threaded by headlights in procession, searching the gloom for invisible dreams. Out in Venice and Santa Monica, the ocean darkens at sunset as restless vagabonds scan the horizon one last time for the perfect wave, as their fathers and mothers did before them. Further east, atop the long slow incline that climbs from the coast into Watts and crests in Hollywood, the Whiskey A Go Go still stands amidst a wreckage of billboards, bottles, and trash, a shrine even now for rock and roll's rootless pilgrims, locked in the communion of youth, with its passionate rituals and vague apprehensions.

This is the Los Angeles of banshee Santa Ana windstorms, of furtive shadows stealing across the green lawns of suburban complacence, of riots on Sunset and rumbles in Venice. Its seductive terrors are recounted in the 1987 movie *Less Than Zero*, in drooling media rehashes of the Manson escapades—and most vividly of all in the words and music of the Doors.

While most young fans perceive '60s bands as amusing relics, the Doors' appeal remains immediate. Their disturbing images and cool style seem more in tune with the post-punk '90s than with the good-time jangle of folk-rock and San Francisco psychedelia. Of course, much of the credit for the public's lingering fascination with the Doors traces to singer Jim Morrison—specifically, to his gifts as a lyricist and to his death at age 27 in 1971, before middle age could tarnish his legacy. The Morrison eulogized by Oliver Stone, by Doors drummer John Densmore in his 1991 book *Riders on the Storm*, by Billy Idol's remake of "L.A. Woman," and by the mourners who still gather at his grave in Paris escaped into posterity without turning into a Fat Elvis.

FROM BLUES TO PSYCHEDELIA

But there's more to the Doors than Morrison. Formidable as his gifts were, his patricidal fantasies in "The End" would probably have languished unread in poetry book bins if not for the musical setting provided by his colleagues. This remarkable experiment in interactive recitation succeeds because Densmore's melodramatic drumming, Robbie Krieger's slithering guitar, and Ray Manzarek's hypnotic organ tune in perfectly with Morrison's text and delivery. The same is true for every cut on the group's debut album, from the nightmarish cabaret lope of "Whiskey Bar" to the hallucinatory "Crystal Ship." Even now, the entire record is as eerie and compelling as the dark side of the American dream.

It was Manzarek who largely defined the Doors' musical identity. No one sounded like him. His fluid lines snaked over pedal drones in mandala-like symmetrical patterns. His tone was deliberately thin, as if to draw attention to the economy of his improvisations. Even on those rare occasions when Manzarek would record with a Hammond organ instead of his trademark anemic Vox Continental, he avoided the emotional excess and hand-me-down churchiness embraced by most rock keyboardists of his day. In his pre-minimalist approach, Manzarek found the pulse of future tastes, as Morrison had done in his free-associative verse.

The Manzarek style was spawned by an interplay of influences: the classical lessons he began before the age of ten in Chicago, the blues he sought out in the city's South Side clubs, the intellectual underpinning of his economics major at De Paul University, and subsequent studies in law and film at UCLA. His encounter with fellow film student Morrison in 1965 led to an oceanside commitment to begin collaborating. As Manzarek put it to writer Digby Diehl, "We talked a while before we decided to get a group together and make a million dollars."

That they did, at the expense of a few indecent exposure arrests and other escapades. Of those who survived the band's rise and fall, Manzarek was best able to pursue intriguing solo projects. These included stints as producer for the L.A. punk band X, leader and keyboardist with a promising proto-stadium band called Nite City in the late '70s, and reorchestrator of Carl Orff's *Carmina Burana*, a '30s-vintage oratorio that Manzarek and Philip Glass adapted for electronic ensemble.

Yet today, nearly four decades after Morrison slipped into unconsciousness in a Paris bathtub, these projects are dwarfed by the Doors, who stubbornly persist as a contemporary phenomenon. Like spirits in an endless séance, they revive again and again in books, on screen, on the radio, in Manzarek's life, and even in his current projects.

But while the group endures, like the City of Night that spawned them 40+ years ago, time won't stand still for Manzarek. He's older now, his hair grayer, his face lined behind the familiar rimless glasses. Gone is the funky flat he shared with Morrison in Ocean Park.

Home [at the time of this interview] is uptown, in Beverly Hills—a spacious place with room for a modest pile of keyboards (Roland D-50 and RD-1000, rack-mounted Yamaha TX816, his son's Dynacord drums), a loudmouthed tropical bird, and shelves groaning with books on art, music, and metaphysics.

Gone, too, is the frenzy of stardom.

Manzarek's activities now involve home studio projects with his son Pablo and occasional appearances as piano accompanist to poet Michael McClure in recitals. He bemoans his generation's yuppification, shaking his head in bewilderment, then in the next breath predicts that today's young musicians can pick up the gauntlet dropped by their parents and "save the world" with rock and roll. His voice, a deejay-quality baritone, sinks into a conspiratorial whisper as he chuckles over old drug experiences and follows free-associative reflections that scatter unpredictably across the landscape of ideas.

Few can evoke Woodstock and marvel at modern materialism while sunk into a couch in Beverly Hills without some loss of credibility. But Manzarek pulls it off for the same reason that Pete Townshend does: He's a believer, a 20-year-old enthusiast in a wiry 60-something-year-old shell. Like L.A., like L'America, the Manzarek that matters remains untouched by time and unrepentant at heart.

In your work with the Doors, and in such later projects as your adaptation of *Carmina Burana* with Philip Glass, you seem to reflect a preference for modernistic, anti-Romantic approaches to music. Didn't you ever go through a Chopin phase as a piano student?

Never went through a Chopin phase. It had to be twentieth-century, outside of Beethoven's *Ninth* and a few other things. I didn't enjoy playing Tchaikovsky. Bach's *Two-* and *Three-Part Inventions* were fun. Their metrical sense was nice: Just keep it on the beat, even if it's not a rock and roll beat. But then Russian classical music got to me, because those guys had so much soulfulness. *The Rite of Spring*, where they hit that rhythmic section—wow, is that powerful.

So even as a teenager, you were into the more adventurous contemporary repertoire.

That and jazz, since I grew up on the south side of Chicago. Blues and jazz— African American music—really got me going. The first time I heard Muddy Waters and those guys, it was the same minor melancholy sense that some of the Russian composers had, but translated into music that had a beat and a blue note—those flatted sevenths. So it was a combination of the blues, and Russian classical, and then of course Miles Davis with his modal stuff. When I figured out what he was doing, it was so much fun to play. Eventually, all of these influences became the way I play the piano.

Were you an annoyance to teachers who wanted you to play traditional pieces?

No. I played what they told me to play until I said, "That's enough of this. I quit." Okay, those pieces are great for your sight-reading, great for your chops. But it got to the point where I said, "Why do I want to play somebody else's music? It's got to have a beat." That's Marlon Brando in *The Wild One*: "Got to go!" It was the '50s, man. In the '50s, you had to go. It had to rock. It had to

With the Doors, Ray Manzarek was most often seen with a Vox Continental organ and Fender Piano Bass keyboard. Here he is—post-Doors—at home in 1977, in his days with Nite City. Photo by Neil Zlozower

move. If it didn't, there was no point in playing it.

Yet your work with the Doors didn't really rock in that sense. Compared to everybody else on the charts in those days, your playing was pretty cerebral.

That comes from being here in California. I always think of the Doors as an extension of the California cool jazz school of [baritone saxophonist] Gerry Mulligan and [trumpeter] Chet Baker. It was the beach, and the Pacific Ocean washing over you, and living down in Venice, but with a Chicago kind of intensity added to the style to put it into a cooler area, and Miles' modality, and John Coltrane working with the same kind of thing in his solo albums. And Bill Evans too. Boy, what a master!

There is a kind of parallel between his sound on piano and yours on organ.

I always tried to play like Bill Evans. If there's one thing I want in my life, it's to be able to play like him, and like McCoy Tyner comping behind Coltrane. They both had that Debussy-like thing that I love so much.

Judging from your remarks about California, you must believe that where you are geographically has a direct impact on how you play.

Absolutely, man. That affects anybody. When you eventually find who you are as a player, a lot of that comes from the flora and fauna of the region where you live.

So if you had stayed in Chicago, for example, you might have wound up playing piano and Hammond organ with the Paul Butterfield Blues Band.

Exactly. I probably would have been playing that Hammond sound. I wouldn't have had that smaller California sound: the Vox, the Farfisa, and like that—what Lester Bangs called "the Doors' cheesy organ sound." It's not cheesy, it's California!

You produced several of X's albums. With your background in relatively sophisticated musical forms, was it difficult for you to plunge into the maelstrom of punk with them?

Yeah. You listened to punk, and you had to say, "For God's sake, would somebody put a major seventh in there, or a minor ninth? Please! Okay, you guys don't do that? Fine, I understand." But their poetry was very sophisticated. John [Doe] and Exene [Cervenka] were doing beatnik poetry. I loved what Bruce Botnick once called their "Chinese harmonies." And Billy Zoom was the king of rockabilly guitar. It was amazing that one guy could get so much noise out of one guitar. So when I got together with them, it was, "I play what I play. You guys play what you play, as long as you play it with the intensity and integrity and power and passion that I love." I'll take any music, as long as real passion is there.

Poetry seems a constant thread in your music, from Morrison through X up to your work with Michael McClure.

If you're working with words, it's got to be poetry. I grew up with the books of Jack Kerouac. If he hadn't written *On the Road*, the Doors would never have existed. Morrison read *On the Road* down in Florida, and I read it in Chicago. That sense of freedom, spirituality, and intellectuality in *On the Road*—that's what I wanted in my own work.

Specifically, how do you attain those elements in music?

Well, let me tell you one interesting story from Kerouac. There's one section in *On the Road* where he goes into a bar, and there's a quartet with a saxophonist—maybe somebody like Gene Ammons, with that big, fat sound. Kerouac listens to the music a bit, and later he writes, "He had it that night. And everybody in the club knew he had it. That was what I wanted to get." I'm reading this around 1957 or '58, and I think to myself, "He had it? Had what? What did he have? And how did everybody in the club know he had it? What is 'it' anyway?"

I never understood what "it" was until the Doors got together for their very first rehearsal. We played "Moonlight Drive." I showed Robbie the very simple chord changes, he put his bottleneck guitar on, we smoked a little cannabis, as people were wont to do in 1965 or '66, and we started to play. By the end of the song, it had all locked in. I said to John, Robbie, and Jim, "Man, I've played for a long time, but I never actually played music until right now." Then I said to Jim, "You know that section of Kerouac where he said the guy had 'it'? I know what 'it' is now: It's what we've just done."

It's an indefinable thing, a sinking down into a lower state of awareness, so that your everyday consciousness is no longer in charge. You tap into, as Jim would call it, a more primordial consciousness. It's the collective unconscious that permeates all of our lives. We all slip right down into it, using all of our intellectual abilities and our knowledge of music to effortlessly play, and allowing ourselves to go into a heightened state of awareness. Boy, it was good.

In a recent issue of *Interview*, Val Kilmer, who plays Morrison in the Oliver Stone movie *The Doors*, said something interesting about your work with the Doors: "I used to say that the organ on the Doors music really irritated me. I didn't get that it was comedy, Brechtian style." Was that, in fact, the effect you were going for?

"I didn't like the organ sound." When I read that, I thought, "Jesus Christ! Where the hell were you, Val?" The truth was that I didn't want to use a Hammond organ, because I didn't want to sound like Jimmy Smith. As far as I was concerned, Jimmy Smith was absolutely brilliant, the master, and I wasn't about to get into a race to play against a guy like him and Charles Earland and all the other great jazz organ players. I could never play that well. Also, the technicalities of hauling one of those damn things around from gig to gig were too much to handle.

What was lovely about the little Vox Continental was that it was a portable suitcase-type instrument. You put it through a good amp, crank up the reverb, and you've got some real power. When we played at the Whiskey, I could split eardrums with that California-style organ. I would squeeze down on the volume pedal until the sound became unearthly and people's heads started turning. I could see their pain, and just at the point where I knew I was going over the edge, I would begin the lick and we would get into "Summer's Almost Gone" or something.

But what about Kilmer's observation on the comic or ironic elements of your organ sound?

There was an ironic edge to the Doors, but I don't think there was necessarily an ironic edge to the sound. "Oh, show me the way to the next whiskey bar . . . I tell you, we must die." Yeah, that was humorous. If you didn't know that came from Brecht and Weill, you'd say, "Why is a rock and roll band playing an oom-pah song? What the heck is that all about? That's gotta be funny." Well, yeah, we were being funny, but we were also saying that death lurks right around the corner, the future is uncertain, and the end is always near, so you'd better make friends with your death. Otherwise, you'll be constantly running from it. What kind of a way is that to live your life—running away from death? Death is coming . . . Val! [*Laughs.*]

That organ sound of yours was instantly recognizable, though, especially since so many other organists were playing the meatier-sounding Hammonds.

My sound was the sound of the instrument. My style was the result of all the studies, all the influences, going to UCLA, reading all the books that I read, and the ingestion of controlled substances, which put it all together and said, "Western civilization is crumbling before your very eyes, Ray. So reinvent your life, reinvent the world, on the basis of the fact that you have three score and ten, more or less, to live on this planet. What are you going to say through your music? How are you going to affect the world through what you're playing?"

Having technique and the knowledge of the structure of music enabled me to take that consciousness and, when I put my finger on a note, let it come through. That's basically what it is: Each person has to find his or her consciousness on this planet. Then, when you play your instrument, you'll get individuality out of it. It doesn't matter whether you've got all the sounds in the world in your synthesizer. If I play the synthesizer, I'm still gonna sound like me. Even if it's the ocarina stop and I'm playing an ocarina piece, I'm still gonna be playing who I am, because every time I put my finger down, the infinite consciousness infuses what I do. That's what every artist has to strive for. All of that stuff that went together to create you is infinite and totally unique at the same time, and it will infuse whatever you do, whether it's playing keyboards, playing guitar, writing, painting, or anything else.

Do you think that the easy availability of killer sounds and samples has made it harder to develop an individual style today than it was in the '60s?

Yes, absolutely, man. I mean, what did I play onstage? I had a Rhodes keyboard bass with 32 to 37 notes on it, and a Vox organ. That's all I had. I could turn on a vibrato or a tremolo, and pull a couple of drawbars to make it more bassy. But all I could do was basically a cheesy California organ sound.

So the sound was the sound; what could I do? Invent the melody! The melody, together with the rhythm, is the most important thing. That's what music is. The sound only augments the melody. As a keyboard player, you must create the melody first.

So you approached your parts with the Doors in terms of lines, rather than chords.

Yeah, although the chords are a melody too. They have a melodic structure. Every *Am7* is composed of the notes that it's composed of. So even if you play a chord, you're playing a melody. Where you voice the chord is a melodic choice. Then it becomes a rhythmic choice: Where do I play that chord?

Do you still have your old Continental?

No. I went through quite a few of them, about a half dozen. They would only hold up for so long. Then the keys would stick when you played 'em too hard, so I'd find myself playing and trying to lift them up at the same time. All my Voxes died. They weren't meant to be in this world for a long time.

You did do some recording on Hammond with the Doors too.

Yeah, on quite a few cuts. We had room for an organ in our rehearsal studio, so just before the last album, John and Robbie and Jim said to me, "Hey, we're gonna get you a Hammond as a birthday present!" I said, "Cool!" And, boom, one day there it was: a good old C-3. The C-3 and the B-3 were exactly the same instrument, except the C-3 had little Maltese cross decorations around it.

Pianos turn up a lot on Doors tunes as well, although frequently you seemed to go for a tacky, vaudeville-type instrument rather than the more elegant and traditional grand piano.

Right. But I never thought of the tack piano as a vaudevillian sound. Elektra [Records] had the greatest tack piano on earth. It was an incredibly bright Yamaha, and somebody had very carefully and laboriously put a tack on the right spot of each of its hammers. When you hit those strings, the harpsichord-like glassiness was just wonderful. I still love that sound.

Although it had a funky, roadhouse quality too.

Exactly. You had both characteristics. But after all, the Doors were basically a roadhouse blues band with intellectual pretensions. [*Laughs.*]

One of the more interesting keyboard parts in the Doors catalog was in the tune "L'America."

A great song. Jim wrote the words, and Robbie and I wrote the music together.

The organ part was unusually dissonant when played against the descending line in the chorus.

It was supposed to be. The piece was written for the movie *Zabriskie Point.* [Director Michelangelo] Antonioni actually came to our rehearsal studio to hear the song, but when we played it for him he went running out and never contacted us. I don't know what the hell he was expecting. Ultimately, he went with Pink Floyd for the movie, which made sense; he was a European, and so were they. But the song was intended to be the opening theme for *Zabriskie Point,* so that dissonance was for the danger of going across the highway. And the blues section, of course, was, "the Rain Man's coming to town. Change your luck. Teach your women how to f-f-f-f . . . find themselves." Ooh, Jim! We thought you were gonna say "fuck." [*Laughs.*] Good lyric!

There seemed to be a lot of variety from one Doors song to the next in terms of how much room you had. On "Light My Fire," for example, you could solo and comp pretty freely, whereas you had to stick to a very minimal part in "Riders on the Storm."

Exactly. That's why Jim objected to doing "Light My Fire." He had to do it the same way every night, but we got to stretch out for 15 or 20 minutes—however long we wanted for our solos. We would do Indian improvisations, we would trade fours and twos and ones with John, anything. And Morrison, unfortunately, had to do the same thing [*in resigned singsong voice*]: "You know that it would be untrue. . . ." There was nothing he could do about it: That's the way the song goes. But everything had freedom within it. Everyone in the band had the freedom to improvise, as long as the basic structure was adhered to.

What about your work with Michael McClure? How much freedom do you enjoy in your duo performances?

We do maybe 15 to 20 poems. Each piece has a rhythmic foundation that I've predetermined: Is this going to be bluesy? Is this going to be lyrical? Am I going to put some Balinese gamelan things in here? I know the rhythmic structure and perhaps the chordal structure for each piece. But I don't know how I'm going to get from one section to another; that's the improvisation, just like when Coltrane would play "My Favorite Things," he knew what he was going to play but he didn't know where it would go. Michael reads his poems and listens to what I'm playing, then gives me spaces. For instance, one of his poems starts with the word "osprey," so I play an osprey; I don't even know what key I'm doing it in, but it's a written part. Another piece starts, "I'm the eagle in the whirlpool," so I play an *Em9* whirlpool kind of sound.

It sounds very similar to jamming on a jazz chord chart.

It's exactly the same thing. The only difference between jazz and poetry as the beats did it in the '50s and what we do is that I'm not blowing. I'm accompanying his poetry. I'm playing his poetry. I've got his poems in front of me, he has his poems on a music stand, and I read the poetry as he's reading it. I've got little notation marks showing where I'm going with it.

Does McClure improvise at all?

He sticks pretty much to the text. He changes tempos, he changes spaces, he changes emphasis, and he changes the tone of the reading. But he's playing the melody, and the melody is his spoken words.

Why are you working with McClure, as opposed to any other poet?

Mainly because he's an American transcendentalist. He's spiritual, he's ecological, he understands the vibrations of the planet and what it's gonna take to heal it. We try to add a little balm to the fractured psyches of the young people who come to see us. It's getting kinda tragic out there. Kids are just lost, man! We play at various universities, and kids come up to me after the concert and say, "We weren't there for the '60s. Do you think we missed out on it?" I say, "No, you haven't missed anything. You can create the same thing we did."

What exactly was created in the '60s? When we were college students in the '60s, we were saying, "Why should we go along with the world the way it is? Why should we go along with rape of the environment and exploitation of the workers? Let's change the world, give everybody a fair break, and nurture the planet." This is the Garden of Eden, if that's what we want it to be. We are the caretakers of this planet. We were not put here to dominate the Earth; we were put here to make sure that it works perfectly in harmony. That's what the intellect can do. That's what our spirituality can do. That whole thing has been lost, but all you have to do is snap your fingers and say, "By God, we're gonna do it!" The future starts tomorrow, and it belongs to us. We can do anything we want with it.

You want to heal the planet? You want to dance and sing and have joyous sex and men and women living together in beautiful loving harmony? Or do you want to fight and have war and chop the trees down? You know you can't chop the trees down. Stop it! Stop chopping the trees down! Stop putting artificial fertilizer on the ground! Stop eating junk foods! Eat what's in season! And the world will keep functioning. It's very simple.

Many of the problems you describe were on the '60s agenda as well. Does this mean that your generation dropped the ball?

That's one of the big questions that my wife Dorothy and I talk about every once in a while. What happened? When we were in college, thousands of people ingested psychedelics and broke on through to the other side and experienced the timeless story of man's quest for enlightenment. Thousands of acid heads joined the ranks of the spiritual people. Then something happened. Materialism turned their heads around or squashed that spirituality out of them.

Maybe all these spiritual acid heads eventually got too old for college and had to start earning a living and paying taxes in the real world.

You're right. When you have to go out and get a job, then the little compromises begin. One leads to another, and pretty soon you've lost your soul, and Kundalini has slipped back down. When that Kundalini power uncoils itself up your spine and your consciousness, and your crown chakra explodes into the universe, and you realize that we are all one and we are all God and we are all the universe, it's a marvelous feeling. But it can slip back down into the lower three chakras, and I guess that's what happened.

Plus, a lot of people wanted to get stuff for free in the '60s. Life was free, therefore everything should be free. People would come to our concerts saying, "Hey, we're hip! Let us in for free!" They didn't want to pay, but you must pay the piper. You can dance to the piper's tune, but you also have to pay the piper. So now the hero's journey is to fight the bastards, to fight the corruption, to fight those subtle things they lay on you for a couple of bucks: "Hey, come on! Ya wanna go for the big bucks?" Well, what the hell are you gonna do with those big bucks? Get a bigger car? You don't need a bigger car. The whole point is to get a smaller car that runs more efficiently. You don't need a big house. You don't need to live in a mansion.

It seems that the Doors confronted this same problem years ago, when you considered selling the rights to "Light My Fire" for Buick to use in a commercial.

We thought it would be a good idea, not so much to make money off of the song but to get rock and roll on television. At that time, in '67, rock and roll was not on television. They had a couple of little Saturday afternoon dance shows, where you could see rock and roll. But for rock and roll to actually penetrate the mainstream, that could be one of the most subversive things you could do. Right in your living room, right in America's living room, here's psychedelic rock and roll! Jim Morrison, God bless him, said, "No, man. Let's not do it, because that's the ultimate trap." And, of course, he was right. Falling in with those guys would have led us to what's happening today. I mean, there's Eric Clapton, man, playing for a beer commercial.

So idealism and naïveté went hand-in-hand in those golden days.

Yeah. We had no idea how terrible it could actually be, and just how powerful the Devil could be—that dark, greedy, rapacious, grasping side of humanity. But now we're seeing it, man. We're cutting down the fucking rainforests! What are we gonna breathe? Where's the oxygen gonna come from? They don't care, man. Nobody cares. They just gotta get more money, so they can get—what? A bigger house? For what? I get scared in a big house. Night comes, and it's spooky. The wind blows. . . .

How does this dark side of humanity manifest itself in today's music?

Well, for one thing, when I listen to songs on the radio, I can't tell who the soloist is anymore. Nor can I pick out the band. I can identify jazz musicians and classical pieces, but with rock I have a tough time saying, "Oh, that's so-and-so." Now, I love what's happened with synthesizers. It's absolutely fabulous. For the most part, urban contemporary music has great dance beats and great synthesizer sounds. But who's playing it all? I have no idea.

Are you saying that's because the emphasis today in mainstream rock is on conforming to commercial ideas, rather than developing riskier unique approaches?

I guess it is. Or is it conforming to what we think reality is supposed to be? See,

I look on this in psychedelic terms, and I see that it goes deeper than just conforming to what's going to sell. I think it's toeing the line of Western civilization—the Judeo-Christian-Moslem myth. Because the Millennium is coming. We're finished.

Exactly how is all this reflected in modern music?

Spiritually, psychologically, you will not go over the line. This is how heavy metal is supposed to be. This is how rap is supposed to be. Contemporary dance music must be this way. You cannot vary that, unless you're an iconoclast. And if an iconoclast actually does vary these standard musical forms, he or she may actually be varying the standard forms of civilization as we know it. I don't think anybody is willing to take that chance, man. I don't think anybody is willing to take the hero's journey, to vary not only the urban contemporary dance mix [*falls into dramatic whisper*] but to vary the whole . . . fucking . . . thing!

So times are even tougher now for creative artists than they were in the Doors era.

Absolutely, because we broke through. For a moment, the young people said, "Hey, we're taking over, man!" It was a real battle. The adult world had no idea how much power we had. Now they do know. Now they know that these kids, these artists, must be stopped. The first thing a fascist regime must do is to stop the artists, because the artists are the free thinkers, and invariably along with free thinking goes free love. The fascists will not allow you to think free. If you think free, perhaps you won't consume. And if you don't consume, then commercial advertising goes down the toilet. Then what happens to our television and radio shows? They have to go off the air. But that's what we've got to do. We've got to have more public access. It's got to be unsponsored. Art should be unsponsored. Either that or give the artist some bucks and say, "Hey, support yourself, man."

Your point is that although speed metal, for instance, might sound raucous and incendiary, it has very little destabilizing impact within a society that has learned to recognize, label, and thereby emasculate it.

Exactly.

So since you can make practically any kind of music these days and still not be perceived as a threat to the social order, what would you do if you were a young musician today? How would you approach playing music?

I would go neo-psychedelic, and I would take every member of the band on Joseph Campbell's hero's journey. I would find the truth of the ancient myths in today's society. Jim Morrison had a great line: "Let's reinvent the gods, all the myths of the ages. Celebrate symbols from deep elder forests." We've got to go pantheist.

Is this a tactic you're following on any specific projects?

Well, my son Pablo and I have been getting the bamboo jungle together. He's my percussionist and computer expert. I'll do sampled and synthetic sounds of the equatorial belt around the world. Here's the good side of what's happening: World music is coming. World beat music is the most exciting thing I've seen in the past 15 years. I can't get enough of this blending of India and Africa and Polynesia.

Of course, people were exploring polycultural music in the '60s too. The difference was that George Harrison bought a sitar and plucked away on it whereas today we're hearing the practitioners of world music first-hand.

Right. We can play with them, and they can play with us. Africa! The power of Africa! And the Nubians, our black brothers! Somebody said to me, "Ray, what do you think of rap?" I said, "I gotta tell ya, I'm waiting for the Nubians."

Are you talking specifically about people from Nubia?

No, Nubia meaning the American Pan-Africa movement. The people who call themselves Nubies. It's a generic term for the seeds of Africa, the pollen of Africa, the shaman of Africa, the pantheistic deities. It's time to let Dionysus and Pan break loose. When that starts to happen, it's going to be very scary for the Establishment, the same way the Doors and the Stones were scary for the Establishment. We, who are getting behind it, are going to say, "This is a music of love and fun and excitement." Sure, there's danger, and there's weirdness in there, and it gets spooky, and you talk about death. But in confronting death, you find an incredible joyousness and strength to live your life in a harmonious way. Music has got to have that spooky element. It's got to have power. The music is gonna have the power, because the baby boom will be relinquishing power soon—certainly aesthetic power. They have financial power, and they'll come into political power, and they'll take over the corporations. But their younger brothers and sisters and their children are the ones who will look back to the '60s and say, "That's what we want to do. That is the spiritual emphasis that is lacking in our lives."

Yet it's the elder siblings and the parents, the targets of this youthful revolt, who defined that spiritual emphasis in their own adolescence.

Ain't that a bitch, man? Robert Frost came to the crossroads and took the road less travelled. And Robert Johnson too! The hellhound is there, and he's on your trail. The city lights are to the right, and the forest is to the left. You can choose to run to the safety of the city lights, where the hellhound can't get you, or you might go off into the forest. As an artist, certainly as a reader of *Keyboard*, since everybody who buys your magazine is an aspiring artist, you have to travel the road less travelled. You cannot serve both God and Mammon.

When you buy a new instrument, you're buying the same package of sounds you hear being played by artists you can't distinguish on the radio. How do you use these tools to follow the less-travelled path?

First of all, you have to play the licks you've heard on the radio. You have to be as good as the guys who are playing, so you go for that. There's nothing wrong with imitating other people's styles when you're starting out. Then, at some point—it doesn't matter what age it happens—you begin to become an adult artist. Now, what does it mean to be an artist? An artist is a person who dares to bring the messages of his unconscious into reality. As musicians, we affect the body more directly than any other artist. The painter affects the eyes, the writer affects the mind, we affect the body. We have the ability to change the vibrational patterns of the body. We can harmonize with the body, heal the body, or put it into a negative state, or a frenzied state. By echoing, through music, the status quo, we can even put the body into a strange consumptive state. But as artists, we have to go beyond the status quo. You do that by examining yourself and by reading some books. Musicians have to read, man. I don't find enough musicians reading poetry. Somewhere in one of those books, either in philosophy or poetry, you're gonna find some passage that says, "The saxophone player had It." That is when you become an individual musician—when you begin to explore what *It* is.

Portions of this article originally were published in the February 1991 issue of Keyboard *magazine.*

FOR MORE ON RAY MANZAREK

Ray Manzarek continues to perform music and spoken word events. He's got a ton going on; you can connect with him at his official website, www.raymanzarek.us.

A SELECTED RAY MANZAREK BIBLIOGRAPHY AND DISCOGRAPHY

Ray Manzarek was and is the embodiment of the creativity of the '60s. If you want to read more about his times and his music, pick up a copy of his book about his experiences as a member of the Doors.

Light My Fire (1999, Berkeley Trade)

Ray Manzarek's work with the Doors remains some of the most powerful and influential music to come out of the '60s. His solo records are brilliant extensions of the philosophies and ideas he expresses in this interview.

AS A SOLO ARTIST
2008 *Ballads Before the Rain*
2006 *Love Her Madly*
1997 *The Doors: Myth and Reality*
1983 *Carmina Burana*
1974 *The Whole Thing Started With Rock and Roll, Now It's Out of Control*

WITH THE DOORS
1972 *Full Circle*
1971 *L.A. Woman*
1970 *Morrison Hotel*

1969 *Soft Parade*
1968 *Waiting for the Sun*
1967 *Strange Days*
1967 *Doors*

WITH NITE CITY
1978 *Golden Days, Diamond Nights*
1977 *Nite City*

WITH ECHO AND THE BUNNYMEN
1987 *Echo and the Bunnymen*

THE
KEYBOARDISTS
OF THE
GRATEFUL
DEAD

BY ROBERT L. DOERSCHUK

INTRODUCTION

IN THESE TIMES OF sequenced grooves and whip-crack backbeats, there is no greater anomaly in music than the Grateful Dead. Everything that makes them unique is precisely the opposite of what makes for success in the modern music marketplace. Their rhythm is as loose as an old pair of shoes. Arrangements seem more a matter of accident than forethought. Solos rummage aimlessly through the instrumental clutter, as amiably unconcerned as an absent-minded lecturer groping for a topic sentence. Voices whine and waver in precarious harmony. Twin percussionists flail manfully yet still manage to accomplish essentially what one drummer with above-average chops could pull off alone.

NOTE TO THIS EDITION: Jerry Garcia passed away in 1995, after which the band ceased to exist as a regularly performing group. Vince Welnick died at 55 in 2006 following a battle with cancer and after a prolonged period of estrangement from the band. Surviving band members continue to perform in a variety of configurations.

Frankly, the whole Dead phenomenon is bewildering. Yet it is also undeniable. They endure. Like hoary old mastodons they tread from venue to venue, long after the rest of their species has vanished with the psychedelic ice age.

And they make few concessions toward changing times. The Beach Boys play Vegas, the Stones hobnob with the hoi polloi. But the Dead do more or less what they were doing in the mid-'60s in San Francisco's Fillmore Auditorium and Avalon Ballroom. They still stand motionless onstage. They still turn their backs and tune interminably between songs. After nearly three decades in the business, they remain—by some definitions, at least—definitively unprofessional.

Clearly, though, they must be doing something right, given the legendary loyalty they inspire. Their fans—the barefooted, serape-wrapped, addled, and organic innocents known to the world as Deadheads—are, like their heroes, a singular breed. That, of course, is part of the secret: To maintain such devotion to a band so oblivious to the ebb and flow of fashion, one would have to be unusual. And, perhaps, forgiving.

For, as the Dead themselves would admit, there can be much to forgive in their concerts. Buoyed by the patience of their listeners, the group takes its time. A song might begin imperceptibly, emerging from a hodge-podge of guitar doodles and drum thumps like a tortoise from a swamp. It might be one of their classics, or it might be something like "Reelin' and Rockin'" or "I Used to Love Her"—songs shunned by even the most retro garage bands. Then, a few minutes later, having more or less reached agreement on what they're playing, everyone might start meandering away from the tune: Typically, Phil Lesh's bass line begins spinning a counter-melody around Jerry Garcia's high, milky guitar lines, while Bob Weir tries stretching the rhythm with off-beat six-string hits, and the keyboardist—most recently, Tubes alumnus Vince Welnick—splatters colors and lines of his own into the mix.

Anyone who saw, say, Janet Jackson's last tour would be mystified by all this. For minute after minute, the Dead drone on over unsteady tempos. Where Jackson fans, their attention spans perhaps truncated by MTV, apparently need some kind of a jolt—a geyser-like flame jet, for instance, or dancers hot-footing like sped-up video holograms—every few seconds, Deadheads are in no hurry. They'll beatifically groove over every second of a 40-minute "Dark Star." In fact, at one recent show this writer saw nearly 15,000 people begin dancing to the Dead's opening count-off. The band hadn't even played its first note, and already its fans were being transported by the anticipated beat.

At every level, from the parking lots filled with time-warped waifs holding signs that read "I need a miracle" to the stage itself, the Dead experience is unique. Normal rules do not apply, a fact that might perplex most keyboard players afforded the opportunity to play with these guys: "After forgetting everything I know about quantizing, editing, orchestrating, and building grooves . . . what do I do now?"

Well, first of all, you don't worry too much about fitting into any kind of a formula based on what previous keyboard players have done with the Dead. For

INTRODUCTION

Tom Constanten with the Aoxomoxoa *lineup of the Grateful Dead, circa 1969. Clockwise, from upper left: Tom Constanten (keyboards), Bob Weir (guitar, vocals), Bill Kreutzmann (drums, percussion), Ron "Pigpen" McKerman (keyboards, percussion, vocals), Phil Lesh (bass, vocals), Mickey Hart (drums, percussion), Jerry Garcia (guitar, vocals).* Photo by Herb Greene

reasons we'll let the mystics ponder, the keyboard position is the only part of the band's lineup that has undergone personnel changes since the group began gigging in the mid-'60s, and each new keyboardist has managed to inject a different stylistic fix into the Dead sound. On their earliest records, Ron "Pigpen" McKernan, the son of a San Francisco disc jockey, manned Vox Continental and Hammond B-3 organs. His playing drew heavily from the blues tradition. Though not technically adept, he was able to adapt his funky riffs and fills to some of the

Dead's more experimental efforts, particularly on *Anthem of the Sun*. Still, Pigpen's main contribution involved galvanizing the band on R&B-style rave-ups through his vocals and benign biker persona.

In 1969, the band recruited Tom Constanten as a supplementary keyboardist. His approach, tempered by extensive studies in Europe and at Mills College with masters of the European avant-garde, differed dramatically from Pigpen's earthy work. In his ten brief months with the band, Constanten left several memorable marks, mainly on *Aoxomoxoa* and *Live Dead*. According to Blair Jackson in *Grateful Dead: The Music Never Stopped*, "Constanten contributed wonderful tonal and harmonic ideas . . . He is the only keyboardist who seemed completely comfortable with the group's free-form interstellar journeys." The verdict was hardly unanimous, though; Constanten's colleague and longtime friend in the Dead, Phil Lesh, would later observe, "TC never got over a certain stiffness. He couldn't swing . . . and that was a problem." By early 1970, he had left to pursue other projects, and Pigpen was once more left in charge of the keyboard parts.

Unfortunately, Pigpen's heavy boozing soon took its toll on his work. By mid-'71, he was missing many Dead gigs; within two years he would be dead at age 27. In part to pick up the slack, pianist Keith Godchaux was admitted to the group during the fall of '71. The son of a professional pianist, he animated many Dead records and concerts with facile piano parts; on such albums as *Mars Hotel*, he was all over each arrangement, adding spice and fire while never disrupting the band's groove. By the end of the decade, though, there were problems here as well. The biggest involved Godchaux's disinterest in playing anything other than piano; beyond that, his lifeless stage demeanor, and his wife Donna's erratic performance as a backup singer, exceeded even the Dead's limits of tolerance. Late in '79, he agreed to leave the group. Less than a year later, after playing with a local Bay Area band called Ghosts and doing some shows with Dave Mason, Godchaux was killed in a car wreck.

Just before Godchaux's death, the next in the parade of Dead keyboardists, Brent Mydland, made his debut with the group. Mydland was, in a sense, a synthesis of all who had preceded him on the job. Trained on piano since age seven and honed on fusion gigs and L.A. studio dates, he had chops that rivaled Constanten's and Godchaux's, yet he played with a feel and sense of drive that evoked memories of Pigpen. Most significantly, Mydland wasn't afraid of music technology. His synth parts were clean, tight, and timbrally refreshing, lending an almost contemporary sheen to late-vintage Dead albums such as *Go to Heaven* and *In the Dark*. His death in 1990 as a result of a drug overdose was perhaps the greatest of all the blows suffered by the band over the years.

Even so, the Dead roll on, as apparently unstoppable as time itself. In the early '90s, they appeared onstage with two keyboardists. One, Vince Welnick, hired on after an audition; other aspirants for the job included T Lavitz and veteran Starshipper Pete Sears. After a long spell with the Tubes and several challenging projects with Todd Rundgren, Welnick played with a sense of discipline that made it easier for him to pick up the 140-song Dead list in less than two weeks of rehearsal. But, on the other hand, discipline can be a liability with this particular band, unless coupled with a willingness to explore the ragged edges of collective improvisation. Judging by his recent appearances with the group, Welnick's progress in this direction is steady.

Sharp-eyed observers will note that there has been another keyboardist working with Welnick on many early-'90s Dead dates. Behind a nine-foot Baldwin planted at the edge of stage left, Bruce Hornsby has been pounding out piano parts with a touch made inimitable on his own hit records. Since his days of playing with a copy band specializing in Dead material, Hornsby has been intrigued by the challenge of finding a way of fitting into their formula. Clearly, he's found that the same method used by every other keyboardist in the band's history works for him as well: Play what you play best, keep your eyes and ears open for cues to solo, and trust that the band's and your instincts will grope together in some sort of synchronous way.

Here, again, is one of the Dead's many paradoxes. Pigpen's gut-bucket organ, Constanten's experimental touches, Godchaux's dancing fills, Mydland's stone-pro polish, Welnick's Tubes-tempered tightness, and Hornsby's powerful crystalline piano chords all affected the sound of the group, but it's the sameness of the sound over the band's lifetime that's most striking. In their flexibility, the Dead have maintained their identity. Even with Welnick driving a complex MIDI rig, a '91 Dead concert is essentially identical in feel and sound to their old acid trip jams. They are flower power's answer to the Glenn Miller Band.

Following are profiles of and interviews with three of the band's keyboardists: Tom Constanten, Brent Mydland, and Vince Welnick.

TOM
CONSTANTEN

THE LONG ROAD FROM DARMSTADT TO "DARK STAR"

AT FIRST GLANCE, Tom Constanten's self-description as an "urban folk pianist" seems to fit. His piano—an ancient upright Pease, replete with nicks, scratches, and rococo case carvings—seems folky enough. And every Saturday morning, he drives into San Francisco to play rambly, new-agey piano segues on West Coast Weekend, a local answer to Prairie Home Companion, complete with genial baritone host and "aw, shucks" vignettes.

Only dedicated readers of the Dead fanzine *Relix* know the truth about Constanten. Before settling into his current comfy routine, he led another life, as a member of the then-infamous Grateful Dead. In fact, Constanten played a key role in steering the band away from its bluesy roots toward a more experimental realm. With former college roommate Phil Lesh, he created the prepared piano and tape music collage on "That's It for the Other One," from *Anthem of the Sun*, conjuring bumps, squeaks, and other noises of sufficient obscurity to dazzle nascent Deadheads. On subsequent albums he added dimension to the band's less adventurous efforts, particularly on "St. Stephen" from *Live/Dead*, where his gently sustaining organ is a tightrope on which Jerry Garcia's quavering vocals teeter.

Before joining the Dead, Constanten led yet another mysterious life, this one as a student of European avant-garde music. With Lesh he took classes from the provocative experimental composer Luciano Berio at Oakland's Mills College. On Berio's recommendation, Constanten pursued advanced study with Karlheinz Stockhausen and other innovators at the Ferienkurse für Musik in Darmstadt, West Germany in 1962 and '63, many of whom had cut their compositional teeth on Schoenberg's serial techniques. The experience remains a milestone in his musical development.

"I was very much influenced by the people teaching there," he recalls.

"But I was already wading out of the serial ocean. I had gotten to the point where I realized that, in terms of the listener's perception, the tone series is not where the piece is happening. It might be a convenient construct to enable you to throw some notes together, but it's not what it is about the piece that communicates. Serialism was like a boat we had taken in crossing a lake. It was now hitting ground, and I was thinking, 'Hey, time to get off.'"

Soon Constanten found himself in Brussels, studying with Henri Pousseur. "He was evolving a post-serialist system whereby he could control interval proportions more directly," Constanten explains. "The thing I had noticed about certain Webern pieces is that while you have major sevenths and minor ninths to contradict the octave and keep the piece atonal, you also have—in the *Concerto for Nine Instruments, Op. 24*, for instance—a lot of thirds. Other Webern pieces—the *Variations, Op. 30*—have a lot of fourths and fifths. But the appearance of these intervals is determined by the series. Pousseur was working with a system that would let you deal with these interval proportions directly. That's what I was getting into."

Constanten did continue to use serial techniques. In fact, one of his larger works at that time, for 23 instruments, was based closely on Webern's techniques. But by the time he came back to the States, the young composer was getting restless within the confines of 12-tone discipline. During a stint in the Air Force, he gained access to an IBM 1401 computer, which he used to compose several post-serialist works. He also wrote several orchestral works, which were performed by the Pops Orchestra in his hometown of Las Vegas. Still, it took a major cultural shock to knock Constanten out of the "art music" loop and into the bubbling cauldron of rock and roll.

It happened, of course, in San Francisco's Haight-Ashbury. While stationed in Denver during the mid-'60s, Constanten visited his old friend Phil Lesh while on leave. Immediately he fell in with the Dead. "I was already planted in the garden by the time I began smelling the roses," he smiles. "The first time I ever went to a rock show, it was with the Dead. They had something that avant-garde art music didn't have, and probably never will: a vast audience. You almost have to be a graduate student to enjoy some of these experimental pieces, but rock music attracted a larger audience, so you could say things from a platform and there would be people there to listen."

Immediately after mustering out of the Air Force, Constanten moved to the Bay Area and joined the Dead. He and Pigpen alternated on keys, depending on the nature of the song; only once, at a gig in Cincinnati where two organs were available, did they play simultaneously. Though perfectly happy to share the keyboard role, Constanten chafed at having to play the band's wheezy Vox Continental. "I didn't like the sound it put out at all," he says. "There was something about the Continental in that particular band that grated. The Dead's guitars were these strands of gold and filaments of light, but the Vox was like a hunk of chrome. I had terribly mixed emotions about everything I was playing because the sound didn't please me. After a bit of moving, shaking, and agitating, I convinced them to let me play a Hammond B-3, which I was able to enjoy a bit more."

Generally, Constanten kept a low profile in Dead shows. His impact on the band, though sizable, was subtle; it nudged rather than overwhelmed, especially on the freer pieces, which seemed like familiar ground to Constanten, thanks to his experiments in Cage-style aleatoric music. "It's no coincidence that there was more organ on records by Lee Michaels or Keith Emerson, because it was their bands," he points out. "The Grateful Dead, as freaky and far-out as they got, were Jerry Garcia's backup band to a large extent. So there wasn't any room. The rainforest was already filled up. I was a seedling, and I couldn't see any sunlight. On top of that, there was the amplification problem. There was always a problem in balancing the keyboard volume. You get Jerry Garcia with four Fender Twin Reverbs turned up to ten; his *mezzo-piano* was louder than my *forte*. My major frustration was not being able to find enough turf to even set up a tent in the sonic texture, and scarcely having time when there was a break to make something happen. I'd get solos sometimes when Jerry would break a string, but even then he'd go back and restring his guitar as fast as he could."

Today, 20 years after parting with the band, Constanten still seems sensitive about his departure. "It's like the monkey trap with the apple and the bottle," he muses. "It's designed so that the apple will fit through the neck of the bottle, and the monkey's hand will fit through, but his hand with the apple in it won't, so you come back at the end of the day and find these monkeys with their hands stuck in bottles. With the Grateful Dead, the keyboard is the apple in the bottle. They want the apple but, to sum it up rather coarsely, I don't think they're willing to grant the keyboardist enough turf to develop as an entity."

Aside from his radio gig, Constanten has plenty to keep him busy these days: He's teaching privately; working on a book; recording solo cassettes; finishing a CD of sonatas by Haydn, Beethoven, and Schubert; touring occasionally with legendary Dead lyricist Robert Hunter; recording with fringe guitarist Henry Kaiser. Yet, inevitably, the past is always in the air. Leaning back on his couch—an old floppy number that may itself date back to the halcyon days of psychedelia—Constanten reflects, "Sometimes it all seems like ancient history, and sometimes it seems like yesterday. At any given moment, it could bounce back and forth between those extremes. Really, those days were like experience bulimia. Part of the excitement and adventure of the '60s was having the freedom to experiment, and to fail. Formats nowadays tend to discourage that. Even on *West Coast Weekend* we're being dragged kicking and screaming toward increased formatting.

"But people forget that the times were just as conservative in the early '60s as they are now. Then it was McCarthyism. Nowadays, just because we don't have as compact a name, that doesn't mean we don't have the same sort of enemy. I say it's time to revitalize the giant and wake him up again."

BRENT
MYDLAND

Brent Mydland: "I used to think that the Dead sounded looser than they sound to me now. I'd think, 'Man, why don't they rehearse?' But now I know the reason."
Photo by Jay Blakesberg

GETTING TIGHT WITH THE LOOSEST BAND IN THE UNIVERSE

ON **APRIL FOOL'S DAY**, 1979, the piano, organ, and synthesizer bench in the Grateful Dead was turned over to Brent Mydland. Born in Munich, Germany, but raised near San Francisco, Mydland took piano lessons for about eight years before deciding around 1967, when he was in high school, to dump the classical disciplines and get into rock and roll. "It was," he recalls, "like learning to play all over again."

His first band, appropriately named Fog, was not quite the Emerson, Lake & Palmer of its day. "We had a tone-deaf bass player," he remembers fondly. "If you had more than three notes on just the roots, he'd get lost. He couldn't tell if he had the wrong bass note to the chord. And we had a drummer who knew two beats, both in four; one was fast and one was slow. The guitar player knew all the barre chords—no leads—and at that time I was pretty much learning too."

But that was all right, Brent explains, because, "I had a small Thomas organ, and nobody could hear it. I ended up getting a Kalamazoo, though. I was so happy when I got it, because you could hear it. Sounded like crap, but you could hear it."

Mydland missed the Haight-Ashbury experience that spawned the Grateful Dead, Jefferson Airplane, Quicksilver Messenger Service, and all the other bands that blasted their anthems of drugs, love, and celebration around the world. He was aware, though, of what was going on. "One of the first dozen albums I got was the first Grateful Dead album," he says. "I got it for the name. I used to go out and buy albums for their covers, like the Mothers of Invention's *Freak Out*. I got ripped off on a lot of albums that way, but I enjoyed a lot of them too. The Grateful Dead was one of the ones I actually liked. I liked the Beach Boys at that time. I probably even liked the Monkees!"

Brent hit the road to L.A. and landed a job with an acoustic duo named Batdorf & Rodney. When they split up, Brent and Batdorf joined with Greg Collier in an acoustic trio; two guitars, one piano. "We didn't have a name," he notes, "until someone at Arista came up with Silver, so we decided, what the hell, it's as good as anything."

The Dead connection came about when Silver's drummer, John Mauceri, managed to play a bit on the side with several well-known performers, including longtime Grateful Dead rhythm guitarist Bob Weir. The Dead being in the midst of an inactive period, Weir was involved with his own band, Kingfish. When Silver split up, Mydland followed Mauceri over to Weir's band, where he stayed for roughly a year and a half. The progression from there to the Dead, after Godchaux's demise, was natural: "I came in, played with them, and that was it. As far as I know, they never auditioned anyone else."

Joining a new band frequently demands a knack for quick musical adaptability, but if the band happens to be well known, and especially if the band happens to be the Grateful Dead, with perhaps the most demonstrative and loyal fans in the world of rock, the transition could be even more complicated. "I think I'm still in a period of getting accepted," he says with a laugh. "When I first got in the band, a lot of people would say, 'Keith. Only Keith.' I think a lot of them are so out of it that they don't really know he's gone. Some of 'em even think Pigpen's still alive."

But by and large there were no real hassles in joining the band. "The biggest challenge was probably the fact that the keyboards haven't had that much of a role in their music," he muses. "On some of the tunes, it doesn't matter if I'm playing or not! What they told me was, 'Don't worry about playing anything you've heard before from Keith or Pigpen; that's not what we want. Just play what you feel, be yourself, and think of dynamics.' So on some songs we do that had Keith's keyboards, if they seemed to have a theme of some kind, I'd cop it, but otherwise I just play my own stuff."

The band's informality is especially agreeable to Brent's tastes. "The Dead is definitely a different kind of band," he states. "With every other band I've been in, we've rehearsed and rehearsed and rehearsed, down to where it's exactly the same every time you play, even right down to the solos. For us, that would be ridiculous. It might be good if the audience that sees you tonight won't see you tomorrow night, but with the Deadheads, you often see the same folks out there one gig after the next."

The band invested in some new equipment for Mydland when he joined, even buying him a Sequential Circuits Prophet-5 when they discovered he didn't have one. Unfortunately, after working a while with it, Mydland decided the instrument wasn't right for the kind of music the Dead would be playing. "Everybody in general is into the idea of having synthesizers on the tunes. The problem is that our music is so spur-of-the-moment," he points out. "I might hear something that gives me an idea to change to a different program, but by the time I'd come up with it, they'd be off on something else. I don't like to be left back there trying to figure out what to come up with. It's not the kind of group where you can work things out in advance."

In the more controlled studio environment, Mydland has contributed synthesizer parts to several Grateful Dead cuts. For example, on "Alabama Getaway," from *Go to Heaven*, he plays a Minimoog, and on "Feel Like a Stranger" he combines Prophet and Minimoog. On "Alabama," in particular, he reveals a fondness for Jan Hammer-like pitch bends in his guitar-like lead line. But, Brent adds, he doesn't utilize the technique that much onstage because of "the difference between the different synthesizers. You don't get the same response from the Prophet and Minimoog wheels, at least with mine. I really feel comfortable with my personal synthesizer, but if you get another one onstage, oops!"

Mydland no longer has his first synthesizer, also a Minimoog, and as far as he's concerned, it's just as well. "Things would just start happening to it," he laughs. "We'd just be playing along, then for no reason the modulation would kick in"—he breaks into a siren-like oscillating wail—"So I took it back to the store. But they wouldn't do anything except tell me where to take it to get it fixed. I took it back to that place for repairs so many times that I ended up writing to the Better Business Bureau and to the Moog people. Between the two of them I eventually got a new Minimoog, but by then the repair people had talked me out of using it, so I said, 'Okay, keep it in the carton, just give me credit,' which I used to buy an ARP 2600."

Eventually, though, Brent went back to a Minimoog. "I had that 2600 for about two years," he estimates, "and I wish I'd kept it for some studio stuff, but at the time I needed money, so I sold it for real cheap and got a Minimoog again. I really like the Mini now. The filter sound is so ballsy and thick, and I love how the wheels are set up."

Despite these synthesizer flavorings, Brent finds organ and piano most appropriate for the Grateful Dead sound. When it comes to picking his favorite keyboard, it's a toss-up between the two; specifically, between the Hammond B-3 and the acoustic piano. The organ goes on the road with the band, played through a miked Leslie speaker, which he shifts constantly through fast and slow vibrato. "I'm always going back and forth with it, whenever my left hand doesn't have anything to do," he says, referring to the vibrato control at the left end of the lower manual. "It's good for phrasing behind a solo. Sometimes I use the tremolo dial on the organ too, usually set on C1, sometimes C3. But actually I hardly ever do use it, because it makes things sound too much like *The Edge of Night*."

Most of the time Mydland keeps the B or B♭ presets down on the upper manual of the Hammond. He especially likes adding a touch of percussion in lower drawbar settings, but, he points out, "as far as percussion goes, you're not going to get any better than a piano." Yamaha is Brent's favorite piano; he enjoys the warm sound of the one he has at home. With the Dead, though, he prefers a sound somewhere between mellow and metallic, and even feels that a honky-tonk tone works best in several of their songs.

On the band's 1980 acoustic tour, from which the live double album *Reckoning* was compiled, Mydland played rented grand pianos, but in the usual electric concert format he uses a Yamaha CP-70 electric grand instead. "The acoustic tour was a lot of fun," he smiles. "I wish we'd do that more. It had more of a back porch feeling than the electric gigs. The piano cut through better there than the electric grand does in our regular concerts, and it felt like there was more space. Also, we did even less rehearsal than usual, so it was even more like a jam. But because I didn't quite know what was gonna happen, I was probably holding back more than I should have. Part of the reason was that we were making a live album, and I wasn't really familiar with what was happening. At that point I just wanted to leave a lot of space and make it as Grateful Dead as possible.

"I'd like to use an acoustic more often, but there's just no room for it," he shrugs. "I like the electric grand better than my Rhodes, though, for rock and roll. If you get into heavy rock stuff, where you're just going all out, the Rhodes comes out sounding too much like bells. I haven't been using it much since I started using the Yamaha. For sustaining stuff the Rhodes is real nice. You don't have to play as many notes on it; two notes on the Rhodes fills the same space as five on an acoustic."

Brent also feels that the Rhodes sounds better with effects devices than the electric or acoustic grands. For example, on his solo in "Easy to Love You," from *Go to Heaven*, he sends it through an Eventide Harmonizer and doubles the line with a steel drum player. He has used a small preamp with both the Rhodes and the acoustic piano, however, though he would eventually like to substitute a graphic EQ for it, since "You could get the same sound and control with it, but without the preamp hiss."

The electric grand, organ, and Minimoog basically constitute Brent's concert setup, all of them EQ'd and miked through the P.A. Occasionally, though, a different instrument may be thrown in. Last December Mydland acquired a Prophet-10, with which he is phasing out the Prophet-5 in studio work with the Dead; possibly it will be brought onstage in the future. "The Prophet-5 I had was a prototype," he notes. "Any time you wanted to change a patch, you had to go back to the beginning. On the updated synthesizers you just turn a knob, but before that you had to turn off the whole section. Now it seems like I'll change each program in it just a little bit. They're all not quite right for me. A lot of times I'll just do something minor, like turn off the sustain, and that'll make the program useful. It's also far better than the 5 as far as tuning goes."

Then there was Brent's first encounter with a harpsichord. This unlikely addition to his keyboard arsenal was rented during the acoustic tour for use on one song, "China Doll"; its tinkling fills can be heard on *Reckoning*. "I never did feel comfortable with that thing," he laughs. "I kept missing the sustain pedal and the control of dynamics. You try to hit something soft, and it just doesn't come out soft. You also have to be real deliberate when you play it. If you want to play a note, you've got to mean it, as if you were trying to play everything loud."

There were other problems with it too. "They brought one into Radio City Music Hall [in New York] for a gig, and a lot of it didn't work," he says. "There were stops on it that didn't do anything, and other stops I'd never seen before. I

BRENT MYDLAND

Brent Mydland onstage with the Dead in 1982. His hands are on a Hammond B-3, and to his right is a Minimoog atop a Yamaha CP-70 electric piano. Photo by Jon Sievert

couldn't figure out how to get the sound I had gotten off the one I used at the Warfield [in San Francisco]. I didn't even have a chance to play it before the gig, so I did all my experimenting with it in the show. It tends not to work for rock and roll too well, so to play the licks that fit the instrument, I kept picturing Bach or somebody like that, with the long gray wig, in my mind."

This devil-may-care attitude is part and parcel of life with the Grateful Dead. "Most of the time we don't get enough people in for a rehearsal," he relates. "Maybe three people come in, and three people don't make it. The rehearsals take place onstage more than anywhere else. The tunes are worked up real loose: 'Okay, that's pretty much how it goes. Good enough! We'll tighten it up onstage.' If it gets too tight, we'd sound the same at each concert, and that's not where the Dead is coming from."

Understandably, performances can vary from night to night. "Sometimes the tunes really stretch out to where I can't believe it," he says. "I'll look over and ask, 'Is it time yet? No? Okay.' Sometimes they'll call a song I've never played with them before. Usually it's something pretty simple that I can pick up; they don't pull anything that's really off the wall—very often. But they have done that. One time they pulled out 'Stella Blue.' For me, that was a case of 'when in doubt, don't.'"

Brent's long-term plans tie in with the Dead. "It's hard to imagine the group breaking up, but then again," he muses, "it's hard to imagine something like this being around forever. Who knows for sure? I used to think that the Dead sounded looser than they sound to me now. I'd think, 'Man, why don't they rehearse?' But now I know the reason. Tightness is not what the band stands for. If things are too planned out, it can take away my interest. But I like the way we work. There are no weirdness trips. It's more like an open marriage, like going out and doing jam sessions for a living."

From the Tubes to the Dead: Vince Welnick with a Yamaha CP-70 supporting an ARP String Ensemble. Photo by Tom Wechsler

VINCE WELNICK

INTO THE AGE OF TECHNO-PSYCHEDELIA

WHEN WE MET WELNICK at the Dead's offices in 1991—an appropriately ramshackle Victorian somewhere north of the Golden Gate Bridge—he brought along the group's MIDI mastermind, former Stevie Wonder tech Bob Bralove, a fine musician in his own right; in addition to doing a virtuoso job of MIDI routing offstage, Bralove has worked closely with the band in the studio as associate producer of Built to Last and as co-author, with Bob Weir and John Barlow, of "Picasso Moon."

Conspicuously absent was Bruce Hornsby, who declined to be interviewed because, as he explained backstage before the previous night's Dead show, he was merely sitting in as a sideman, whereas Welnick was a permanent and full-fledged band member. So, hunched over a kitchen table crowded with coffee cups, bits of cheesecake, and overflowing ashtrays, we got to know this latest traveler on this leg of rock and roll's longest, strangest trip.

Although you've put together a huge MIDI system for the band, most keyboards in the show play traditional sounds, usually Bruce's piano mixed with organ samples from Vince. Why weren't there more adventurous combinations of sounds, given the band's resources?

Bralove: We've got a new organ sound, which is probably why you heard so much organ. It's actually a system I put together. Vince uses his controller to drive a bunch of [Hammond] B-3 sounds which are played by a rack of Voce DMI-64 modules and then bussed into a Niche audio-control system that's remotely controlled by the little Lexicon MRC faders. He ends up being able to play organ sounds and use these faders like drawbars to bring in harmonics, because each preset has its own overtone series. That all goes through an electronic Dynacord CLS 222 stereo Leslie simulator, with slow and fast controls in his foot pedals.

Welnick: With this system, instead of just getting the fundamental, you're getting the entire organ sound with the fundamental predominant. It's basically the sound of four organs instead of one.

Bralove: Some of the organ sounds are distorted too, like an overdriven B-3, so when Vinnie lays into it he can get that quality.

It sounds like a pretty elaborate system.

Bralove: When I started with the Dead, there were only two or three MIDI sounds onstage. As I recall, there was an E-mu Emulator II. Now there's a 32-track board for the electronic drums alone.

Welnick: Every guy in the band has got some elaborate MIDI thing going. Bob goes around and oversees it all.

What kind of MIDI system is Phil Lesh using?

Bralove: He has an MB4 MIDI Bass wired-frets system for his bass, which was built for him by [New York custom bass designer] Ken Smith. He uses it to play flute sounds or whatever else he wants.

How has MIDI affected Jerry Garcia's playing?

Bralove: The issue for a guitar player, especially for a guitar player like Jerry, is whether you can communicate finger movements, like vibrato, through MIDI. Jerry's guitar has a little sparkle to it all the time. Nothing ever sounds flat. So that has to translate through MIDI: When he's playing a trumpet sound, for instance, do his pitch-bends still sound like the way he plays?

Welnick: I love the way he can get those trumpet mouthpiece sounds by pulling up on a string. He really gets the *pfft*.

What's the source of that trumpet sound?

Bralove: Probably a Korg M1. But a lot of work goes into customizing the sounds so that they become expressive for each person using them. One of the great things about the Grateful Dead is that every member of the band has his own completely different musical world. Everyone has a different agenda for what they want from their systems.

How do the guys in the band let you know what they need from their MIDI systems?

Bralove: Everybody is different. Vinnie is an unusual case because he's jumping in on the fly, so in a way I'm taking advantage of that. He's incredibly responsive to the sounds. With everybody else, except for Mickey [Hart, drummer], if I throw some sound in as a complete surprise, it's got to be a lot more subtle. But Vinnie is right there, responding. He'll be playing something, sitting somewhere in a fat groove, and I'll hear it as horns and lay them in. All of a sudden it's twice as good as I imagined it, because he hears the horns.

Welnick: And I start thinking like a horn guy.

Bralove: In other words, it's not just layered on what he was playing before. **In effect, you're improvising along with the band.**

Bralove: Orchestrationally, yeah.

Welnick: So I don't have to go groping for sounds. I can just dedicate my mind to playing whatever the sound is at any given moment. I see a lot of synth guys who are pretty much one-handed players. Most of the time they're selecting patches and screwing around with the sounds. I don't have to do that. I let the sound somewhat dictate what I play.

There aren't many bands that will let their MIDI techs get into the act to that extent.

Welnick: Some don't have the luxury.

Bralove: And not everybody can do it. From both ends. Our songs grow by what happens onstage, especially with Bruce on piano.

Welnick: Like last night, "Foolish Heart" went into 25 minutes. We set a record. [*Laughs.*] I heard from a couple of guys that that was the best all-time Dead performance of "Foolish Heart." So the arrangement changes depending on who jumps out in front. We've even dumped the set list, so what we play is up to the whim of the band at any given moment.

Is that a new approach for you? Did you work that way with the Tubes?

Welnick: No, with the Tubes it was like, "Get your own sound. Good luck. Make it loud, too." [*Laughs.*] I had to learn to operate an Emulator and a few synthesizers, but Mike Cotten was really the synth man. He actually had the first ARP 2600, which he modified greatly. He invented a lot of really wonderful sounds. He could play better with his left hand, because his right hand was always patching. And he put together one of the first sequencers. I was never very into the technology of arriving at a sound. I wanted to go out and have it there, and just drive the damn thing. I didn't want to know about all the specifics, like electricity. I just wanted it to go. So this has turned out to be perfect. All I have to do is make sure the pedals are all down and I don't turn off the Leslie switch. There's not a whole lot I can do to screw it up. I came to this band with no gear at all. I just sat down at the stuff that Bob set up, which was mostly Brent's.

So you're working mainly with Brent Mydland's old sounds?

Bralove: That's erroneous. It's Brent's modules. Brent and I did come up with some of the sounds together for certain orchestrations, but we were only using them just after Vinnie came along. Now it's him. The more you develop the sounds, the more obvious it becomes that certain aspects of these things have to be dynamically controlled by Vince. I can't second-guess where he's gonna go. Once he's there, I can enhance it. But he's got to be able to pull those strings.

Welnick: He'll give me, like, a three-combi sound, with strings added. But those strings will be on a separate pedal, like off to the side of your plate, so you add them at will or take them out.

Do you split your controller, the Roland RD-300 keyboard, between different sounds a lot?

Welnick: No, because our sounds can be removed or added in any combination with faders and pedals.

Bralove: Some of the sounds are designed to move over the keyboard, depending on how Vinnie plays them. They have dynamic characteristics. I know, for instance, that he plays certain low-end things with a certain kind of dynamic.

Welnick: Sometimes it does sound like a keyboard split. One sound might be like a guitar on top, but it gets bigger as you move into the low end. There are other sounds where, with touch-sensitivity, it's more ethereal on top, or you have less modulation on the low end. But we don't put, like, a tuba, a calliope, and a harmonica on one keyboard.

Why did you choose the RD-300 digital piano as your controller?

Welnick: I was playing with Todd Rundgren, and he had one. I used it recording live to digital with him, and it worked out okay.

On *Nearly Human*?

Welnick: Yeah, and his new one, *Second Wind*. It seemed great because it's got 88 keys and they're weighted, and I grew up on piano. I had a [Yamaha] CP-80 electric grand with the Tubes, but those things were pretty wimpy, with no triple unisons all the way down.

How does your experience of working with the notoriously meticulous Rundgren compare with your routine with the Dead?

Welnick: The difference is that there's a lot more soloing with the Dead. In Todd's music, most of the solos were for guitar. The keyboards were dominant throughout the albums, but they were structured, with no solos. With the Dead, they'll nod at me and Bruce, and say, "Hit it!" Then we have to decide which of us is supposed to play. Sometimes we both stop at once, and neither of us hits it. [*Laughs.*] But they're very forgiving, so that inspires you to reach for the brass ring.

How did you get this gig?

Welnick: I was selling my house, and my real estate agent told me about Brent's death. At that time, for the first time in 20 years, I was free to do anything. The Tubes weren't happening. I had just finished Todd's last album. I'd never met Brent, never even saw the band with him in it. Anyway, I called Mimi Mills, who worked for the Tubes a long time and now works for Bob Weir. She got me in touch with Bob, and he said, "We are auditioning. Bruce is in the band, playing piano. We need a synth guy who can sing high harmony." So I checked out what Brent's gear was, and then I met Bob Bralove and Jerry.

That's when I realized that these were real people, and that this could be a family kind of thing. I was totally sold at that point. It was nothing about money; I just wanted to do it. So I tried out. I practiced at least an hour a day. [*Laughs.*]

Bralove would give me tapes with maybe 10 percent live cuts and tell me to check them out. I also had the CDs, but they preferred that I listen to the taped jams to get the gist of the way they play nowadays. And I started hearing more songs. It was like getting a bunch of Christmas presents. There was something in them of every style I had gone through since I was a kid—a lot more diversity than I expected, because after the '60s I was off with the Tubes and I lost track of what was going on with a lot of bands. So I was amazed at the wealth of wonderful material. Simple, yet complex and wonderful.

What about their loose approach onstage? The Dead are among the very few major league bands who get up there and essentially wing it each night.

Welnick: This is new to me, too. With the Tubes we had a production that was like a travelling circus. We had songs that ran in sequence throughout the entire tour; that was the only way we could get our props on and off. And Todd, on his gigs, would even tell the same jokes sometimes—actually, every night. [*Laughs.*]

So this is great. Everything is reproduced clearly, but nobody's lip-syncing, there's no click track going down, and no added effects. It was hard to convince myself that I was allowed that much freedom, and that I should just go for it at will. I kept waiting to seek permission to do stuff, and finally they got it through to me that I should just play. I think Bobby told me that the key emphasis with the Dead is fun. I can relate to that, so I started from there.

The toughest material must have been the really free stuff, such as "Space" and the improvised segues between songs.

Welnick: Actually, I like being in that space, when it gets to be a jam and you just take off. Being a synth player now, not playing piano that much, the jams are a lot easier for me to deal with. I have a tougher time with country tunes. The really simple is complex for me, since I'm constantly trying to change it or do something different, when it ought to stay stock in the first place. Something like "Ramble On, Rose" is very difficult for me, because you have to keep in the frame of a specific style. It was a lot more challenging to figure out what to do in a song like that than to figure out what to do with, say, "Terrapin Station."

Because "Terrapin" sticks to a relatively tight arrangement?

Welnick: Yeah, and because there's also a lot of mileage in it in terms of sounds that change between sections.

Bralove: But it's tougher for me to give you good sound when certain songs have been piano to me for such a long time. And I have to say that Vinnie is coming up with some great stuff on the country songs. To me, the fiddle things he does are some of his greatest playing.

These are single-note fiddle samples, which you play in idiomatic fiddle-like fifths?

Welnick: Yeah. It's a convincing little fiddle, too.

Bralove: Those samples are from a Kurzweil 250 RMX. Sometimes I enhance them with strings. Sometimes a single fiddle will grow into a section.

Is there any sequencing in the show?

Vince Welnick: "The arrangement changes depending on who jumps out in front. We've even dumped the set list, so what we play is up to the whim of the band at any given moment." Photo by Tom Wechsler

Welnick: Yes, there is. Bob does a lot of stuff on "Drums" and "Space."

Bralove: The drum solo has a lot of processing, and some sequencing happens. The only thing that's really new is that "Victim or the Crime" opens with a sequence, which came about from a performance of "Drums." Bobby [Weir] came up to me that night and said, "You know that sequence you're using? Let's try to throw it in front of 'Victim or the Crime.'"

So the group has no philosophical objection to sequencing?

Bralove: Not for the drums.

Welnick: I don't think you're going to hear computer-style keyboards, though.

Bralove: You have to remember that the systems are the slaves. Always the slaves. As long as it's responsive to what's happening onstage, I don't think there's any objection to anything.

What kind of sequencer do you run?

Bralove: I started off with an Alesis HR-16 drum machine, and now I have that slaved to an Akai MPC-60. I've been using software sequencers for recording; sometimes I'll record Bruce's and Vince's MIDI information for my own purposes.

Do the percussion sounds in the "Drums" sequence come from the Akai?

Bralove: Yeah, but we try to go someplace new with it so that you don't always recognize the source. It's processed and harmonized. That section of the show is meant to be a drum solo. I never want to give the impression that I'm doing something with sequencing that they [drummers Kreutzmann and Hart] couldn't do on their own.

Welnick: It sounds like it's all triggered from the drums. It's a pattern that sets up a rhythm, but the drums can vary it.

Is Bruce's piano MIDIed?

Bralove: It is. Sometimes he uses it or his accordion to drive a [Roland] Juno-106. He's got an M1 on top of his piano too, which he uses on "Stander on the Mountain."

Have you played any Dead gigs without Bruce since joining the band?

Welnick: When we started to tour last September, we did the first five or six gigs without him, then we got to Madison Square Garden for a six-show run. I did the first one alone there, and then Bruce came in. He's been with us every show since then with the exception of a couple in Europe and one recently in Denver.

How do you compensate for his absence during those shows?

Welnick: We stick the piano sounds back into what I'm doing, as many as two or three layered together to get that fat sound. That's the only difference. It doesn't affect what parts I sing.

Bralove: When Bruce is out, I make sure that Vince has got a piano all the time.

Welnick: For every song, there's at least one piano somewhere.

Bralove: If he turns on the piano sound, I'll realize that this tune is now going to be about piano. Then I might bring in, say, the huge piano.

Welnick: The twelve-footer. [*Laughs.*]

What's the source of your piano sounds?

Bralove: Well, there's the RD-300. Then there's the Kurzweil RMX, which has kind of a Steinway sound. There's the Roland MKS-20. I EQ them different- ly, depending on what's going on. Sometimes, for example, it's good to have a bright edge an octave down. There are so many things you hear from a real piano that don't quite make it on the digitals. Throwing something down an octave, just hinting at it, fills out the sound.

So Vince has to keep listening to what kind of piano sound you're giving him, in order to know how to voice his part.

Welnick: Right, especially when we get the octave-down part. You only have to touch the keyboard once to know you have to move up an octave. [*Laughs.*]

By the way, it looks like you're sitting on an actual old piano bench onstage.

Welnick: Is that what it is?

Bralove: It's a regular old piano bench, with a lift-up top.

Welnick: The very first night I played with the band, we had just finished soundcheck, and one of the guys in the crew slid over to check out my micro- phone. As soon as he sat down, the bench splintered into a hundred pieces. That would have been me on my first night out. It looked like somebody had sawed it.

Bralove: Maybe it was Brent.

Welnick: Yeah: "Look out, kid." [*Laughs.*] But before the show was on, it was magically restored, and it hasn't given out yet.

Have you studied much of what the keyboard players who preceded you did in the band?

Welnick: I would like to get a full knowledge of that in time. Unfortunately, I know very little now about what Keith [Godchaux] played. I just heard a CD they're making of a show the band did with Keith in '75 at the Great American Music Hall [in San Francisco]. Brent, of course, I heard a lot on those live tapes. I love the way he played "Foolish Heart"; I've kept true to that in how I play it. On some of the other stuff I've forgotten what he played, or even what instrument he played, so I just go for what I know. The earlier organ sounds, before we got the [Dynacord] Leslie down, were reminiscent of Pigpen, especially on "Cold

Rain and Snow." I added that Vox touch and got that sound pretty much nailed. But that's evolved too. The sounds change all the time. Also, I'm changing my style of playing all the time as I listen to the tapes and learn about what Bruce is doing. I definitely don't want to tread on what he's doing, because that Baldwin is his signature. There isn't a digital piano in the world where I can't hear the difference between it and a real grand.

Did you bring in many of your own sounds when you joined the group?

Welnick: I didn't bring anything except a big tablet of blank paper.

How is playing for Deadheads different from playing for Tubes or Rundgren fans?

Welnick: Well, for one thing, there are lots of Deadheads. But also, there's so much love out there, especially for the lowly keyboard player who normally sits in the back line and is seldom even heard over the rest of the band. With the Dead, of course, everything is so impeccably done that you could turn off the stage monitors and still play perfectly. These audiences give you great feedback, though. They really know the songs.

Are they too loving? Is it too easy to please them?

Welnick: I used to think that maybe they'd suffer from the too-easily-amused syndrome, but not since I've read some of the Deadhead magazines. They write reviews for every show, and they really put you under a microscope. If you drop a note in any given song, that's gonna be published. They love the band, no question about it. But they're critical and they're truthful. They call 'em as they see 'em.

Bralove: When I started working with the band, Brent and I were creating some new presets for different songs. We tried them out about three times. Then, at one show, I went out and took a walk through the audience.

Now, I was brand new. And somebody I had never met before walked up and started talking to me about Brent's presets—which ones he used in which songs, how we'd changed them. At that moment I realized that there were people out there listening to everything.

What about the unconverted? How would you advise listeners raised on Madonna or Depeche Mode to begin developing an appreciation for your band?

Welnick: Dump the word "quantize." Do you always want everything to be like hands going around a clock, with alarms ringing at regular intervals? That's in the Grateful Dead too, but it's done humanly. The sounds we're getting are as rich and wonderful as anything you could sequence, but we're all players putting in on the songs. A lot of quantizing and sequencing in music today stems from there only being a couple of players in a band that's putting out product, which makes that sort of thing necessary.

Sequenced pop hits usually build grooves around strong backbeats. In Dead music, the backbeats are part of a more polyrhythmic structure, so you probably have to build your grooves in a completely different way.

Bralove: I had a hard time initially with that issue, because I had been making a lot of dance records with Stevie, doing a lot of sequencing. I still love that music. A 2/4 groove, when it's done right and it has that huge feel, is fantastic. But with the Grateful Dead, the function of rhythm is slightly different. It's more alive. It's allowed to change. Tempo can move. Feel can change from one section of a song to the next.

Welnick: We don't have to sit up all night in a studio and re-sequence stuff to get our backbeats tight. I always thought the amount of energy you have to put out to work in the studio that way is brutal. I've done a lot of sequencing with the Tubes. I love doing it, but rather than try to do something tricky in programming the beat, it was usually easier to have a tricky drummer like Prairie Prince do it naturally. It's far more rewarding to get a couple of chaps together and play.

You mentioned fluctuating tempo as a characteristic of Dead performances. Frankly, that continual speeding and slowing, subtle though it is, can drive some listeners crazy.

Bralove: That's the bridge you have to cross in putting the Dead in perspective. Once you realize that tempo is allowed to live in its own form, it becomes another exciting element to music. It can change even in the middle of a solo, if somebody's starting to move and everybody else is listening.

Welnick: Bill and Mickey can change at a moment's notice. They'll grab onto something and, boom, it's the next new arrangement.

So you wouldn't consider asking the drummers to play to a click, for example.

Bralove: Well, if you go into working with this band with the idea of changing the identity of the Grateful Dead, you must be nuts.

Portions of this article were previously published in the September 1982 and March 1991 issues of Keyboard *magazine.*

FOR MORE ON THE GRATEFUL DEAD AND ITS KEYBOARDISTS

Of all the keyboardists who were associated with the Grateful Dead on a long-term basis, Tom Constanten is the only one still making music in this earthly realm. He is constantly in motion, and you can connect with him at his official website, www.tomconstanten.com.

To connect with the Dead themselves, and to see how their creative energies have manifested since Jerry Garcia's death in 1995, visit www.dead.net.

A SELECTED GRATEFUL DEAD BIBLIOGRAPHY AND DISCOGRAPHY

Books of the Dead. How cool is that? These are the best of the best, written by those who were closest to the band.

Ben Fong-Torres, *Grateful Dead Scrapbook: The Long, Strange Trip in Stories, Photos, and Memorabilia* (2009, Chronicle Books)

Blair Jackson, *Grateful Dead Gear—The Band's Instruments, Sound Systems, and Recording Sessions, From 1965 to 1995* (2006, Backbeat Books)

Jay Blakesberg, *Between the Dark and Light: The Grateful Dead Photography of Jay Blakesberg* (2002, Backbeat Books)

Listing all the Dead's studio recordings isn't hard; deciding which among their live recordings are the best examples, however, is an exercise in futility; there are so many. And that's not even including the bootleg tapes! This selection, then, contains the greatest recorded examples of the Grateful Dead live and in the studio, in our humble opinion, covering the time that they existed as a creative entity with Jerry Garcia, who died in 1995.

1991 *Infrared Roses*
1989 *Built to Last*
1987 *In the Dark*
1981 *Dead Set*
1981 *Reckoning*
1980 *Go to Heaven*
1978 *Shakedown Street*
1977 *Terrapin Station*
1975 *Blues for Allah*

1974 *From the Mars Hotel*
1973 *Wake of the Flood*
1970 *American Beauty*
1970 *Workingman's Dead*
1969 *Live/Dead*
1969 *Aoxomoxoa*
1968 *Anthem of the Sun*
1967 *The Grateful Dead*

THE PIANO
ICONS

BILLY JOEL

Billy Joel: "You want to reach those people in the back row at someplace like Madison Square Garden, and for some reason this makes you feel like you have to pound the hell out of the piano. I break bass strings constantly."
Photo courtesy of Photofest

THE PIANO MAN ROCKS ON

BY ROBERT L. DOERSCHUK

ROADSIDE JUKE JOINTS, down-home blues, and teenage sock hops—the spiritual birth-places of rock and roll. But as the audiences that were weaned on rock grow older, new roots to this musical family tree take hold and funnel fresh strains into its genealogy.

When Billy Joel first appeared on the national scene with the hit tune "Piano Man" in 1974, he introduced concepts that had previously been unfamiliar—even unwelcome—in the rock format. Earlier keyboard rockers had followed the frenzied footsteps of Jerry Lee Lewis and Little Richard, but Joel, playing perhaps to a slightly older audience, was, as his song titles indicated, the Piano Man, the Entertainer. He didn't assault the piano; he actually played it, though with enough panache to qualify him as a rock pianist through and through.

In their different ways, people like Keith Emerson, Leon Russell, and Elton John had also softened or sophisticated the traditionally pneumatic rock piano style, but Joel was a transitional figure in a different sense, providing a segue from the instrumental pyrotechnics of '60s performers to the classic song-oriented approach of the older pop composers. In his uptown New York image, not to mention his ability to write memorable tunes like "Just The Way You Are" and "New York State of Mind," he seemed a kindred soul to the Gershwins and Cole Porters of the past, and a candidate to carry on their tradition in the rhythm of the rock generation.

Was this progress or retrogression? Certainly Joel's life was easy to identify with, especially for garage band alumni now anesthetized into the cocktail piano circuit, except in that he returned to rock after paying his tip-jar dues in a Los Angeles lounge gig. Born 32 years ago in Hicksville, New York, Joel was shuttled off to his first piano lesson at age four when his parents observed his delighted reaction to a Mozart piano piece. His studies laid the groundwork for his chops on the keyboard and for his self-assurance even in the difficult times: "I had a lot of confidence in myself," he told a reporter for the *San Francisco Chronicle*. "I had been playing piano since I was four years old, so when it came to musicianship I knew I could play an instrument really well. Whatever was happening commercially didn't bother me. It was my own ideal of excellence that I had to live up to. The only thing that would let me down was if I let myself down."

Billy continued with his lessons until 1964, when the Beatles' record "A Hard Day's Night" jolted him out of scales and arpeggios and into his first band, the Echoes. Suddenly he was playing gigs several times a week with teenage intensity, and catching up on his sleep in school. The Long Island rock scene, which spawned the Young Rascals, Vanilla Fudge, and other raw-edged outfits, offered the young keyboardist an exhilarating training ground.

Billy did his first recording with the Hassles, a group he joined in 1968 after his long stretch with the Echoes (who had since transmogrified into the Lost Souls and then the Emerald Lords). They cut two albums in two years before Billy and their drummer Jon Small formed a duo. Calling themselves Attila, they recorded an LP on Epic in 1970, then vanished into history and $1.98 record bins.

The first Billy Joel solo album came in 1972. *Cold Spring Harbor* was released on Paramount, but after a six-month tour promoting the LP, Joel abruptly packed up and moved off to Los Angeles. He had had a financial dispute with his label, and decided to solve the problem by disappearing to the West Coast, where he played cocktail piano under the pseudonym Bill Martin following the breakup of his band, and buckled down to some serious songwriting. Columbia records tracked him down and signed him in 1973; *Piano Man* followed in 1974, the title cut cynically recounting his experiences as a barroom pianist.

Fast-forward 15 years to 1989, and take into account some of Joel's biggest successes in the meantime: *52nd Street, Glass Houses, The Stranger, Turnstiles,* and *Streetlife Serenade*. As with these releases, *Storm Front* showcases Joel's full-lunged vocals and, here and there, double-fisted keyboard accompaniment, mixed into a variety of musical settings. Like much of his work in the past, the songs on Storm

Front often seem more like imitations of other artists than distinctively original statements. But those who fault Joel as merely derivative miss the point. After 25 years of weathering mediocre material by bands more interested in sounding unique than sounding good, Joel seeks excellence in the work of those he respects—in the spirit of modern rock and the craft of the great songwriters from the era of great songs.

The clue to Joel's attitude lies in the title of his debut album: *Piano Man.* Though he doesn't play on every cut of *Storm Front*, Joel—like Gershwin, like Berlin, like such modern throwbacks as Burt Bacharach and Marvin Hamlisch—carved out his understanding of music on the keyboard. To pop composers raised on the 88s, the best songs are the ones most firmly rooted in the kind of voice movement, structure, treatment of theme, and other principles handed down from piano-based classical composers. Flashy guitar leads over blues riffs represent a foreign, less satisfactory, approach.

This may explain why some rock critics have enjoyed slagging Joel over the years. Never mind the thumping beat of "We Didn't Start the Fire," the first single off of *Storm Front*; the percolating organ jabs in the Major Lance-flavored "When in Rome"; or the funky shuffle of the title cut. To guardians of the rock aesthetic, Joel smells suspiciously like a poseur. "There simply isn't any way to deal with him except as a lightweight," sigh Dave Marsh and John Swenson in *The New Rolling Stone Record Guide.*

Wrong. One deals with him as a pro in the old sense of the word. Armed only with a piano, he can hammer together sharp hooks and sophisticated changes, and flavor it with some genuine streetwise soul. Need a deathless ballad? He'll give you "Just the Way You Are." A more inspiring alternative to "New York, New York"? Here's "New York State of Mind." Something that evokes the Beatles? The Stones? The classic Stax records? You got it, and with anchovies if you wish.

As we sat face-to-face with Joel last September, shortly before release of *Storm Front*, we recognized him as a stubborn perfectionist, proud of the work he puts into his music. He answers questions quickly and easily, at times heatedly when pressed. Despite his stupendous success over the past 16 years, Joel is sensitive about his rock and roll credentials: When we suggested that some of his work paralleled the hard musical sell of the proverbial Tin Pan Alley song plugger, he bristled.

"Which songs did I do that on?" he demanded, an annoyed edge in his voice. "Look, everybody who gets in front of a microphone has to sell the damn song, one way or another. Let's not kid ourselves. It's just that I've never thought of myself as doing that."

Yet few do it better than Joel—in his soaring vocals on "The Downeaster 'Alexa,'" the whispered intimacy of "And So It Goes," and the Peter Gabriel-like inflections and keyboard licks on "Storm Front." He straddles two musical worlds—pre- and post-rock—and leaves his mark in each. Perhaps this is his real significance: While his contemporaries ponder the exotica of compositional software, sampled textures, and sequenced grooves, Joel stays rooted in the tried and true. As much as he was in his formative years with Long Island bar bands and on the L.A. lounge circuit, Billy Joel remains a Piano Man—happily, defiantly, successfully.

When you do your songs that were originally for solo piano and voice, do you notice that your piano style has changed a lot since the days you were working alone in little clubs?

No, my style hasn't really changed at all. That's probably the one thing that's stayed pretty much the same. If I do a song that's just me and the piano, I do it now just like I would have ten years ago.

Don't you play differently in front of thousands of people than you do in smaller surroundings?

I think I just play harder. It doesn't really make any sense, because hitting the piano harder doesn't mean you're gonna get all the way to the back of the room any more than if you play softer, since you've got all this amplification. But you want to reach those people in the back row at someplace like Madison Square Garden, and for some reason this makes you feel like you have to pound the hell out of the piano. I break bass strings constantly, at just about every show.

How would you characterize your keyboard style?

A lot of it is actually based on ideas I have for the guitar. I've always wanted to play the guitar, so what I do in a lot of my writing is to compose the guitar part on the piano, then come into the studio and say, "This is what I want. I'd like to hear this on the guitar." The producer or somebody will say, "Why don't you play that on the piano?" And I'll say, "But it's not supposed to be for the piano!" See, I've never really thought of myself as a stylist. I think I'm a lousy piano player.

Many of our readers, who voted you Best Rock Pianist in our *Keyboard* Polls, would disagree.

Well, I took classical piano when I was growing up, and I know how good a really good pianist can be. My left hand pretty much plays octaves all the time. My right hand can play some flashy stuff, and I can play choppy chord things pretty well, but I don't really ever step out of a certain number of keys, like $B\flat$, to me, is really adventurous. And $E\flat$? Wow!

Why, then, have you always played the keyboard parts on your records? Why not hire a more accomplished session player?

I found that extremely accomplished keyboard players tend to get outside of the original conception of a song. We're going for a simple band sound most of the time, like the Beatles. Everybody looks at the Beatles individually and goes, "Ringo wasn't so hot." Well, I think he was fantastic, because he didn't try to play like Ginger Baker. Paul McCartney is a great bass player because he doesn't try to play like Stanley Clarke. I never really felt the need for fancy instrumentation, except for once in a while like on "Zanzibar" [from *52nd Street*], which was begging for [trumpeter] Freddie Hubbard, or with [saxophonist] Phil Woods on "Just the Way You Are" [from *The Stranger*]. Maybe that's another admission of defeat.

Not if you consider yourself a songwriter more than a keyboard virtuoso.

Yeah, but that still takes us outside of our little rhythm circle, and we're all very jealous about that. When we're in the studio the arrangement isn't even there a lot of the time. There'll just be a melody and a vague idea. The drummer, Liberty DeVitto, will yell at me, "Stop playing! What you're playing stinks! Don't play anything!" I'll say, "Okay," and just sit there. Or he'll yell at the guitar player [Russell Javors], "You're playing too much! Stop! Cut it out!" See, the rhythm tracks should be done by the guys who've been working together for a long time. I write with that in mind a lot of the time, and anything after that is gravy.

Do you write songs in certain keys to fit your vocal range?

They go through a cycle. When I write a series of songs I usually start in good old *C*, because that's safe. Then once I get that knocked out, I might want something a little alien to *C*, so maybe I'll go to *E*.

And the guitarists go, "Thank you."

Right: "Whew, it's finally an *E* song." Then I'll go to *D*, and then *B♭*. I'll try to keep changing keys as I write songs. I'm usually aware of my limitations as a piano player while I'm doing that, so I try not to overextend the piano parts. To me, it's not the singer or the instrument; it's the song. And that attitude seems to get in the way of a lot of people: "Gee, I didn't hear enough piano on the last album." But sometimes I think it's effective to underplay the piano, like in the midsection of the song "Don't Ask Me Why" [from *Glass Houses*], there are 15 pianos overdubbed on top of each other; which I thought was especially effective because you didn't hear that much piano before then.

You also seem to go out of your way to cover lots of different styles, from bluegrass to jazz to whatever, and you probably can't adapt the piano to every single format.

Right. I think it should be held in reserve for when it's meaningful and when it's going to have some impact. A whole album of piano-based songs can get real tiresome. I think Elton pulled it off pretty well because his style was novel. He was playing a lot of arpeggio-type stuff with a lot of rhythmic things too.

Is there any solo you've recorded that you're especially proud of?

Let me think. There's a pattern I like a lot, in a song called "Summer, Highland Falls," on *Turnstiles*. It's a series of bits, starting on *F*, with the left hand playing riffs. It goes up to a *C*, drops back a fourth, goes up a fifth, back down a fourth, up another fifth, and somehow or other it resolves itself. I didn't know what I was doing when I wrote it. I didn't set out to do anything particularly clever, but after I finished the song and saw the symmetry of it, I said, "Hey, that's really neat!"

What about the repeated note in the "Prelude" to "Angry Young Man," from Turnstiles? Was that hard to do?

Not really. The piano is essentially a percussion instrument, so I just took the

Billy Joel: "I have a great inferiority complex about my voice, I'm always trying to hide myself in a character. I do what I call 'method singing.' It's like, 'How can I not sound like me again?' So one day I'll hide in Hendrix, and the next day in Ray Charles." Photo courtesy of Photofest

thumb of the right hand and the index finger of the left hand and drummed away. You could do it on bongo drums.

There were some chords interspersed within that single-note rhythm, though.

Yeah. That was kind of a challenge, like, "I can do that on one note, but it gets boring real quick. What else can I do?" So I threw in a chord here and there, and once in a while I'd drop off the *C* and go to a *B*. Then there's a piano part in a song called "Cold Spring Harbor," which is on *Songs in the Attic*. It's not a solo, but the piano is doing a rhythm guitar part that's really hard to play. It always makes my hand ache, but I get a kick out of the fact that I can do it. It goes back and forth from *C* to *F* in real fast arpeggios. Then when it comes to the bridge I start banging with both hands like I'm playing bongo drums. I call that particular style "lucky fingers," where you should be hitting every wrong note in the world, but somehow or other your fingers are trained to go to the right ones.

Do you correct any wrong notes that might show up in your live recordings?

Oh, no. There are mistakes all over, and we decided to leave them all in. We had to choose between going for a technically perfect record or some accurate representation of a live performance. In "Streetlife Serenader" on *Songs in the Attic*, there's this left-hand arpeggio that's absolutely, totally wrong. It makes me cringe every time I hear it, but Phil [Ramone, produc-er] said, "Look, leave it in, 'cause that's what you did."

You used to play organ in rock and roll bands.

I'm a better organist than I am a piano player. I can scream when I'm play-ing an organ! When I got my first Hammond organ—I think I was 17—I bought every Jimmy Smith album there was, every Jimmy McGriff album there was. I got all the Groove Holmes records. I'd play that stuff with my eyes closed. Actually, I have more fun playing organ than playing piano.

What organ did you play when you joined your first rock band?

It was an Estey, one of these little wooden things that had air blowing through it; it sounded like a big harmonica. No, more horrible than that; it sounded like a sick cow. I got it for Christmas when I was about 14. I thought, "Wow, this is the hottest thing!" Back then everybody played guitars, and there were really no key-boards developed, so we took an old Kent microphone and stuck it in the back of the Estey when I wasn't singing. When it was time for me to sing, we pulled the mic out and I used it. After that I got a Vox Continental, which I considered top of the line until I heard a Hammond organ, and that just wiped me out.

Do you write much away from the keyboard?

No. I've got to have the piano there. I'm always finding stuff out on it. See, I took classical piano for about 11 years, and a lot of what I learned there got in the way of my writing because I got hung up in these rules: "I can't do that. That doesn't make sense. I can't make that change, because that's too obvious." Then one day I just said, "Why can't I do all these things? Forget the theory! Forget everything I ever learned and try to get innocent again." And I'm still working backwards to this day, still trying to write without any rules. Who says that when you go from a *C* you have to end up on *A* as the tonic? What's the word they use? The pivot chord? You have to hit a chord to get back to the tonic. The chord before the resolution.

You've got the tonic, the dominant, the subdominant.

I forgot all this stuff. [*Laughs.*] But before I forgot it I always would get hung up. How do I get back to the tonic? Finally I said to myself, "Why don't I just play any chord I feel like playing, if it pleases me?" You lose a certain amount of feeling when you intellectualize.

Does that apply to your piano playing too? Is there any conflict between your classical training and the way you play rock nowadays?

Yeah. My fingering has suffered with rock piano. I played a lot of the clas-sical stuff by ear anyway. I got tired of reading the music, so I'd go out and buy the record. I had to learn the *Beethoven Sonata in D Minor, Op. 31*, so I went out, got the record, and learned it pretty much by ear. I'm sure I missed a lot of notes; the teacher looked at me and said, "What arrangement is this? That's not on the music!"

How long did it take to learn it that way?

About two or three days, I suppose, if I sat down and listened for an hour and a half each day.

That's incredible.

Well, it was really laziness. When you're lazy you become very ingenious in certain ways. I just got tired of reading those black dots. To this day I can't sit down and sight-read. When I was about 12 I was able to sight-read great, but I just can't do it anymore. It's too slow. My ear's a lot quicker.

Do you ever check how accurately your songs are notated on commercial sheet music?

Yeah. A lot of times it's wrong, because I don't go in there and oversee it myself, since I've forgotten how to read. Instead, I'll make sure the key is right and check certain chords once in a while, but often I wouldn't know whether it was written out correctly. I notice that the phrasing is loused up a lot. Some of the guys who do copy work, when they can't figure out a phrase, they just put a stock pattern in there. The worst thing I've noticed was in the sheet music to "Just the Way You Are." The second chord in the intro is absolutely wrong.

How is it supposed to go?

It's in *D*, and it starts with *D-A-D* in the left hand, then a *G* minor chord in the right hand, with the *G* on top. Then there's a *G* major and a *Gsus*. But I hear it played wrong all the time by people who learn it off the music, and it drives me nuts! I've always played by ear, and that's how the band works too, but people who depend on the music too much are missing a lot of how the song was conceived. It wasn't written on a piece of paper. It came out by ear.

Does your musical self-image still stem primarily from being a keyboardist?

For the full range of expressions, to me, as a writer, nothing beats the piano. But it's not the ultimate instrument anymore in terms of writing, because there are alternatives. There are softer alternatives and harder alternatives. I did a good amount of writing for the new album on Hammond organ. I did a good amount of writing on synthesizer—not with experimental sounds, but basically Clavinet stops, harpsichord stuff. I still don't enjoy the feel of synthesizer. I just don't get any feedback from it. I still enjoy the percussive timbre and resonance of the piano.

Because you're such a physical player?

Yes. The possibility of snapping a string still appeals to me. But my favorite axe in the whole world, just to play for virtuosity's sake, is still the Hammond B-3. I can scream on that thing. I've done David Letterman shows just to be able to play it, just to get my rocks off. Paul Shaffer was going, "Wow, he's doing sixteenths!" One of my fantasies was always to be just an anonymous Hammond organ player in some roadhouse blues band. I'd wear a hat and sunglasses—nobody would know who the hell I am. And I'm just groovin'—not singing, not doing nothin' but playing.

There are some chorded organ textures on the bridge to "That's Not Her Style."

Yeah. That wasn't really Hammond organ. That's what I call the sick hybrid between a Farfisa and a Lowrey. I was looking for something that hinted at being a bent church/Iron Butterfly thing, like bad B monster movies from the early '60s, before they had synthesizer technology, and they used Lowrey organs to get eerie and creepy sounds.

Craftsmanship is especially obvious on a tune like "Leningrad." It takes craftsmanship to know when a particular inversion of a chord will make the progression move better, rather than just hitting the root all the time in the left hand.

You're talking about the *E* minor substitution for the *G*? It's in the key of *D*. At the end of every verse, I have an option: Because it's in *D*, it can go *G-A-D*, but I have the option of going *Em-A-D*. To me, going to the *E* minor makes such a huge difference that I held it back, and only used it twice in the song. To me, using the knowledge that you have these differences creates something magical, something really strong.

That same awareness of options animates many of the bridge sections to your tunes.

Bridges are my forte. I think I'm better at writing bridges than I am at writing verses and choruses. You've really got to challenge yourself. If you come up with something that you think is ingenious or really clever, and it's the impetus for completing the song, you often find that you've painted yourself in a corner: "How the hell do I get out of this?" That's where the real creativity comes in. The bridge is often looked upon as an unimportant part of the song, but I always ask myself how I can make it just as good, just as strong, as the rest of the song.

Without detracting from the power of the theme.

That's right—without going so far afield that you're not even dealing with the same theme. The first bridge in "Storm Front," which is in the key of *C*, starts with the minor third to the tonic in an old blues mode. But the second time we go to it, as an instrumental breakdown, it goes into the key of *E*. I don't know if anybody picked up on this, but the melody in the guitar is "Stormy Weather." Then we got away from it. It was like "Sunshine of Your Love," where Eric Clapton actually played a variation on "Blue Moon" in his solo. To me, this is a little bow to a master songwriter, like, "Hey, this is such a well-written piece of music that I can translate this into a modern idiom."

You seem to have paid attention to key relationships even in segues from song to song on this album: "Leningrad" leads nicely to "State of Grace."

It's interesting that you picked that up, because I thought about that. "Leningrad" is in *D*, and when it goes to the instrumental section at the coda, it goes to *A*. "State of Grace" is in *A* too, so I was thinking, "Where's the tension? Where's the release? Where's the dynamic in going from *A* to *A*?" But I spent such a short amount of time in *A* on "Leningrad" that I thought picking up on it to go to "State of Grace" was a nice segue. Also, "State of Grace" dallies so little in the tonic. It makes left turns, and it keeps going left and left and left, then it gets back to home base. It goes *A*, then *E* with a *G♯* bass, *F7*, then to the *D* minor, which is related to *F*, to *D♭*, which is sort of related to *D* minor. Getting out of that was like a *B* demented—I don't know what the hell to call it—to *E7*, and back to *A*. Home free! God knows how I figured that out. I found myself crying for my mother at times while I was writing that song: "Mommy! I've gone to Egypt! Where the hell am I?" But I love that challenge. It's like an Escher painting, where the lizards are climbing up a staircase going up but they end up down at the bottom. And the melody still holds up!

Duke Ellington did that same thing a lot. The end of the bridge on "Sophisticated Lady" is a masterpiece of meandering chords.

Yeah, and he gets back to where he started. You can't intellectualize that. You actually have to figure it out with your fingers.

The interesting thing about "State of Grace" is that you go through these backflips on the verse, whereas on most other tunes the verses are kept simple, and the more complex changes are explored in the bridges as a contrasting device.

Yeah, the tension and release are built into the verse. Then, when I finished the verse, I said, "Well, this seems complete to me. Where do I go from here? Haven't I pretty much covered everything you can do?" That's why there are actually three bridges to the song: There's a B bridge and a C bridge.

What tunes did you write on the organ?

"Storm Front" and "Possible Light," which is the B side of "We Didn't Start the Fire." It's what I call "biker bar blues." See, I'd always kind of downplayed my soloistic stuff. Everybody was saying, "When are you going to play something where you really show off your organ playing?" I'd say, "Ah, that's really not important. The big picture, the material, is more important." But it is important for people to hear some really good stuff. So on that B side, I'm playing sixteenth-notes on the organ, and jumping to thirty-seconds. I'm not smearing the keys: I'm literally picking the notes out. That was a gas. I really wanted to do that, because there's not a whole lot of great musicianship nowadays. Even though people think they're hearing some flailing guitar solos in heavy metal, it all comes out of the same videotape.

Did you have to get your chops back up for this album?

I worked back up to the playing part of it, because this is the first time in a long time that I had the amount of material that I had together before I went into the studio. Usually, when I go to the studio, I have three or four basic ideas—maybe an embryo here, a fetus there, whatever—and it gets written in the studio. It's a pretty expensive process. But Mick Jones [producer] said, "Why don't you come in with ten or eleven things?" "Ten or eleven? What about that creative process that happens where I finish everything in the studio?" And he said, "Just do me a favor. Come up with ten or eleven tunes. And while you're at it, why don't you rehearse them with the band?" So now I'm doubly horrified! "What about spontaneity? My God, doesn't that count for anything? What if we hit the peak during rehearsal? Are we condemned to forever do what I call 'Top the Demo,' which is an exercise in futility?" Once you've done a certain performance on a demo, you're never going to get the same thing again. It was what it was at that particular moment: Even the clams count for something.

But Mick said, "Just go rehearse." Well, you know what? I used to do that, back in the early days, before I had money to spend in the studio, before there was this big-time rock and roll album budget crap. We had to rehearse. We had our act together. So I went back to doing that, and I started by throwing out five songs.

Why did you get rid of those five old songs?

They didn't fly. They weren't happening. They sounded good live, but when we came into the studio, we realized that it was a live wank. There is a particular amount of wanking that goes on live.

Was there also a question of finding songs that fit into your album concept?

Well, here's the thing. I've found that it's not always a good idea to limit yourself to what you think the album concept should be. Once you get a certain distance into writing and recording an album, it begins to take on a life of its own, and you become a captive of that. You're no longer the master of what the concept is. You're chained to it: It takes on a certain momentum, and you have to go with that flow. So to try to force it back into that initial concept is to do yourself a disservice as a musician and a composer.

For you, then, the song, not the album, is the governing element.

The material is the dictator. And I've always tried to sublimate style. I don't even think of my voice as being an I.D. I'm always changing my voice. I have a great inferiority complex about my voice, I'm always trying to hide myself in a character. I do what I call "method singing." It's like, "How can I not sound like me again?" So one day I'll hide in Hendrix, and the next day in Ray Charles.

You've definitely unleashed a John Lennon voice on several songs, such as "Scandinavian Skies" and "Laura" from *The Nylon Curtain*.

Yeah, there's a lot of that on *Nylon Curtain*. It's scary. See, I don't think of myself as any kind of a stylist at all. I may have gotten a certain amount of critical abuse because I'm such a non-stylist, but I don't think that's necessarily a bad thing.

Many of your records do seem to be based on the styles of other artists. Do you write many of your songs with the Beatles, the Four Seasons, or whoever in mind?

I don't know if I necessarily write the songs that way. When the actual composition is going on—it's all me. A lot of times it happens during the recording process: The admiration I've had for the artists I've always idolized will come out. I reinvent myself every day, so on one particular day, maybe I'm Hendrix. On this album, for example, "Shameless" is an unabashed imitation of Jimi Hendrix. It is *screaming* Hendrix. I've never heard anybody recreate what Hendrix did. I don't know if I pulled it off, but I wanted to hear that myself. "That's Not Her Style" owes a great deal to the Rolling Stones. "Storm Front" is steeped in either Sam and Dave or an Otis Redding groove. Or maybe it's more of a Steve Winwood/Peter Gabriel approach. On "State of Grace," I was thinking of Percy Sledge on "When a Man Loves a Woman." I could probably find somebody else for every song, but those are the ones that jump out to me.

Was all of the piano sound on *Storm Front* real piano? Were there any electronic pianos on the album?

When you hear a piano, it's an acoustic piano—either a Baldwin or a Yamaha, good 7' grands. Much of the time there was a MIDI hookup with another sound, but whether it was the Clavinet or some other sample or synthesizer sound, it is a mix with piano you're hearing, except for the solo in "I Go To Extremes," which is what I call straight-ahead psycho piano—just grabbing clusters of notes and letting your fingers do the walking.

That solo is one spot on the album where a definite Billy Joel piano style comes through, in terms of how you syncopate and voice your chords.

To me, it's like playing the congas. I'm using the piano as a set of congas, just praying to God that my lucky fingers will bail me out.

Did you write "Leningrad" based on your Soviet experience?

The music was conceived, before the lyrics, as a classical piece, way before I went to Russia. Sometimes I just write classical pieces for my own enjoyment. I love classical music so much. It goes back to when I was a kid taking piano lessons. Rather than read what the teacher had given me—the Beethoven sonatas, the Kuhlau, the Clementi, or the Mozart—I'd just make up my own classical music, just challenge myself and see whether I could do anything like Chopin or Brahms or Schumann. I got to be pretty good at it; I actually started enjoying the pieces I made up. I rarely show this stuff to people, but once in a while it does surface in a song. I'll bet you I've used them without even knowing it. That's where "Leningrad" came from.

The intro does evoke a Rachmaninoff flavor.

Actually, Tchaikovsky, with the suspensions and the descending bass line. In the back of my mind, I had a title for it: "Stalingrad." The lyric is based on a true story. This guy was always in the front row, a clown in the circus named Viktor. I took some liberties with the year he was born: He's younger than me, but I wanted to place him in World War II. As anybody who knows Russian history knows, they got creamed in the war. Twenty million were wiped out. If anyone who's prejudiced toward the Russians had any inkling of how those people suffered, they wouldn't be worried about dropping bombs on these folks to stop them from attacking us. The last thing they want to do is have a war with us.

I wanted to write a song about the Soviet Union because everybody we met there, all the musicians and artists, were begging me, "Please don't let this be the last experience you have with us! Come back, or write about us, or something!" The biggest emotional experience for me was the fact that my daughter was there. It was such a matter of trust for them that I brought my own child. I remembered the relationship between her and this guy who was a clown. She was enchanted by him. It didn't matter that he was Russian; she didn't know. She just responded to him instinctively. I mean, here was a guy who was sobbing in a heap, when we left the Leningrad Airport and flew back to the States. He was going to pick one of my photographs, which I was going to give him as a gift; in the end, I gave him the whole pile. We were all crying when we left, because over there, when you say goodbye, it's not "See you later." It's "Good-bye. I'll never see you again."

So I started writing, and the song pretty much wrote itself, because the story was there.

On "We Didn't Start the Fire," there are some heavy percussion interludes. Were those sections sequenced?

No. That was actually me playing a cowbell and something else, Liberty [DeVitto, drummer] on timbales, and Crystal [Taliefero], the percussionist in my new band, playing congas. And we're not Tito Puente. To tell you the truth, I wasn't going for a virtuoso percussion force. I was going for what I call the global drum. Having people who are not experts at percussion but could beat out some good stuff on instruments that maybe they weren't used to created that sound— not necessarily African, not necessarily Latin, not necessarily Oriental, but a combination of a lot of drums.

On the *Storm Front* tour, will you be playing your piano parts on a real grand or an electronic piano?

Here's a sick thing: I want to play a goddamn 9' grand. I've never done that before onstage. We've always used somewhere between a 5'8" and a 7' grand piano. But the piano has become almost an anachronism in modern music. I want to scream piano. I'm gonna have it MIDIed. I'll either utilize the MIDI or I'll just go with a straight piano sound. I'll also be playing accordion and synth, although Jeff [Jacobs] will be handling all the heavy-duty electronic parts.

Do you plan to have a Hammond organ onstage?

That's a good question. You know, we played with Winwood on *The Bridge*. He didn't have any of his synths; he just played Hammond. And we jammed Spencer Davis and Traffic stuff for eight hours. When we recorded with him, we did it live too. He was kind of blown away. He said, "Geez, do you record live all the time?" I looked at him absolutely befuddled and said, "Didn't you do that when you were with Traffic?" And he said, "Yeah, I suppose I did!" He had so much fun playing the Hammond organ. It's an anachronism, an inconsistent instrument. It takes wear and tear on the road: Drawbars disappear, tone wheels don't spin right. Each Hammond organ is unique. They're all quirky. Every one of them is a monster. But that's what gives them depth: They're prone to fallibility. There's also something about the physical presence of a B-3 that screams a certain rhythm and blues tradition. It's even in the body language of how you play it.

How will you set up the piano?

As usual, I'll set it up backwards. I always have the wrong side to the audience, because I sing to the left. It's sort of like being a left-handed bass player, I guess. Sorry, folks, but you get the straight side of the piano.

Wouldn't it be simpler to go with, say, a sampled grand than a concert-sized acoustic piano?

I've tried them, but there's something about being able to play this acoustic beast. I can't replace it with anything else. A 9' grand is going to be a pain in the ass to mic, because of the resonance from the bass strings. We don't just use pick-ups; we use mics, because it's very important to me that the piano sound like a piano, not some amplified electronic instrument. So we use all kinds of nefarious combinations of pickups and microphones to get that across. It is a pain in the ass. But I'm gonna do it, because I'm a piano player, and I'm damn proud of it.

Portions of this article originally were published in the December 1981 and January 1990 issues of Keyboard *magazine.*

FOR MORE ON BILLY JOEL

Billy Joel hasn't slowed down a bit since these articles first appeared. In fact, Billy and Elton John continue to tour together extensively. You can connect with him at his official website, www.billyjoel.com.

A SELECTED BILLY JOEL DISCOGRAPHY

Billy Joel's recordings are packed with great songs and performances. If you want to concentrate on his plethora of hits, he has several "Best Of" collections out, as well as an anniversary re-release of *The Stranger* containing lots of fun bonus material.

2006 *12 Gardens (Live)*
2001 *Opus 1–10 Fantasies & Delusions—Music for Solo Piano*
1993 *River of Dreams*
1989 *Storm Front*
1987 *Kohuept (Live)*
1986 *The Bridge*
1983 *An Innocent Man*
1982 *The Nylon Curtain*

1981 *Songs in the Attic (Live)*
1980 *Glass Houses*
1978 *52nd Street*
1977 *The Stranger*
1976 *Turnstiles*
1974 *Streetlife Serenade*
1973 *Piano Man*
1971 *Cold Spring Harbor*

ELTON JOHN

BY ROBERT L. DOERSCHUK

THE CAPTAIN CONQUERS

NEVER IN THE HISTORY of rock and roll has so unlikely a star as Elton John captured the loyalty of so many fans. Elvis was tall and surly, the Beatles were schoolboy cute, the Stones short and surly, and all of them were guitar players. Elton John is almost none of these things. Nor does he pretend to be. And in this respect, he is perhaps most different from the rock star stereotype.

For Elton John is Reg Dwight in disguise, a grown-up English lad, undistinguished in most ways except for an extraordinary musical talent. He is the living fantasy of fame-starved rockers everywhere, who see themselves in his frolics through the pop music pantheon, daring to wear outfits as extreme as the stretch of his imagination, smashing the post-Buddy Holly taboo against wearing spectacles by donning wide-screen frames complete with window-washers, and otherwise celebrating the license that success allows.

He was one of us, his legions whisper, and that is a key reason for his popularity. Elton hasn't forgotten; in fact, he enjoys reminding himself as well as his public from time to time that his roots dig down to levels of family and community familiar to us all. In a remarkable pair of booklets included with his autobiographical album *Captain Fantastic and the Brown Dirt Cowboy*, he lays out his life in a scrapbook of cartoons and old photos. In them we see the story of a lost love in ten comic-book panels, mixed in with pages torn from an old diary and snapshots showing him in his days as Reg Dwight, out of focus with narrow tie and thick specs in 1964, fashionable in Sgt. Pepper attire in '69, teenaged and tiny behind a Vox organ, unnoticed and alone in a rock festival crowd. No stylish angst, no dues-paying recollections; his story is too close to ours for that to be necessary.

In his Elton John incarnation, this young fellow has become the

Elton John: "I used to stand in front of the mirror and mime to Little Richard and Jerry Lee Lewis records. Little Richard was just an ace." Photo by Jon Sievert

Everyman of rock or, more precisely, Everyman's dream come alive. All that separates him from most of those who never will bring this dream into reality is his talent, the other crucial factor in his success. This is what took him and his songwriting partner Bernie Taupin from behind the gray door of their basement flat in London to the mirrored world they share now with other showbiz heroes.

From his first appearance on the American charts eleven years ago, Elton has shown himself to be more than a fantasy symbol. At a time when rock music was still

hung over from its fling with psychedelia, he stood apart as an individual, presenting thoughtful tunes in musically sensitive arrangements, which centered around his piano work and singing. *Saturday Review* described his early release *Tumbleweed Connection* as "the only out-of-left-field surprise pop album of 1970" in that it was filled with "music that is organic, intensely human, and capable of an elusively intimate effect," and that managed even so to become a hit.

From the keyboardist's point of view, he had the added significance of bringing the piano back to the forefront of rock instrumentation. Various organists of the Emerson or Billy Preston mold had preceded him into the spotlight during the late '60s, and of course the rock piano tradition dipped back to the '50s and before, but it had withered with the ascension of the guitar as the premier solo instrument. When it revived in the hands of Elton John, it had been reinvigorated with a sense of melody and texture unprecedented in the style.

Time noted the significance of this contribution in the keyboard area when it observed back in 1970 that Elton "plays piano with the urbane primitivism of a Glenn Gould thumping out variations on Jerry Lee Lewis." But more importantly, "Elton John also symbolizes a subtle but highly significant change in a field where once no composer worth his suede jacket would be caught dead without a guitar. Slowly, surely, the piano is gaining ground. Many of today's leading rock composers find the range and nuance of the piano more suitable for the personal, diverse, and poetic turns rock is taking." And much of the credit for that must go to the influential Mr. John.

The piano has been a part of Reginald Kenneth Dwight's life as far back as he can remember. He began his piano studies at the age of four in Pinner,

Middlesex, England, where he was born. The lessons were classical, and he advanced far enough to be enrolled in London's Royal Academy of Music at age 11, but after his mother brought home two pop singles one day—Bill Haley's "ABC Boogie" and Elvis Presley's "Heartbreak Hotel"—his heart was captured by the beat and feel of rock and roll.

By the time he turned 14, he was playing R&B tunes with a group called Bluesology. They started out working in local pubs on weekend nights, doing songs by Jimmy Witherspoon, Mose Allison, and Ray Charles, among others. In time they were being booked to back up visiting American soul singers. Their first important job was with Major Lance at the State Cinema in Kilburn; later they would play behind Patti LaBelle, the Drifters, the Ink Spots, and similar acts. Elton was strictly a pianist in those days. He would eventually save enough to buy a Hohner electric piano, but his only vocalizing was done at one Bluesology recording session, when the song was found to be out of their regular singer's range. "We were considered to be a pretty good ensemble, although we played in Scout huts and at Youth Group dances with just one ten-watt amplifier and an unamplified piano," Elton recalls. "But we were always playing the wrong stuff— always too late or too early."

Stanley Dwight, a strict former RAF squadron leader, was appalled at his son's interests. In a letter to Elton's mother after their divorce, he insisted that the 16-year-old boy "get all this pop nonsense out of his head; otherwise he's going to turn into a wild boy. He should get a sensible job with either the BEA or Barclay's Bank." But nothing could slow down the young pianist's momentum. Two weeks before his final exams he quit school to work as an errand boy at a London music publishing company, while also picking up more jobs with Bluesology. They played with exhaustive dedication—Elton remembers one night when they backed singer Billy Stewart at four separate clubs—until they were signed by the pioneering British blues singer Long John Baldry as his regular band. Baldry not only gave the group new opportunities to perform throughout England and abroad; he also helped provide his pianist with a new name, a marriage of first names borrowed from him and saxophonist Elton Dean. (Elton would later pay back the loan by co-producing Baldry's 1971 recording, *It Ain't Easy*.)

Bluesology backed Baldry on his biggest hit single, "Let the Heartaches Begin," in 1967, but the success of this commercial ballad led to the singer's decision to dissolve his group and pursue a solo cabaret career. Suddenly desperate for work, and armed only with his new identity, Elton answered a newspaper ad placed by Liberty Records announcing a search for new talent. His audition, in which he made his first real attempt to sing, didn't bring down the house, but one perceptive executive did hand Elton a package of lyrics written by Bernie Taupin, another unknown respondent to the ad. Elton constructed songs around the words provided him by his invisible accomplice; the two didn't even meet until six months later. Soon after that the two were rooming together and establishing their rhythm as a songwriting team. The songs were done quickly—Taupin would often knock out the words in an hour, with Elton finishing the song in thirty minutes—and, after a two-year string of forgettable efforts, they were well crafted. By 1969, Elton was ready to enter the studio and record one of their works as his first single, "Lady Samantha." A debut album, *Empty Sky*, followed, and in 1970 his first high-selling releases, *Elton John* and *Tumbleweed Connection*, clambered into the charts.

The rest of the story, beginning with his auspicious American debut at the L.A. Troubadour, is already modern folklore. The cold numbers tell part of the story. When MCA signed him in 1974, they guaranteed Elton $8 million in royalties against all albums produced over the following five years. By 1975, he had sold 42 million albums and 18 million singles. His eleventh LP, *Captain Fantastic and the Brown Dirt Cowboy*, went platinum with 1.4 million advance orders not only before release, but before the tapes were even shipped to the pressing plants; eventually sales passed the 2.8 million mark. *Elton John's Greatest Hits* would top these figures by going quintuple platinum, with 5 million copies sold. On his 15-date *Rock of the Westies* tour in '75, Elton drew 250,000 fans and grossed more than $2.2 million. Of all concerts staged anywhere during one six-month period of 1976, the top four in terms of ticket sales and gross receipts were Elton's, rating him above Elvis, Paul McCartney's Wings, and other top acts.

Blessed with this sudden and awesome pile of money, Elton distinguished himself from his arty or blue-jeaned confreres by romping his way merrily through the '70s, his inhibitions disintegrating as his energy and capacity for enjoying himself ballooned to mythic proportions: What other rock star zillionaire would accept a high school student's invitation to play at their prom for free? Or perform an adaptation of Tchaikovsky's *Piano Concerto No. 1* in Leningrad before swooning devotees and befuddled bureaucrats? Or give away Rembrandts and Rolls Royces as birthday afterthoughts? Or fly his relatives, his friends, the staff of his London-based Rocket label, and the staff and fans of his professional soccer team to Los Angeles for a one-week vacation as his guests? Or sing "Your Song" onstage at Disneyland in shorts and Mickey Mouse ears?

But as we contemplate the legend that Elton has fashioned for himself, we see that there is more to it than this. His music may be more accessible than much of what fills the airwaves nowadays, but at the risk of suffering accusations of old fogeyism, one may admit that it is at least *musical* music. It may not offer much nourishment to some, but compared to the thudding nihilism that occasionally passes for art, Elton's efforts are a fun-feast for the soul as well as a relief for the ears. Few other keyboard players have been able to bridge the gap between ballads and up-tempo pounders as successfully, and despite charges of his selling out to rock muzak, his credentials as a classic rock pianist are intact: "I bang the piano a lot," he admitted to Rolling Stone. "It's hard work. Like the start of the tour, the first three days, my hands were hell. They bled every night. And my nails broke. Once you've got over the first three or four dates, your hands harden up."

Other aspects of Elton's artistry are also noteworthy. His melodies are punctuated by irresistible hooks, his taste in production is often impeccable, and his studio technique in general is quite remarkable: He began and finished his double album *Goodbye Yellow Brick Road* in just 15 days, and *Caribou* took no more than four. As a performer, his love of entertaining the crowds—in which he was a nameless face himself not so long ago—is obvious, and his sense of obligation to his fans is endearingly real. This interview, for example, was set up after extended periods of phone calling, letter writing, and note passing; only after we had confirmed the time and place did we learn why it had taken so long. The word came back to us through his liaison at MCA that Elton was aware of his influence among young keyboard players, and of how many of them read *Keyboard*. For him, then, this was not just another interview. Before getting together with us, he wanted to make sure he was clear about what he had to say, so that he could communicate his ideas as clearly and directly as possible to those most interested in reading them.

And so we met Elton John in one of his Southern California mansions, a white Spanish spread perched high above the smog in Beverly Hills. There, in a den filled with tour souvenirs, memorabilia, and an Elton John pinball game, we discovered that the one available electrical outlet didn't work. Where could my tape recorder be plugged in? Elton, fresh from the shower and relaxed in robe and slippers, remembered that there was another one in the far wall, behind a massive couch. Suddenly he sprang to life, jumping onto the couch, taking the extension cord, and disappearing from view as he burrowed back toward the plug. After considerable grunting and straining, he pointed to the recorder. I pressed the start button. Triumph! The cassette was rolling, Elton reappeared, laughing, a winner, and ready to go at last.

You said that you had always considered yourself primarily a pianist. Is that still your view of yourself?

Well, I consider myself a much better singer now than I used to be. It's gradually coming together, but I suppose I consider myself mostly a pianist. I mean, when you're onstage you try to sing the right notes, but you also have to hit the right chords. When I first recorded as a singer it was because no one was recording Bernie's and my songs, and somebody just suddenly pushed me into a studio and said, "You can do it." "Lady Samantha" [a single released in 1969] was the first really decent record I ever made as a singer. When I was in a semiprofessional band I hardly used to sing at all. I knew I could sing—I always used to sing in the bath and things like that—but I had to be pushed into doing it on *Empty Sky*, and then I was pushed into getting a band together to go out on the road and sell the record. Everything was sort of an accident, a falling into place. So right now I'm probably 50-50 as a pianist and singer, although there was a time when I would concentrate on my playing rather than my singing.

Is that one reason why you did a solo piano tour back in 1979, accompanied only by percussionist Ray Cooper, to even out that 50-50 balance?

That was done mainly to get me back into playing live. I never really thought I'd go back on the road after having come off of it in 1976. I had enjoyed everything we did in that tour. I had really good bands and very rarely played bad concerts, but I felt a little stale both singing-wise and piano-wise because the last thing I was thinking about onstage was singing and playing. I was thinking instead, "Can they hear the band? Are the monitors right? Is the lighting right? Is the audience getting beaten up?"

Everything was becoming a little mechanical, so I decided to try a little tour of Europe, doing a couple of solo concerts in England and another one with Ray Cooper. Of course when you go out alone you have to play and sing the right bloody notes, so I concentrated real hard and I actually enjoyed the discipline, every single minute of it. Throughout the 125 gigs I did in 1979 I never got fed up, not with one of them, because without a band you're free to extemporize whenever you want, within certain limits when you've got Ray onstage with you. But there was no real framework, and it was quite exciting. It also gave me my confidence back as a musician. I had become lazy, and after '76 I didn't want to see another piano. The solo tour gave me a good time, though, and it was the only thing that could have gotten me back into touring.

Well, what actually brought me back was when I came to Los Angeles to do some tracks for the *21 at 33* album, and I played again with Dee [Murray, bassist] and Nigel [Olsson, drummer]. There was a certain magic. It was like never having been away. We had been the only piano, bass, and drums trio on the road in the early '70s, I think, and I thought, "Right, you're 33; let's get the band together for a few years, give it one more shot, and see how it goes." The solo tour was just what I needed, though, because I was able to pay more attention to Bernie's lyrics than I had done in the past. And anyway, I certainly don't want to be trucking around the world with a rock and roll band forever [*laughs*].

Was it harder to reproduce the full flavor of the songs without a band?

No, it was much easier, because you don't have all the problems. It's much easier to mic the piano. It was an absolute bonus for Clive Franks, who produces my records and has been doing my sound for the last six or seven years, because he was able to concentrate much more on the piano and vocal sound than when you've got six people onstage.

Did you carry your own piano on the road?

I always do, yes. It was the old 9' Steinway, the same one I've had for five or six years now.

Are you a Steinway artist?

No. They've been most unhelpful in placing ads and things like that. They don't really need to have anybody advertising them; they're like Rolls Royce in that respect. I play Steinway because I've gotten used to the piano, but I've also played great Yamahas, and the best piano I've ever played on is a Bösendorfer Imperial. That's my favorite. It's incredible. That's what I used on *Tumbleweed*.

How long does it take you to decide whether you like a certain piano?

I think that when you first sit down at a piano, within a minute you can tell whether you're going to like it because of the tone quality, but the action is really even more important to me. The piano I have now has been doctored so much that the action is ridiculous; it's just like an electric piano.

How so?

It's real fast. The action on it now is absolutely incredible. But when you buy a Steinway, I think you have to live with it a couple of years to let it settle down. I knew it was a great piano to start with, but it's a question of easing into them when they're brand new. Like any instrument, they can be temperamental sometimes. If you're a guitarist, you've got to have your one guitar, but for pianists I think it's even more important to have your one piano. If you're going to be doing concerts all around the world, it's important to know exactly what you're going to get. I mean, I played on the worst pianos in the world back in the early days, from '70 to '74. We used to have a separate piano every gig. It was potluck. You're there to play and you should be able to play on anything, but it's a soundman's nightmare. My piano is also completely miked and wired inside—not that I'm electrically minded, because I'm not, but they don't have to set up any mic when they get there. It's all on the inside already. Eleven years ago, when I first came to the States, miking a piano was a real problem. I remember when I got my first Helpinstill. And in the early '70s I used to play on uprights with two mics hanging down the back.

This was after your first albums had become successful?

Oh, yeah. Yes indeed. I've played on many one-legged grands in England. I've played on some dreadful pianos here as well. In fact, when I came over in '70 for my first American tour, I played with Tracy Nelson and Mother Earth at the Electric Factory in Philadelphia, where the piano was held up by orange crates! Having your own piano is a real luxury, especially when you can travel with someone who knows it inside out and takes care of it for you, like it was his Rolls Royce. My piano has gotten to the point now where there's really nothing much wrong with it.

Christine McVie of Fleetwood Mac told us that they often had trouble getting good pianos on the road, since piano companies felt they would jump up and down on them or set them on fire because they played rock and roll.

Well, I've jumped on a few, I must admit. I mean, if anyone jumped on a piano, I did, not Christine McVie [*laughs*]. But then, I was a solo act, so people probably tended to think of me as not having to jump on pianos. We never had trouble with Steinway in that sense. Some places just don't have Steinways. For example, in Hawaii, I think you can only get a Baldwin or a Yamaha. When we played there the first time, we had to borrow a piano from some doctor and physically take it out of his house. If you play in Ames, Iowa, you may have to put up with a 9' Baldwin or whatever, and it's okay, you do what you can. But that's part of the fun of it when you look back: "Oh, do you remember that piano we had to play on there?" Sometimes it's like working in a disaster area, but if you've got the right attitude, you can get up on the stage, play on uprights with the notes missing—as I've done in England—and still put on a good show. It's just a matter of making do with what you've got, which fortunately I don't have to do anymore.

You said a while back that you were involved in one of the only piano trio acts in rock back in the early '70s. Did you see yourself then as a harbinger of a keyboard renaissance in the decade to come?

Well, I sort of arrived at the same time as the Carole King album *Tapestry*, which probably had more to do with it than I did. I was trying to think of other piano, bass, and drum acts, and there weren't any then. There was Emerson, Lake & Palmer, which was mainly organ, and there was Lee Michaels, which was just organ and drums.

Not much piano, though.

No, and that probably had something to do with our popularity. When we came to the Troubadour the first time, people honestly thought that because of the *Elton John* album I was going to come out with an orchestra. Then when we came out and played rock and roll, everyone just went. "Huh?" And afterwards they said, "We didn't expect that!", even though I've always been a rock and roll player. But I don't know how much of a new thing I was, because back in '70 I'd been influenced by Leon Russell, the Band, and people like that. They were already around. It's just that in the '70s a whole lot of people who played the piano came up, like Billy Joel, Steve Bishop, and loads of others.

Have you played many other keyboard instruments in recent years?

That's one side of the keyboards that I really don't understand too well. I'm not the most technical person. There are only two records I've used them on that I'm really proud of: "This Song Has No Title" [from *Yellow Brick Road*], on which I played all the electric things, and "Song for Guy" [from *Single Man*]. I could do it if I had more patience, but usually I don't because I don't understand programming and computers. The guy who plays synthesizer with us, James Newton Howard, can play five things and four pedals at once; I envy him, and I'd love to be able to do it, but I just don't understand it. He adds so much dimension to the band.

Even when we played in 1976, we'd come into rehearsal and he'd have a huge rack of synthesizers. Somebody brought the Prophet-10 in recently and said, "Look, you can do away with all of that." He'd gotten to the point where we'd just finished rehearsal and he'd just programmed everything, and it was very tempting to say, "Yes, we'll use it," but we couldn't.

Do you work with him in getting the sounds you want?

No, he does that entirely himself. He's one of these infuriating keyboard players, much better than I will ever be. You can play any chord on the piano in any shape or form, and he will tell you each individual note. He's a classically trained pianist with perfect pitch—I mean, he's brilliant. We're hoping to do an instrumental album together this year, with nothing but keyboards and drum machines; James and I have been talking about that for years. He really is a genius, but geniuses, I've always found, are pretty untogether, so he just needs to be pushed.

Has the synthesizer become a vital part of your current sound, then?

Oh, yeah. After going on the road solo, I couldn't take a band out without a synthesizer player. James was one of the first persons I thought of for the current band, and I only found him by accident. Ironically, [L.A. studio keyboardist] David Foster was going to be in my band—he's not doing badly for himself. But I never even gave James an audition. He just came up at the eleventh hour, and I said, "You've got the job if you can play one." We've been friends ever since. He's a great string arranger as well. On the next album he'll be conducting the London Symphony Orchestra again.

When had he done it before?

On the *Blue Moves* album, on a track called "Tonight." He's a clever boy. I know that if I record an all-keyboard album with him I'll actually sit down and make more of an effort to play an electronic keyboard, because he'll make me. He's good for me. He'll say, "Come on, you can do it." As a pianist I can manage. I know the technique to use in the studio and onstage when it comes to piano, but even so, in this day and age there is a technique to playing a Rhodes that is far different from a grand piano technique. I can play a Rhodes and make it sound okay, but James has got a certain technique. Instead of me playing it on, for example, "Little Jeannie" [from *21 at 33*], I'll give it to James.

Did you write "Little Jeannie" on the Rhodes?

I wrote that on the Yamaha CP-80 with a four-track tape recorder. I love the electric grands. They're amazing things, actually, a revolution for piano players. I wrote most of the stuff for *21 at 33* and the next album on the electric Yamaha. We tried it in the studio on the CP-80, but it's a gentle number and it needed the Rhodes sound. The Rhodes is a bastard to record with, really. Finding a good Rhodes sound is like finding a good piano. It's very, very hard. I mean, they're all good, but to find one that records and plays well on the road is not easy. They need just as much looking after as a grand piano does. And a Wurlitzer like that, which is my favorite, is even harder to find. They're like gold dust.

You've played the Wurlitzer on records, haven't you?

Yeah. There's a Wurlitzer on the next album. I used it on my second single,

ELTON JOHN

"Lady Samantha." I'll always remember that, because the tune was in Bb, and a Bb key went out of tune, so I had to play around it. I loved the sound of the Wurlitzer because it was on the Small Faces record "Itchycoo Park." Now, of course, Supertramp uses it.

Do you still play sessions occasionally for other artists?

Yeah, if they ask me. If I have the time, I love to play sessions. I think people are afraid now that I will say no, but I've played a lot of dates. I played piano on the Hollies record "He Ain't Heavy (He's My Brother)." At that time I was just a struggling new artist in England. Then when it was a hit they said it was their bass player playing! I was so mortified [*laughs*]! And I played on the follow-up, "Can't Tell the Bottom From the Top." I used to sing on a lot of records.

Weren't you on a copy record of Stevie Wonder's "Signed, Sealed, Delivered" in the '60s?

That's right. It was one of those cheap cover versions that were being put out in England. I used to do that all the time. They were great fun, really hilarious. That record was too high for me. Every time I hear it, it sounds ridiculous. I was singing like I had a pin sticking in my backside. I played or sang on a lot of records by English groups: the Scaffold, the Baron Knights. I sang on Tom Jones sessions. I've done the whole works, from crazy people down to Tom Jones.

When you play a session now, do people ask for Elton John-type piano, or do they ask you to adapt to some other style they're working toward?

I usually go in and play the way I feel on the track. The only problem is that I sometimes overplay when I should underplay, so they might ask me not to play so much. But most of the time it works. I usually tend to take over a session when I get in there. With studio musicians there's usually no problem, but when you get a bunch of musicians from groups coming in to play for an artist, and they've never played together before, someone's got to take the lead, you know? Someone's got to say, "Come on, let's do it." Otherwise it's going to be a disaster for the producer.

When you're backing another singer, do you play differently as opposed to when you're backing your own vocal?

When you back someone else, I think you tend to play better piano. In my concert set now, Nigel Olsson does a little song of his own in the middle and I play background for him on piano. During rehearsal I really enjoyed it because all I had to concentrate on was piano, whereas if you've got two things going on at once, it's really hard to do your best on both of them. I like to play piano for people.

Do you ever get insights as a composer from playing other people's material?

Oh, yeah. It's all just good fun. I mean, I'm not one of those people who'll stay up until four in the morning playing "Twelve O'Clock Blues," but I do like to play with other musicians. You have to take risks. You can't play safe all the time. There are things I'd love to do in the future, like just go to the studio and do a mini-Keith Jarrett—extemporizing and using the best of it—because I can sit at the piano and play for hours and hours. Even with Taupin, when I was working off of lyrics, I'd just play around till I found a chord structure I liked. I know I could do a really good album that way. There's something within me that would love to do an album solo, just absolutely raw, with maybe some singing as well. It's just a matter of finding the time and place to do it.

Are there any problems you can foresee in a solo project?

I think you can get carried away with yourself. When Clive and I are mixing, I tend to mix my voice down and Clive will always mix it up again and say that's what people want to hear. As a musician you want to hear the other things on the track, so you have to make a compromise. I've never liked some of the mixes on my albums, but everybody else thought they were great, so as a musician you can sometimes be wrong. You might look for a certain bass part or rhythm guitar part, or an electric piano thing you like, to lift in the mix to the detriment of your own vocal performance. Knowing the best road to take is very hard.

How do you choose your own sidemen in sessions? For example, what made you decide to use Rick Wakeman on one song?

Yeah, on "Madman Across the Water." He played organ. I got him for that because I'm the world's worst Hammond organ player. I'm more used to playing my old Vox Continental, and that very badly as well. I couldn't even understand the drawbars on the Vox. I played with the same setting for three years [*laughs*]!

There was a photo of you in *Captain Fantastic* at a Vox organ.

Yeah. In the early days, when I did the *Elton John* album, the songs were planned down to the smallest point, where everything was written down, even the bass parts, note for note, so most things were played by session guys, and I'd have to play with string players sitting in the studio at the same time. *Tumbleweed* was more or less written down note for note because there was a budget in those days. The *Elton John* album cost about £6–7,000, which was enormous back then, like about $15,000. At that time the idea of investing that much of my money in it was just incredible.

You were putting out a lot of records back then too.

That was because we had a contract for two albums a year, and we stuck to it. We didn't find that hard to do. I remember too that everyone was amazed that we could do two albums per year. People like Santana were in litigation at one point for not delivering albums, Linda Ronstadt was when she left Capitol, and Dylan was when he went to Asylum. I never wanted to get into a situation where I owed some company albums. Most of our albums were so easy after *Elton John* and *Tumbleweed*, but when I wanted to stop using session musicians and start using my band all the time, [producer] Gus Dudgeon didn't want me to. I fought hard enough to get one track for the band on *Tumbleweed*, called "Amoreena," but by the end of *Madman Across the Water* I really wanted to start using the band.

Do you find working with your band less efficient in terms of time than working with session players?

Oh, no. We always recorded quickly. I just hate wasting time in the studio.

Nowadays, of course, recording has gotten a little more prolonged and scientific, and with the advent of 24 tracks and 48 tracks the temptation was to go crazy. But you do your best work when you have discipline. We used to do three or four tracks a day at Caribou Studios in Colorado, for example; I used to do 11 vocals in one day. When we did *Caribou*, the basic tracks had to be finished in ten days because we had to go to Japan. And two days were spent getting a drum sound, so we had eight days to record the album.

Are you more satisfied by your later albums than your earlier ones, because of more sophisticated studio facilities?

I don't know. Look at the old Beatles records. All the original things we did were on 8-track, then later 16, and I'm constantly surprised by how good things like *Tumbleweed* and *Elton John* sound when I listen to them now. It seems that sophistication hasn't really improved things much. I don't know how people can take a year to do an album. Everybody to their own sort of thing, I suppose; nobody works the same way, but I'd just go mental if I had to spend a year over an album, hearing those things over and over again. No way. I have to work fairly quickly in a studio.

Do you ever record the piano and voice simultaneously?

No, hardly ever. The only time we did that was on "Ticking," which was on *Caribou*.

That sounded like a pretty complicated piano part too.

It was, but playing the piano without the voice was harder: I would think so much about the voice that I wouldn't play the piano right. Gus was always a stickler for separation, but I had to tell him, "Look, the only way we're ever going to get this thing done is by doing the voice and piano together, and forget about the leakage." It would only be the voice leaking anyway, so why care? When we're doing the instrumental track, though, I usually whisper a rough vocal into the headphones, because it's helpful for other people to play if they can hear a guide vocal. That can be frustrating, though, because you have to whisper it to avoid leakage into the piano. But we've also done things like "Saturday Night's Alright for Fighting," which was recorded without the piano, but we put it on later because we couldn't get the right feeling.

When you compare your earliest albums to the ones you're doing now, can you hear any changes in your piano style?

Not really. I haven't picked up any new influences. I like Keith Jarrett, but I would hate to say that my piano playing is at all like his, because it's absolutely not. Over the last years the only guy who's really influenced me has been Bill Payne. I love his sort of time-signature changes in the middle of things; he does all the "don'ts" and I love that.

When you're playing alone for your own enjoyment, do you often extemporize freely?

Oh, yeah, all the time. I very rarely sit down and play—I don't just get up every morning and play the piano—but when I'm in the mood to do it, I can play for hours. Just playing "Stand by Me" for hours is wonderful; those chord changes are so fabulous. But I mess around all the time, and then out of something like that comes a song. My songs aren't planned; they just come out of the blue. The only time we've written planned songs in the last few years was when the Beach Boys asked us to write something for them. It took me six months, and nothing had ever taken me that long before! It's called "Chameleon," and it's on the *Blue Moves* album. They hated it [*laughs*], so I said, "Right! That's the last time I'm going to write a song for anybody. Forget it."

How did that uninhibited performing style evolve? You weren't leaping around in your days as a pub pianist, were you?

Well, I was always physically held back from wearing what I wanted to as a teenager, so being able to put on any clothes I liked helped to evolve that style, I suppose. People used to say that it detracts from the music, and I can understand their point of view, but I was just having a good time. I enjoyed it, and I think people did too, because I didn't take myself too seriously. When the singer/songwriter thing did evolve in the early '70s, a lot of musicians were starting to get very intense about what they were doing, and people did take them maybe a little seriously. I mean, look at the cover to the *Elton John* album. It was so confusing, all dark and mean and mysterious, yet there I was onstage, popping along with Mickey Mouse ears. I've always been a rock and roller, so maybe if that album had had a different cover, it wouldn't have been so confusing.

So there was never a moment when you kicked over your first piano bench and decided to change your style.

Not really. I used to do that in England before we came over to the States. Pete Townshend [of the Who] used to smash his guitar and amplifier on some nights. I can't remember how it evolved. I think maybe one night I just kicked the piano stool over, and it got to be a regular part of the act. But I haven't had too many scenes like that lately. You can't really argue with a piano stool too much.

You once described yourself as a rock pianist of the Little Richard school, as opposed to the Jerry Lee Lewis school. Could you explain how you differentiate between these two styles?

Well, Little Richard was more of a straight vamper, and Jerry Lee Lewis had more technique. He did those long runs, so he was probably a better piano player in that sense, but little Richard had more soul. I mean, they've both influenced my life and I love them both very dearly, but Little Richard was the king for me.

That's interesting, because you also play in a much more mellow arpeggiated ballad style that has nothing to do with either of them.

Absolutely. I don't know where I got that from at all. But I used to stand in front of the mirror and mime to Little Richard and Jerry Lee Lewis records. Little Richard was just an ace. And to play the piano standing up like he did is not easy, because the piano keys are quite low down, and he never used to look at them either. When you analyze the sound of their records and take it separately, it's crap, but when you put it all together, it's wonderful.

Portions of this article originally were published in the February 1981 issue of Keyboard *magazine.*

FOR MORE ON ELTON JOHN

Elton John continues to write, record, and tour. In fact, Elton and Billy Joel continue to tour together extensively. You can connect with him at his official website, web.eltonjohn.com.

A SELECTED ELTON JOHN DISCOGRAPHY

Every single year, from the time of his debut in the U.S. market in 1970 until 1996, Elton John had a single in the Top 40 charts, a feat unequalled by any other artist. His remake of "Candle in the Wind, 1997," as a tribute to his great friend the late Princess Diana, became the fastest-selling hit single of all time as well as the biggest hit of his career. His collaborations with Tim Rice on the Disney animated film *The Lion King* garnered Grammys, and the soundtrack of their collaboration on the live stage show *Aida* went gold. Oh, yeah, and he recorded all of these albums full of great songs and piano playing, too.

2006 *The Captain & the Kid*
2004 *Peachtree Road*
2001 *Songs from the West Coast*
2000 *The Road to El Dorado*
1999 *Aida*
1999 *The Muse*
1997 *Big Picture*
1995 *Made in England*
1994 *The Lion King*
1993 *Duets*
1992 *The One*
1989 *Sleeping with the Past*
1988 *Reg Strikes Back*
1987 *Live in Australia*
1986 *Leather Jackets*
1985 *Ice on Fire*
1984 *Breaking Hearts*
1983 *Too Low for Zero*

1982 *Jump Up!*
1981 *The Fox*
1980 *21 at 33*
1979 *Victim of Love*
1978 *A Single Man*
1976 *Blue Moves*
1976 *Here and There (Live)*
1975 *Rock of Westies*
1975 *Captain Fantastic and the Brown Dirt Cowboy*
1974 *Caribou*
1973 *Goodbye Yellow Brick Road*
1973 *Don't Shoot Me I'm Only the Piano Player*
1972 *Honky Chateau*
1971 *Madman Across the Water*
1971 *Tumbleweed Collection*
1970 *Elton John*

TIMELESS
TALENT

MICHAEL McDONALD

BY ROBERT L. DOERSCHUK

DUES WITH THE DOOBIES

IT'S NOT NEWS TO *Keyboard* readers, but keyboards are on the ascendancy in rock and roll, and there is no better way to demonstrate this than to cite the case of the Doobie Brothers and their singer/songwriter/keyboardist, Michael McDonald. His husky voice and funky piano work have helped propel the Doobies not only to the top of the charts in recent years, but onto the sacrosanct pages of *People* magazine, where he received official blessings as a "new sex-symbol star."

Michael was not a founding member of the group. In the early '70s, thanks to a string of hits that included "Listen to the Music," "Jesus Is Just Alright," "China Grove," and "Long Train Running," the pre-McDonald Doobies established themselves as one of the biggest acts in the business. Their roots were in the lively San Francisco Bay Area music scene of the '60s, and like most bands from that place and time, they built their sound around the guitar. Their trademark, in fact, was the folk-oriented electric strumming of Pat Simmons, which anchored their clean, high vocal lines.

Then came the mid-'70s, heralding some new directions for music in general and the Doobies in particular. As the aggressive raunch of the earlier era began to smooth into a tighter, more controlled style, keyboards often started taking over the guitar's role as the typical group's rhythmic and textural terra firma. The Brothers' invitation to McDonald to sub for ailing guitarist and singer Tom Johnston on their 1975 tour was therefore especially well-timed. Fresh from a live stint with Steely Dan, where he had worked with Doobie-guitarist-to-be Jeff Baxter, the 24-year-old newcomer plunged into two days of practice with the group, then took to the stage before 18,000 fans as the first ever official Doobie Brother keyboard player.

It didn't take long for his influence to broaden the focus of the band. Keyboards began to appear at the forefront of their most popular songs, especially those written by Michael, like "It Keeps You Runnin'," "Takin' It to the Streets," "Minute by Minute," and their number one single, "What a Fool Believes," a collaboration between McDonald and singer/songwriter Kenny Loggins. The contributions of Pat Simmons continued to echo the earlier sound of the Doobies, but more and more McDonald added strong shots of rhythm and blues, tempered with an apparent knack for reeling off one hit composition after another.

All of this made McDonald a hot item in Hollywood. His works have been recorded by Billy Paul, Quincy Jones, Pablo Cruise, Jack Jones, and O. C. Smith, among others, and he joined with singer Carly Simon to co-author one of her recent hits, "You Belong to Me." And he puts in long hours backing up other artists at recording sessions, usually as a vocalist, an important part of his musical life since he arrived in Los Angeles in 1970 to record an album of original material and sing behind everybody from Jack Jones to David Cassidy.

Offstage Michael is soft-spoken and shy. His self-deprecatory attitude with regard to his keyboard skills marked a refreshing deviation from the horn-tooting posture often affected by many rock celebrities. After five years of international success with the Doobie Brothers, there is still more down-home St. Louis than Beverly Hills glitter in the modest McDonald personality.

What kind of musical training did you receive as a child?

Well, in short, I really had very little formal study in my background. I took piano lessons when I was a little kid from a guy in St. Louis who was a friend of my father's. He played piano, and my father was a singer, an Irish tenor. Dad never sang professionally, but he sang in every bar all over the city of St. Louis. In all the years I knew him, my father never took a drink, but he was in more bars than any drunk, because he loved to sing. My whole family is like that. They're music freaks. They're brought together by music, and they love it. I learned about it at that level, as a kind of basic human habit from just being in the family. They're thrilled to death at what I'm doing now.

So the John McCormack style of singing was the first kind of music you were exposed to?

MICHAEL McDONALD

Exactly—old World War I songs that my uncles would sing as they sat around. My grandmother and her brothers were all World War I age. I'm sure that my father was my first real influence, in the sense that he wished he could have become a singer. I think that was the one thing he might have really wanted to do, but somehow he never saw fit, with the Depression and getting married, to pursue that as a career. But he did drag me in and out of every bar in St. Louis; my mother wouldn't let him out without a hassle unless he took me with him.

Do you remember your performing debut?

Oh, I remember it explicitly. I was real little, four years old, and it was a typical Saturday. My father was a bus driver, so on Saturdays he would go by the bus station, then he'd go by the bars, and I would hang out with him. Like I say, he never drank; he just met his friends, and he liked to socialize. Anyway, on this particular Saturday, they got me up on the bar, and I sang "Around the World in Eighty Days." I couldn't even hold a tune, but I loved it. More than anything, I think I enjoyed the recognition from him and all the people. It was a very young age to be hit with such a positive reaction to something, so I was hooked. From that moment on I wanted to be a musician for the rest of my life, truly because of that experience.

Did you primarily want to be a singer?

I pretty much always wanted to be a singer. I really don't consider myself much of a piano player. I played to write songs, more than anything else. I have a certain knowledge of harmony and chord progressions, but I wouldn't call myself a pianist, really. I mainly decided to pursue it so that I could sing and play at the same time, but studying the technical part of it just didn't appeal to me as a kid, so I let it go and I didn't really pick it up again until I got into rock and roll.

Did you do any more formal studying after that?

Yeah. I took lessons recently from a guy named Fletcher Peck, a teacher who was living in L.A. He's such a great teacher. First of all, the guy is an excellent pianist, but he taught me more about the piano than I'd ever known before. I was much worse at the keyboard before he got to me than I am now [*laughs*]. During the year I knew him, he expanded my horizons as far as my writing was concerned, too. What he did mainly was to give me harmonic exercises and things that got me better acquainted with the piano—scales and stuff I never knew I was doing before. Not that I know now about everything I play, but I just took a huge leap forward by knowing that guy. A lot of the inspiration for the writing and playing I did on our last album [*Minute by Minute*] sprang from working with him.

Is it true that you played banjo for a while when you were a kid?

I played some banjo, but in my first rock and roll band I played guitar. I went from that to just working as a singer, and that was a disaster. I never made it performing as a stand-up singer, so I started playing the piano and writing then.

So you took up the piano largely to have something to do onstage?

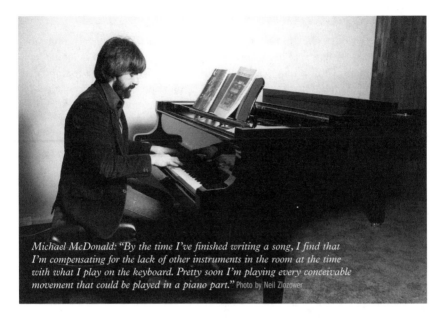

Michael McDonald: "By the time I've finished writing a song, I find that I'm compensating for the lack of other instruments in the room at the time with what I play on the keyboard. Pretty soon I'm playing every conceivable movement that could be played in a piano part." Photo by Neil Zlozower

Well, that was one reason, plus it just slipped back in there when I started writing. It felt more natural for me to compose at the piano than at the guitar.

You can often tell with the Doobie Brothers whether a song was written by Pat Simmons on guitar or by you at a keyboard.

That's true. What I notice about that is that piano songs don't travel in such a straight line all the time, because with the piano the relationships of the tones are all laid out in front of you. I think more ideas come to your mind when you can look at it like that, whereas with the guitar you tend to write more abstractly; more of the music is square or geometric, somehow. With me and the piano, though, the main thing I've always noticed is that some of my better songs are written out of ignorance, based on what I didn't know. Chord changes that I really enjoy and like now I have no basic reason for coming up with, other than pure accident.

Are you saying that your creativity has at times been inhibited by what training you've had?

No, never by what I did have, but miraculously I've been taken in another direction by my lack of it sometimes. If I knew more about what I was doing, I don't honestly think I would have written some of the songs I've done. I shouldn't really say that, because the more I learn about the piano the better are the songs I write, there's no doubt about that. But as I look back on a lot of the earlier stuff, I find a certain charm and I realize I wouldn't have written things that way if I had known what I was doing. It's not a question of being musical; it's just the spirit and the simplicity of these songs. I would hate to lose those qualities in trying to incorporate all my chops into songwriting.

Did you once compose songs on guitar?

I used to write a little on guitar, but I was such a terrible guitar player that it was kind of senseless to just sit there and hammer away. The chances were pretty slim that I would be able to come up with a tune all the time on piano, but I was really making the odds unbearable when I would sit with the guitar.

What kind of process do you usually go through in writing a song?

A lot of times I'll start with the chords first. I have a real affection for chord changes. Once I have them down I'll try out a melody that revolves somewhere around the root, and then I'll try to write a melody over the same changes that is like a third up, just to see if I can find a melody that accentuates the changes. I would have to say that what I enjoy most about writing songs is trying to come up with interesting changes. That's why I used to love Burt Bacharach's songs. I always enjoyed his use of chords, like the way he'd change keys for a chorus.

How did you write your first hit with the Doobies, "Takin' It to the Streets" on *Takin' It to the Streets*?

The chords came first on that one. I heard the chord changes as I was driving in my car. I wasn't sure if I could play what I was hearing when I got to a piano; I didn't know if it was one of those ideas that sound great in your head, but once you sit down and try it out it doesn't sound right. I guess it worked all right, though.

How about your collaboration with Kenny Loggins on "What a Fool Believes" from *Minute by Minute*?

Kenny called me out of the clear blue sky one day. I'd never met him in my life, but he said that he enjoyed our records and would love to write something with me. So I said, "I'd love to write together with you too. Why don't you come over this week or something?" We made a date for the next night. I knew that I wanted to work with him on this song, which I'd been trying to finish but had kind of reached a dead end with. To make a long story short, he came over and we worked on it until around five in the morning for a couple of nights, and on nights we didn't get together we talked on the phone about it. In about five days we managed to write the song. I was glad I had worked with him, because I don't think the song would be anywhere near as good had I not gone to him with the basic idea I had for it. He's an amazingly musical guy, and there's a lot of music in that song.

There are a lot of keyboards in it as well. Did you have the keyboard arrangement in your mind as you wrote the tune?

No, it was hashed out later. Billy Payne [of Little Feat] and I just did it by head. I'd already cut the track with either electric or acoustic piano, I don't really remember which, and I just had Billy bring in his synthesizers. It was mainly a matter of us sitting around going, "Well, you do this and I'll do that." I'd start to show him the part I wanted, and I'd wind up playing it myself on his synthesizer. Then he just sat around and came up with the string part on the Oberheim Eight-Voice. During the course of the session he was working with sort of a half horn and half steel drum program on the Yamaha CS-80. Patrick came up with his guitar parts later. I really enjoyed some of the stuff he played on it; I think they are hooks that really add to the record. It was basically a day of sitting around the studio and having a pretty good time.

How do you evolve your own keyboard parts?

The tune kind of dictates them itself. By the time I've just about finished writing a song, I find that I'm trying to compensate for the lack of bass and other instruments in the room at the time with what I play on the keyboard. Pretty soon I'm playing every conceivable movement that could be played in a piano part, so a lot of times I'll have to go back later to force myself to play a lot less and let the band start playing the song.

Often there is a lot of left-hand work in your piano playing.

Yeah, and sometimes there's even a lot more before I get through doing it with the band. I have to let go of some of that and let them come up with their own parts.

What led you toward that R&B style on the keyboard after being raised on Irish songs?

I really don't know. I've always loved that music. I grew up in St. Louis, and that town is pretty predominantly oriented towards rhythm and blues; Stax/Volt records was right down the river in Memphis, and Chess records in Chicago wasn't too far away, so St. Louis was really a pocket for that kind of music during the time I grew up.

Were there any particular piano players who influenced you in those days?

I don't think I really ever listened too intently to anybody, like I hear some guys say they have. They'll say, "Hey, have you heard Art Tatum, or Oscar Peterson, or blah blah blah?" They give you the impression that they do a lot of listening to other people's styles. Well, whatever style I have was derived in a general sense from being surrounded by different kinds of music. I never was much into sitting down and listening to one record or album many times. I've always worked as a musician, so most of the music I got, I got in my day-to-day work; I was always learning somebody else's songs, and I got more education and knowledge from the people I was working with than from anywhere else.

Since you used the piano a lot to accompany your own singing, did you learn to play easily in whatever odd keys your voice happened to fit?

Mainly I started out in *C*, because for some reason it seemed to me like the easiest key for playing. I always felt I could sing wherever I had to, which I think is a good philosophy for singers, because it lets you stretch your capacity beyond your limits if you thought you were straining your voice all the time. You either have to have a throat that can take your sitting there and screaming, or you really have to build yourself up to it. When I'm off for a while, I don't try to kill myself during the first couple of days of rehearsal. I might sound like a dying dog, but I'll let myself go through that, and if it doesn't feel right, I won't sing the whole song. After a few more days I'll be ready to sing again. I work my way up to it gradually that way, but usually I keep my voice in enough shape to at least be able to get up and yell.

What were your first recording experiences in L.A. like?

I was brought out by a producer named Rich Jarrard. He was producing [guitarist/singer] Jose Feliciano, the first couple of [singer] Harry Nilsson albums, and [Jefferson Airplane's] *Surrealistic Pillow*. I was with him for five years, doing a lot of sessions as a piano player and backup vocalist, and we recorded two albums together featuring me as a writer and singer. I was writing a lot of songs then; I was very young, and I sounded like it [*laughs*]. Those records were me at the time. Neither of them made it big, but they were good albums. I had some good times with Rich, and I learned so much from working with him that I don't think I'd be able to even do what I'm doing today if it weren't for what I learned then. I'm sure I wouldn't. So it was a very good learning period.

Did you absorb a lot in your sessions with artists like Jack Jones that has helped you in your current career?

Oh, yeah, I picked up a lot. I worked with some great musicians there. I really had no business doing those gigs, as far as that goes, but nevertheless I learned so much, primarily about how to make records. I made the most of the opportunity I had in those situations.

Were they helpful in learning how to adjust your playing to other styles of music as well?

Yeah, although I learned a lot about that in playing piano at various club dates. Playing clubs is a whole other aspect of growing musically, and it deals with things like how to build your endurance, how to play with an ensemble, how to keep up your energy, and other elements that don't really come into play all the time when you're doing sessions. You can do a lot of sessions and still not experience the kind of playing you go through live onstage with five other musicians in terms of being inspired or playing behind somebody's solo, just using your creative mind spontaneously to build dynamics together with the soloist, and trying to relate to other players so you can guess where they're going and figure out how to meet them there.

Did you ever record on keyboard with Steely Dan?

Oh, no, I've never played keyboard with them, except onstage. I sang on *Katy Lied* and on a lot of their albums since then, but they've just used me for background. Those guys are the all-time greatest for me. I think they're the best songwriters I've ever heard in any category. I just enjoy working for them, and I always look forward to the next session.

Do you feel that your arrival signified a change in direction for the Doobies?

Things did change, but kind of naturally. It's not that I just showed up and changed everything. The band has changed me a lot too. I really started out just filling in for Tom Johnston, who was kind of ill, by doing some singing. I think Pat had originally intended to do all of Tom's vocals, but then we wound up splitting them between us. When "Takin' It to the Streets" came about and it was time to do another album, things got kind of chaotic. Tom was still ill, so anybody who could write a song came up with something.

How has being in the Doobie Brothers changed your personal musical tastes?

Well, I've gotten in touch with a certain kind of energy that I've never felt in playing with bands before. My old band had more of a funky, low-key energy, but the Doobies play a different kind of full-out energetic music. I think it's a real fun experience. I enjoy playing with the band, and I enjoy playing with the new line-up the way it is.

Have you and Pat collaborated on any material?

We collaborate at different stages—arrangement stages, mainly. In terms of writing, Pat pretty much writes his stuff and I write mine. Then we get it together and the band gets in on it. Our music is pretty simple. It gets kind of complicated in funny ways sometimes, but if you just strip the songs down to their basics—a piano and a voice—our music is pretty much pop material. I've always wanted to write songs that I'd like to hear on the car radio, and that's where our music is at. That's what gets us off. There's just something about the feeling of American music. It's what I grew up with, and it's what I dig playing.

How has your onstage keyboard setup changed through the years with the Doobies?

I've gotten it down to a pretty simple arrangement now. I used to get up there with an Oberheim Eight-Voice synthesizer, which was silly because I never got the chance to use it too much, since I'm always singing leads. I was using a Yamaha 6' grand piano until I switched over to the Yamaha CP-70 electric grand. Now I've got a Rhodes, a Clavinet, and a Sequential Circuits Prophet-5 synthesizer.

Where was your first contact with synthesizers?

It was with this band, actually. I did a demo with a Minimoog on "Losin' End" [from *Takin' It to the Streets*] in Tiran's [Porter, bass guitarist] basement.

Did you ever use the Minimoog onstage?

I never really played it live. I never soloed on it or anything. I don't take many solos now, but when I do it's usually on piano. I'm still not really comfortable with any of the synthesizers. I go from song to song and learn what to do in each case to get what I need. I haven't really spent any time sitting around trying to figure them out. When I first joined this band all I had as a setup was a small Wurlitzer electric piano going through a Twin Reverb or something, and that was it. That's all I used. I'd just throw it in the back of my car, haul it from club to club, set it up, and play.

What interested you in the Oberheim?

I was mainly turned onto it by our road crew. I just liked the sound of it. It was also very adaptable to pretty much anything you wanted to do. You could do a lot with it as far as programming each VCO module separately, and with all the switching mechanisms, it just seemed like the state-of-the-art synthesizer at the time to me. Mainly, though, I went with it because it was one of the first polyphonic synthesizers I even knew of at the time.

Why did you switch to the Prophet?

Mainly because I found myself not getting into synthesizers so much. It just wasn't me to be that involved with them. Most of my preoccupation was with writing. The Prophet was just the easiest of all the polyphonic synthesizers to play. A lot of things attracted me to it: I liked the tuning mechanism live, I thought it sounded great, and I thought it would just be easier for me to deal with on the road.

Do you play the 88-key stage model Rhodes?

Yes. It's been modified somewhat. Dixie Swanson, our stage manager, got inside and rewired it, and put a little preamp right behind the input to give it more of that suitcase model Rhodes sound; the high end has a sparkling kind of sound now.

Do you run the Rhodes through any effects?

I like to use the Vox Chorale on the Rhodes; that's a nice pedal. I don't use much else. For a long time I'd just take the Rhodes direct, and Grey Ingram, our engineer, had an Eventide Harmonizer. Now I use my Rhodes with a Leslie in a small wooden cabinet, like a 147. We put it inside a road box when we're on tour and just mic it through the board from offstage. It really sounds neat, and I've found that that's the best sound we can get with it so far.

Do you do a lot of keyboard overdubbing in the studio?

Yeah. I usually play only the piano or electric piano on the basic track with the bass and drums. We generally then build the tracks with a guitar player, but most of the time we just start with that basic rhythm section, and then I put other keyboards on later if I'm going to use them. It's a hassle sometimes to have to figure out how to play all the stuff at once when we go out live, but we cover for each other. When we do "What a Fool Believes," the guitar players take over one of the synthesizer parts, and it works out real well. Onstage I play the string lines and the piano part.

How will you and Cornelius Bumpus, your other keyboardist and sax player, interact on your instruments?

Corny and I may develop some kind of exchange of solos or coordinate our synthesizer playing, but I don't know; it's tough sometimes to add that much synthesizer stuff into a live show. I'm just not that quick-minded with synthesizers, and I think that's the main thing that keeps me away from being a real expert with them. I mean, my style is a whole different bag. I like to sit down and sing in front of people. I like to rock and roll, and I like to just relax and perform, as opposed to having too much going on at once that distracts me from simply enjoying the song and doing it the best I can.

Is that how you view the Doobie Brothers—as purely a goodtime rock and roll band?

Well, I see us more as a manifestation of a lot of elements, more so than as an input into what direction rock and roll is going or anything like that. I think that we, like I guess everybody else, stem from what has gone before us. We play rock and roll as good and better than most, and sometimes it's even better sounding live than it was on record. But it's tight, you know, and we try to keep the band as solid, tight, and impressive as we can. None of us are virtuoso players or anything, but as a band we have a certain talent. We're entertainers in the sense that we have a good time when we play in front of people, and that's always a very relaxed situation for us. I enjoy live performing very much. It's a chance for me to sing out all night long, and it's a big release. I don't think I could live without it.

Portions of this article originally were published in the August 1979 issue of Keyboard *magazine.*

FOR MORE ON MICHAEL McDONALD

Michael's on the road constantly, and he puts together interesting collaborations and projects quite often. You can connect with him at his official website, www.michaelmcdonald.com.

A SELECTED MICHAEL McDONALD DISCOGRAPHY

Michael embarked on a solo career after he left the Doobie Brothers in 1982. Though his solo albums are few and far between, and not all of them have charted as well as his initial release, *If That's What It Takes*, Michael's amazing talents are in force on each one. He achieved success again with his duets with other artists, such as "On My Own" with Patti LaBelle in 1982 and "Ever Changing Times" with Aretha Franklin in 1992.

AS A SOLO ARTIST
2008 *Soul Speak*
2004 *Motown Two*
2003 *Motown*
2001 *In the Spirit: A Christmas Album*
1997 *Blue Obsession*
1993 *Blink of an Eye*
1990 *Take it to Heart*
1985 *No Lookin' Back*

1982 *If That's What It Takes*

WITH THE DOOBIE BROTHERS
1983 *Farewell Tour*
1980 *One Step Closer*
1978 *Minute by Minute*
1977 *Livin' on the Fault Line*
1976 *Takin' It to the Streets*

Steve Winwood and Minimoog: a soulful voice with a soulful synth.
Photo by Ebet Roberts

STEVE WINWOOD

BY ROBERT L. DOERSCHUK

DIVING INTO DIVERSITY

EARLY THIS YEAR, A familiar voice was heard again on the radio after too long an absence. It had changed over the years, grown deeper and developed more control where it had once been wild and driven beyond its limits by the singer's elemental talent. And where it had drawn strength from a powerhouse blend of jazz and blues piano and organ, it now floated in a more subtle sea of synthesizer colors. The keyboards and the vocals together brought their message to the '80s: Steve Winwood is back.

Winwood has faded in and out of view throughout his long career, always resurfacing in different guises, from the psychedelic esoterica of early Traffic to such ambitious superstar adventures as Blind Faith and percussionist Stomu Yamashta's project Go. Now, with the success of his latest solo album, *Arc of a Diver*, he shows another persona, this time as the consummate solo rock artist, with something fresh to say as a singer, songwriter, and, of course, multi-keyboardist.

After watching Winwood in his various bands and solo efforts for some 17 years, one is struck by the fact that he is only 33 years old. It is easy to forget, when listening to his classic early records with the Spencer Davis Group, that behind the searing organ work of "Blues in F," the gospel funk piano of "Can't Get Enough of It," and the wailing vocals of "Gimme Some Lovin'," was a slightly-built boy in his mid-teens.

Born in Birmingham, England, in 1948, Steve received his taste for music from his father, a semiprofessional saxophonist. He began piano lessons as a child, and attended music college for a year as a young teenager, studying theory and composition. Steve's first gig was with the Muff Woody Jazz Band, a Birmingham-based group led by his bass-playing older brother Muff. Steve was 15 when he joined the group in 1963, but despite his youth he was already an accomplished instrumentalist and singer. Spencer

Davis, then a 22-year-old teacher at Birmingham University and guitarist with his own R&B band, recalled hearing him for the first time at the Digbeth Civic Hall that year: "I'd heard rumors about this guy named Steve Winwood," he told *Crawdaddy* magazine. "When I saw him it was a revelation! Steve, who was about 15 and still wearing short pants, was at the piano playing an Oscar Peterson-type thing. Then Steve got hold of a melodica, and did a version of 'One Mint Julep' that sent shivers down to the bottom of my spine."

In 1964, the Winwood brothers joined Davis and drummer Peter York in their gig at the Golden Eagle, a Birmingham pub. They honed their gritty style on material lifted from records by John Lee Hooker, Betty Everett, and other American R&B artists; their first album, now out of print, reflected this orientation largely through young Steve's impassioned versions of "Nobody Knows You When You're Down and Out," "Georgia," and other chestnuts. One of the newer songs from that LP—"Keep on Running," written by a West Indian tunesmith named Jackie Edwards—broke into the British hit lists, lodging at the number one position in 1965. (Their first single, "I Can't Stand It," recorded in November 1964, ran aground in the lower end of the charts.) The band's third release—another Edwards song, "Somebody Help Me,"—likewise featuring Winwood's startling vocals, also climbed to the top shortly afterward.

Their first international smash, though, was "Gimme Some Lovin'," which reached number two in England and the American Top Ten in December 1966. Written by Steve and Spencer, the song was based on the bass riff to a Homer Banks record, "Whole Lotta Lovin'," but it took a flavor of its own in Winwood's hands. His growling Hammond tone and effective use of the Leslie vibrato were especially important elements in making this one of the most stunning records to come out of the '60s—in spite of the fact that prior to this recording session, according to Spencer Davis, Winwood had never even touched a Hammond organ!

There would be one more worldwide hit by the Spencer Davis Group: "I'm a Man," co-written by Steve and producer Jimmy Miller. But by the time of its release early in 1967, Winwood was already preparing to explore a different musical direction. For three months in 1966, he rehearsed and recorded several tracks with guitarist Eric Clapton and bassist Jack Bruce, later of Cream; although three of their cuts appeared on the Elektra anthology album *What's Shakin'*, their band, called Powerhouse, never got off the ground.

Instead, Steve's energy was funneled into a search for new ideas with some old friends: saxophonist Chris Wood, a veteran of the Birmingham jam session circuit; drummer Jim Capaldi, whose father had played with Winwood's dad at local pubs and weddings; and Dave Mason, who played guitar with Capaldi in a group called the Hellions and had since gotten a job as a roadie with Spencer Davis. They were exploring the possibilities of working together even in early 1966, when they played their first job at a venue called the Elbow Room.

Mason has even stated that it was they, not the Davis Group, who recorded "I'm a Man." As the year went on, Winwood began getting more restless with Spencer Davis' strict R&B format and more interested in the looser, more improvisatory potential of this new quartet. In April 1967, he played his final gig with Davis, on singer Cliff Richard's TV show. The next day, he moved off to a cottage that he and his new partners had leased in the Berkshire countryside. There, the seeds of what would become Traffic were planted.

After six months of living and practicing together, the band emerged in June '67 with a hit single, "Paper Sun," and an album, *Mr. Fantasy*, which showed a combination of spontaneity and innovation missing from Winwood's earlier work. The complex interplay of personalities in Traffic produced several flavors of music, from acid rock with an English accent ("Hole in My Shoe") to beerhall shoutfests ("Feeling Alright," recorded, crudely but effectively, on a cassette machine). In their early material, Winwood was a less dominant figure than he had been with Davis; the influence especially of Dave Mason seemed to soften his approach, stimulate his composing, bring out his skills as a guitarist, and diminish the importance of his keyboard playing. For those fans who expected more soulful virtuosity, this new Steve Winwood was a surprise.

Mason's revolving-door relationship with the band had a deleterious effect, however. Personal tensions among the four led to the dissolution of Traffic after a period of carrying on without Mason as a trio. Once again Steve and Eric Clapton got together, and with bassist Rick Grech and drummer Ginger Baker, they formed Blind Faith. The optimistic title and promising LP weren't enough to hold the talent-laden band together, though, and after a debut concert in London's Hyde Park before 100,000 enthusiasts and an American tour to mixed reviews, Blind Faith came to an end.

But musically, this group had a strong effect on Winwood. On their LP, *Blind Faith*, he stepped forward again as a keyboardist, even taking a long solo in Baker's 5/4 showcase "Do What You Like." When Steve re-formed Traffic in 1970 to record *John Barleycorn Must Die*, it was as a three-piece again. Mason was gone, the production was less experimental, and once again Winwood stood out as the focal point, with lengthy improvisations on organ ("Mother Nature's Son") and electric piano ("Empty Pages"). This balance was preserved in the final batch of Traffic albums, like *The Low Spark of High Heeled Boys*—a more conservative product than the group's first releases, despite the amorphous looseness—and their farewell record, *When the Eagle Flies*.

Since then, Winwood hasn't involved himself in any permanent group situations. Throughout the '70s, however, he has participated in various one-shot efforts, including a pair of albums in 1971 with American bluesmen Muddy Waters and Howlin' Wolf [*London Sessions*]; Eric Clapton's comeback concert at London's Rainbow Theatre in 1973; and Stomu Yamashta's two ambitious per-

Steve Winwood playing an RMI electric piano in 1970 with drummer Ginger Baker's Air Force. Photo courtesy of Keyboard magazine

formances with Go, a pickup group that featured Winwood, synthesist Klaus Schulze, and drummer Mike Shrieve. He also came out with his first solo album, simply titled *Steve Winwood*, in 1977. Backed by a relaxed lineup, including Traffic alumni Jim Capaldi and percussionist Reebop Kwaku Baah, Steve still echoed the latter-day Traffic in the unhurried and unstructured air of tunes like "Vacant Chair" and "Luck's In," while balancing out his keyboard soloing with long guitar fills. But there were also indicators of changes to come, especially in the tentative first steps toward using keyboards for coloristic background textures, and even in chord voicings; some of the seventh chords in "Midland Maniac" can be heard intact on "Spanish Dancer," from his latest album.

With the release of *Arc of a Diver* this year, Winwood has taken firm steps beyond his past in Traffic, and has planted himself solidly in the '80s. The success of this album—up to number one in the Billboard charts as we went to press—showed that even though he hadn't played onstage in several years, Steve had been growing musically. The increasing prominence of keyboards in modern rock is reflected here, along with the contemporary preference for tight arrangements. *Arc of a Diver* is also a complete Winwood work; although he wrote all the tunes in collaborations with others, each drumbeat, every note, and every vocal phrase was his own. More than most recent self-styled solo albums, this was a genuinely singular tour de force.

On the edge of what may be one of the musical comebacks of the decade in rock, Steve Winwood, a soft-spoken veteran of the music scene when many his age are only beginning to define their interests and careers, met with *Keyboard* during a recent trip to Los Angeles.

Why did you decide to do *Arc of a Diver* by yourself? This was the first album you've ever done with no sidemen at all.

That's right. The first one I didn't use an engineer on as well. It's something I've always wanted to do, but I'd never been able to. I always found it difficult. Also, I'd built this studio in my house that finally enabled me to do it myself. I don't think I would have been able to do it completely alone in a commercial studio.

Because of the costs?

Because of the costs and the pressure and everything. I've always enjoyed messing around with tape machines and overdubbing, but it's very difficult to do that if you're working with other people, because they need the patience of Job. If an artist is doing all the overdubbing, it's a long time before anybody who isn't directly involved can see that there's anything worthwhile happening. A producer is not going to sit around for three days with nothing happening, then suddenly wake up when it comes together on the third day and say, "Oh, yeah!" He's going to keep saying, "Why don't you do this? Why don't you do that?" That's why I prefer working totally alone if I'm going to overdub. If you're going to work with other people, you have to work with other people; it's one or the other.

Was it also hard to create the kind of groove a live band can generate, when doing all the tracks alone?

In a lot of ways that was the main problem, but I really did the album in such a way that the tunes could be played by a band, and to a certain extent it sounds like a band, so I'm happy with it.

How many of the bass lines were done on bass guitar, and how many on keyboard?

It's keyboard on all of them, even the ones that sound like a bass guitar.

What instruments did you use for the bass?

I used a Multimoog, and I think I used a Minimoog on a couple of the cuts. My basic education on synths was with the Minimoog. It was one of the first mono synthesizers, and I got used to it. I did get the Multimoog, which I suppose is just an updated version of the Minimoog. It has more voices, and the triggering is not always from the same place; it goes up the keyboard. It has a ribbon instead of a pitch wheel too, but that was basically the only mono synth I used.

For solos as well as bass lines?

Yeah.

Were you trying to phrase the bass lines like a bass guitarist?

Yes. Had there not been a synthesizer that sounded like a bass guitar, I would most certainly have played bass guitar. I wouldn't have been able to play the stuff I did on the album, but I certainly would have had a go at it. I did play bass guitar on some Traffic stuff, but I could never play it with the technique I know and understand on the keyboard.

To bend notes with a string-vibrato effect, did you prefer the Multimoog ribbon to the Minimoog wheel?

Yeah. I'd gotten used to the Minimoog technique, and going to the ribbon was a bit of a changeover; but now the ribbon feels a lot better, in fact, than the wheel. I only use Minimoogs for patching into sequencers now. I play very little on them, because the Multimoog ribbon just seems so much better; when you let go, the pitch goes straight back to center without you having to push it back. It's a lot quicker.

Did you use a Multimoog for that solo with the hard-edged tone in "While You See a Chance"?

Right. I can't remember the wave shape. It was fairly square, but I did use a filter pedal to give it kind of a phased texture. I've found that synths can very easily lack natural sounds, so you need some kind of chorus effect to fatten the tone up and give it some life. Basically, a synth is not an actual instrument. It has sounds of its own, but mostly it's based on the sounds of other instruments. Even people like Klaus Schulze, who do abstract music, base their sounds on strings or voices, things you're familiar with.

Did Schulze, whom you worked with in Go, and other modular synthesists influence your work on this album?

Well, firstly, yes, because I think they're fantastic and I love to listen to them, but secondly, no, because I don't know what the hell they're doing or how they do it. I think it's amazing that someone can take a Debussy piece and orchestrate it for the synthesizer. It's a fantastic achievement, but I don't use things like oscilloscopes and voice prints. To a certain extent I think you can't reproduce certain sounds so exactly unless you use that kind of equipment, but I still go by ear.

Are you comfortable on modular gear?

I'm not very comfortable, no. I'm on the level of the factory presets, which are made for people like me who have to start with some sound. To me, these are the greatest things around. I would very much like to concentrate more on synths, but I don't like to get buried in books about electronics; they confuse me a bit. I'm the kind of synthesizer player who never reads the manual. I just kind of mess around with the instrument, then maybe three or four weeks later I'll read the manual, and by that time I understand what it's talking about. I find that's easier for me than wading through these thick manuals; it's not so forbidding. So for someone like me, who has never been satisfied with his piano technique, the presets are great because suddenly they give you these instrumental sounds.

Were there any keyboard players who helped introduce you to synthesizers when you started getting into them?

In a word, nope. I just played around with them until I could make them do what I wanted them to. In some cases I went for years before I realized a synthesizer could do something else [*laughs*]. Chris Wood had a way of seeing some control that didn't seem to do anything, then thinking, "Well, I'll have a go at the manual and then go on." But basically, no, nobody really helped me.

One of your earliest synthesizer solos was on the title cut of *The Low Spark of High Heeled Boys*, with that buzzy tone. Or was that a saxophone going through a fuzztone?

Actually, it was an organ through a fuzz box.

Fooled me twice!

Yes! But I think that was the idea. We had been looking for something like synths for a long time, I suppose. I wish they had been around ten years ago. I suppose they were, actually.

Now that they are around, do you find them effective, as tools to bring out your musical ideas into sound?

Absolutely. In fact, I find that I'm able to do things that I otherwise might not have been able to do. I've always made vague attempts to produce different sounds on instruments, like you mentioned on the *Low Spark* album. I've even tried to do that on instruments I can't play! There's one track on that album, in fact, where I played sax with Wood, and I've never ever played saxophone in my life!

Which track was that?

"Rock & Roll Stew." I played a line where I just stayed on one note. I just found it, and then Chris and I played the line: *bup bup bup*, or whatever it was [*laughs*]. I'm still trying to find simple music where I can do things like that. I mean, I can't play the drums, but I was able to make it sound like I could by writing the drum parts on *Arc of a Diver* within my limitation on the instrument.

You also used rhythm boxes on that album, didn't you?

Not on every track, and even when I did use a Roland CR-78, I overdubbed drums on it. On one track I used the sequencer, and on another I used a tambourine loop.

Why combine electronic rhythm devices with actual drum tracks?

I'm just not able to play drums unceasingly for seven minutes when there's nothing else playing, and you've got to start somewhere, so the rhythm boxes would be the first track.

How carefully did you plan the synthesized orchestrations? Was it fairly spontaneous from track to track, or did you sketch it all out in advance?

Well, rock and roll music is basically a spontaneous medium, and while I might have planned in certain cases to do something, there were other occasions when that didn't happen, where I surprised myself and was able to use whatever came up. What tends to happen is that it all gets put off to a later date. In other words, when I'm doing the final mixing, it becomes necessary to put everything in order, which is certainly taking it to the other extreme. I'm not saying that I just pull out anything that comes into my head and mix it all in at the end; it would be mad to do that, because you'd be presenting yourself with too much work all at once. It was necessary to mix some ideas in and out at the end, though.

What do you see as the real challenge of producing quality rock and roll?

Well, I know this is a musician's magazine, but I personally have an ultimate faith in the listening public. That's not to say that I'll do anything as long as people say it's good, but I think I'm saying that people who aren't musicians somehow know instinctively what is good music. I think it's wrong when music, or any kind of art for that matter, gets so complicated that it becomes a plaything of some elite intelligentsia. Music is a very natural thing that's inside everybody; it just happens to be something that some people are able to make and some people aren't, but that's only a question of organizing sound.

One striking thing about *Arc of a Diver* is the fact that your Hammond organ work, particularly your choice of registration and your phrasing, seems to have been practically unchanged despite your explorations into synthesizer playing,

Yes. The organ has its sound, but it's limited as an electronic instrument, and it's hard to do anything with it. Possibly if poly synthesizers didn't exist, I'd try to do more different things with the Hammond organ, but you could never use it in place of strings, for example. I just treat the organ as an organ and put it into its compartment, like Pierre Boulez writing a score and saying, "Horn would sound good there, and piccolo would sound good there."

Are you playing the same organ you had years ago?

Yeah. In fact I'm using the same C-3 I brought over with me on my first trip to the States in 1969. It's not in very good shape. It's held together with gaffer tape [*laughs*]. I've got a B-3 as well, which I've boarded for some time in L.A.

You've played the Hammond foot pedals.

Not on the album, but I used to do that with Traffic. It was necessary when we were a trio.

How could the old Traffic play live with such a limited instrumentation?

It was limited, almost suicidal, but we used to make it work. We used to make up for the differences in sound between the records and what we could do onstage by changing around the instrumentation. We'd do a couple of tunes with organ, sax, flute, and drums, and then I'd play the guitar and Chris would play the bass or the organ, which would give the trio a very different sound, and then we'd do an acoustic thing with the flute. We tried to change often enough so you didn't get tired of the organ/sax/drum sound.

Your work with Traffic was a dramatic change of pace from the rhythm and blues style that had first brought you before the public with Spencer Davis.

Well, the Spencer Davis Group started out just copying the blues. Later, after "Gimme Some Lovin'" and those kinds of records, we did develop more of our own style, but even then we were still basically emulating rhythm and blues, which was a music no one in England had really heard of before the early '60s. We were part of a clique of people who felt we were discovering some new kind of music for ourselves, and we had to take it to other people.

That period of imitating a certain style was probably something you had to go through before clarifying in your own mind the kind of music you really wanted to do.

Yes, I think that's it. Against all opposition I left the Spencer Davis Group when it was, as they say, hot. The band was selling hit singles, and I left it, not just wanting to withdraw from rhythm and blues, but wanting to do a much broader thing within Traffic. We wanted to draw from different areas, like classical music, country music, folk, all kinds of things.

When you listen to your old records, do you hear any major changes in your keyboard style?

Strangely enough, I think I've changed the least in my keyboard playing. There are changes in the way I sing, the way I write, and the way I produce, but like you were saying, my organ playing sounds very similar to the stuff I was doing ten or 15 years ago. Obviously I can hear a development in my keyboard playing. I'll play a piano solo or an organ solo on an old record, and I'll realize that I was hung up on something then, which I'm not hung up on now. But it's hard to pinpoint exactly what it is that has changed. I'd like to think that now I have more awareness of doing things more tastefully.

And of course you've got more instruments to develop on.

Right. I've got the same full-sized Steinway concert grand I had ten years ago; I bought it as an investment, and it seems to have paid off. I recently bought a Jupiter-4 from Buzz Music, which is quite a big keyboard store in London.

With your interest in unusual tunings, were you attracted to the potential of using the Jupiter's filters to obtain microtonal tunings?

That's right. That's a fantastic instrument. It also has a bend lever I like, which you can use to determine how much bend you've got on the tone, and to bend either way.

Do you have many volume pedals for your synthesizers?

Yes, I do. I have the pedal option on the Jupiter that works the filter volume, I use it mainly on the filter. I like filter pedals. There again, I've gotten used to working with a Moog pedal on the Minimoog, and I use it now on the Multimoog. It makes the sound a bit more human.

How did you set up the repeated-note pattern in "Spanish Dancer"? Did you use a sequencer?

No, it was played. I overdubbed a Polymoog after finishing the track, with a Roland Space Echo. That way I only had to play one of every four notes in the pattern. It was easier than sitting there playing the same note over and over—just one quarter of the work [*laughs*]!

Do you write songs with a particular instrument in mind?

No, I don't. I try not to be taken by certain instruments, although there again I don't like formulas or rules. On some occasions it might happen that I would record a keyboard and then put some vocal line over it that sounds good, so in that respect, yes, but I don't think generally that a certain kind of keyboard will affect the way my songs come out. And for that reason I try to write on different instruments, on guitar, keyboards, even drums. I sometimes write with no instrument at all. Writing all the time on keyboards can get you imprisoned into doing certain changes, although maybe that's because my piano technique isn't as varied as I would like it to be. I talk a lot with the guy I'm writing songs with, Will Jennings, about ways of writing songs, and he's taught me something that's very valuable: that you can sometimes rely too much on tunes you've written, for fear of not being able to write one as good. But if you don't write anything until the time comes, it can be incredibly productive, because you get carried on the enthusiasm of it. It's not a spread-out process.

Have you had to change keys on some songs to accommodate your changing vocal range as you get older?

Yeah, I have. I've done a few odd gigs with friends and other bands in the last two or three years, and I've found that I've had to bring "Gimme Some Lovin'" down from *G* to *E*, for instance.

Is it easy for you to reconcile the entertainment aspect of your work with the musical or creative aspect?

It hasn't been a problem, but it probably has stopped me from reaching wider audiences than I would otherwise have reached had I put more emphasis on theatrics or visual arts. I haven't done that, because I don't know as much about that as I do about making music. But I don't think I'll get too much of a negative reaction if I just concentrate on playing. In other words, I've got nothing to live up to as far as showmanship is concerned, so that's okay; that's not going to be a problem. I'll play the stuff that's good as well as I can, and it'll be interesting because, as I say, equipment has gotten so much better, and I'm really looking forward to that. And if I could do a few dance steps. . . . [*laughs*].

Portions of this article originally were published in the June 1981 issue of Keyboard *magazine.*

FOR MORE ON STEVE WINWOOD

Steve Winwood and Eric Clapton have partnered up lately for a series of extremely successful live shows, the Madison Square Garden one of which wound up as an extraordinary CD/DVD set. You can connect with him at his official website, www.stevewinwood.com.

A SELECTED STEVE WINWOOD DISCOGRAPHY

Steve Winwood has appeared as a sideman on hundreds of recordings, and he continues to do so. His solo works and the recordings with the following groups and artists represent the best of his astounding recorded output.

AS A SOLO ARTIST
2008 *Nine Lives*
2003 *About Time*
1997 *Junction Seven*
1990 *Refugees of the Heart*
1988 *Roll with It*
1986 *Back in the High Life*
1982 *Talking Back to the Night*
1981 *Arc of a Diver*
1977 *Steve Winwood*

WITH THE SPENCER DAVIS GROUP
1967 *I'm a Man*
1967 *Gimme Some Lovin'*
1966 *Second Album*
1966 *Autumn '66*
1965 *Every Little Bit Hurts*

WITH TRAFFIC
1974 *Where the Eagle Flies*
1973 *Shoot Out at the Fantasy Factory*
1971 *The Low Spark of High Heeled Boys*
1970 *John Barleycorn Must Die*
1969 *Heaven Is in Your Mind*
1968 *Traffic*
1967 *Mr. Fantasy*

WITH BLIND FAITH
1969 *Blind Faith*

WITH ERIC CLAPTON
2009 *Live from Madison Square Garden*
2005 *Back Home*
1993 *Stages of Clapton*
1988 *Crossroads*
1984 *Backtrackin'*

TRANSFORMING
PROG
INTO POP

Tony Banks onstage with Genesis in 1978, surrounded by an ARP 2600 in the foreground and at left, a Mellotron 400 under the ARP 2600 keyboard, a Yamaha CP-70, and a Polymoog behind Tony. Photo by Jon Sievert

TONY BANKS
and GENESIS

BY DOMINIC MILANO AND
ROBERT L. DOERSCHUK

PROG GIVES WAY TO POP, CHOPS GIVE WAY TO PARTS, AND PHIL COLLINS GIVES WAY TO DRUM MACHINES

KEYBOARD SPOKE TO Tony Banks for the first time in 1976, during the tour that supported the release of *Trick of the Tail*, Genesis' first album without Peter Gabriel. When we next spoke to Tony, Genesis had just released *And Then There Were Three*, the first Genesis album to go gold in the United States, which included their first-ever hit single, "Follow You Follow Me." Guitarist Steve Hackett had just left the band (hence the name of the album), and it was the first conscious attempt they had made to record shorter tunes. All of which gave fans of the early- and mid-'70s progressive movement (of which Genesis was a major part) an excuse to entertain the notion that Genesis was selling out.

However, Genesis continued covering even their most ambitious material live by hiring sidemen Bill Bruford and later Chester Thompson (on drums) and Daryl Stuermer (on guitar and bass) to play the parts that they overdubbed in the studio as a trio. This left Collins free to devote most of his time onstage to singing and fronting the band.

Tony's keyboard parts have continued to be tastefully interwoven and subtly applied to the music, the antithesis of the gonzo-keyboardist styles of Rick Wakeman. This fact, along with the emergence of Collins as a charismatic pop star, is probably one of the reasons why Genesis has been able to flourish and grow while so many of the progressive dinosaurs bit the dust as we entered the '80s.

On its two most recent albums, *Abacab* and *Genesis*, the band has been exploring different ways of collaborating on writing. Where before they had collectively developed ideas presented to them by one another in demo tape form, they were now jamming together in the studio, developing ideas together from scratch.

In the years prior to our interview, Tony had been involved with scoring several films, though he had mixed feelings about the process. We spoke to him about the improvisatory collaboration of the band and his unique approach to chord voicings, changes, and modulations, as well as the evolution of his keyboard gear and the role it plays in the Genesis sound.

Has your interest in exploring instrumental music in films been influencing Genesis? Your live set has more instrumental tunes in it than ever, more than you'd expect, given the emphasis of the last few records.

Yeah, well it's a weird thing really. The emphasis on the last two albums has

Tony Banks onstage with Genesis. Photo by Ebet Roberts

been more towards the vocal thing. We never plan these things, they just happen. So our albums don't necessarily prove that we're changing direction, they just show what we're doing on each particular record. We just like to make sure the live show includes a balance of things from throughout our career.

It's also true that certain songs work much better live, and some albums don't give us that much live music really. Like *And Then There Were Three*. I think the only song we're doing off that is "Follow You Follow Me," and we only do that because it was sort of a hit, I suppose. *The Lamb* and *Trick of the Tail* produced so many live songs, like "In the Cage" and "Los Endos." Even "Mama" and "Home by the Sea" from *Genesis* are probably two of our best live tracks. It appears that there's something about the slightly longer, more extended tracks that suits the live format better. There's no doubt. I don't get any pleasure out of going to see a group, even if they're very good, who just play a string of three-minute hits one after the other. You get bored. Extending songs makes them feel more like you're seeing a live performance. Of course, the light show helps.

It also seems that the music has been heading back towards the dramatic on the last two albums.

I think there's a little bit of everything on the last album. It's just that the emphasis is slightly different from what it used to be because we've had hits with the shorter songs, whereas in the old days we didn't make hits at all. If you go back to albums like *Nursery Cryme*, you'll find short and simple songs, but they weren't hits. They didn't get much emphasis. Everyone's attention was concentrated on "Musical Box."

Then there's "Home by the Sea" and "Mama" from *Genesis*. "Mama" was a big hit in Europe, but it only got to number 70 over here. The nature of the new album is such that you get your main act on side one and you get the character pieces on side two. I've always felt that side one was the stronger of the two, and that's the side with "Mama" and "Home by the Sea."

Is there any particular reason why it turned out that way?

It's because of the way the album was done. It was all done from improvisations. You start with a doodle and then you work on it. So you tended to get quite a strong identity on each track. They'd stay in one mood, like "Illegal Alien," which has a very strong Mexican feel to it. And "It's Going to Get Better," which has a funkier kind of feel. It's fun for us to explore different areas the way we did with "No Reply" [from *Abacab*], whereas "Home by the Sea" and "Mama" are more rooted in a traditional Genesis kind of thing.

You've stopped listing individual credits for each tune, crediting the group instead.

That was a conscious thing, really. We felt that on *Abacab* and *Duke* the most exciting things were things written by the group, Things that were developed in the studio. So we decided to try to do a whole album that way. This time, we didn't play each other anything we'd had before. And the songs just kind of evolved. We started putting things down on tape as soon as they took any kind of shape. It was an exciting way to work. You can get more spontaneity that way.

Sometimes, when you get a song beforehand and go into rehearsals with it, develop parts for it, and end up changing it, you overwork it. This time we didn't really develop things in quite the same way. We tended to try and get them down in the freshest form possible. That's why some of "Mama" is so simple. We started from a drum box, and everything else was added to enhance that. We just organized the first few jams we had on the thing and made a song out of them.

What about vocals? Did you have a melody line and add the lyrics later?

Phil was sort of singing along as we went. That phrase "Can't you see me, mama" was there quite early. So it all evolved together. That's one advantage to using rhythm machines when you haven't got an actual drummer in the group. Phil can sing and you can still get a feel for where everyone's heading, right from the word go.

What happens to the bass parts in situations like that when Mike is playing guitar?

In that particular tune, I put a drone E all the way through, because Mike was making sound effects on the guitar. Then I got this chord sequence that couldn't have the E all the way through it, and Mike couldn't play it on the bass pedals, so I just put the E on the [Sequential Circuits] Prophet-10 all the way through until the middle section. It depends on the song. We don't worry too much about it because we know the bass will be there one way or another.

There are quite a few songs over the last couple of albums where I've been playing the bass, because Mike's playing a sort of synthesizer guitar sound, and it's natural for me to head straight for the bass part. "Keep It Dark" [from *Abacab*] is one example. I don't play any chords on it for the entire last half of the song. And that's quite nice. The advantage of having three people is that you don't fill up everything. It doesn't matter if a certain person isn't playing, because they're always doing something else. In the old five-piece days, there were songs where Steve [Hackett] felt he had to play something, but it really wasn't necessary. There are two or three examples of that on *The Lamb*. "Colony of Slipper

Men" and "Lamb Lies Down on Broadway" itself didn't really need the parts he was playing.

Your keyboards have been changing over the years, but the roles they've been playing haven't changed all that much.

There is a tendency to do that. Live performance tends to mean that you've got to cover the old sounds even if you have new keyboards. And once you've got the old sounds, you find yourself using them in new songs as well. I suppose it has to do with the approach. I like certain things, and they tend to come back. I probably do go for certain similarities. But hopefully, you get something new and that becomes part of the sound.

For instance, the first time I used an ARP ProSoloist. That was something I hadn't done before, but now it's obviously part of my sound. I still have instruments that do the same job. I think the biggest differences now are that I'm using keyboards, the [E-mu] Emulator in particular, for sound effects. Since you can record anything you like and then play with it, you can get some things that are quite bizarre. "Illegal Alien" has a lot of that sort of thing—car horns and phones. It was quite fun recording all of it. It's a lot easier to lay that into a track than it is to get tapes going all the time. I've got some great disks full of sounds for that.

And then you've got the more musical approach to that same thing, where you go around and record sounds to be played as notes, so the sound isn't anything like what it started out as. There are all sorts of things that everybody does with the Emulator for that—like blowing across the tops of bottles and glasses. There's quite a bit of that sort of thing in "Home by the Sea." It's nice to be able to use sounds like that in a musical way, rather than limit yourself to reproducing them in a strictly representational way.

You've been playing the same solo in "In the Cage" for quite a while now. Do you ever get the urge to break out of it and do something new?

For me, the solo is as much a part of the song as the melody line. You could vary it, but it's kind of difficult, because either you've got to change it completely because of the way the bass and the drums work with it, or you've got to leave it alone. Playing the same thing has never really worried me. I see it as part of the composition. I don't get particularly bored. The things I get bored with, I cut out. Like lots of parts of "Cinema Show" [*Selling England by the Pound*] I couldn't stand playing anymore. So we only do the three best parts of it. I think "Cage" is a good song, so it's nice to do it. I think it's time to start giving a lot of thought to giving these songs a rest. We've been doing "Cage" since 1978, probably. It only started to sound good in '78, and it's become one of our classic songs, but we've rested classic songs before. When we first dropped "The Knife" [*Trespass*], we thought we'd never be able to drop it. But we dropped it and no one seemed to notice. I think audiences' favorite tracks are probably always an album or so ago. The most recent stuff is always too recent for them.

What kind of processing are you using on your Prophet-10 to get your Hammond sounds?

I'm using an MXR Phase 100 for those organ sounds. And chorus. But I use chorus on the Prophet all the time. I use chorus on lots of things all the time. I use chorus on the Prophet to get the size. I use quite a lot on the piano. I put a good strong mono signal up the middle on the piano [along with the chorused stereo image]. I really like that. I only put a very little bit of it on the Synclavier. If I was doing more chord work on it, I would put more chorusing on it. I don't tend to put any on the Quadra. It does have a phase shifter on it that I use for some things.

But to produce the Hammond sounds on the Prophet-10, you've got four oscillators and you tune them in octaves. Sometimes you put a fifth in there, depending on the sound you want. Another thing that helps is the Prophet-10's EQ controls. An organ sound is all middle, so you take off a lot of bass and you get that sort of sound that's distinctly organish. Putting it through a phase and chorus gives it that Leslie kind of sound. I started putting the Hammond itself through the phaser instead of a Leslie at the end. The only trouble with the phasers is that sometimes they tend to make the chorus too noticeable. Some nights they go wild and seem to make the instrument sound out of tune. That's what the chorus is doing anyway, but sometimes it's more active than I'd like. I can get away with it most nights, though.

You use the CP-70 on records a lot. Why it instead of an acoustic piano?

Yeah, I hardly use a real grand. I did use one on *Abacab*, for "No Reply." But I started to forget about grand pianos. I don't know why, but I got so used to playing the CP-70 that when I play a real grand, it sort of feels funny. It doesn't sound chorused [*laughs*]. No, I still play around with them, but it's much easier to fit a CP-70 on a record. In a group situation, when you're playing with the other guys in the room, you can actually get the levels right with the CP-70 much more easily. So I end up using it on records. I suppose I will get back to the acoustic sometime.

Do you find yourself gravitating to any one instrument during group improvisations?

I use anything in the group. It really depends on the sort of thing we're doing. I can do more playing on the piano, but sometimes the actual sound of a synthesizer can set you off in the right direction. I wrote most of the things on *The Fugitive* on the synthesizers. It was the first time I've done that. I did a lot of things where I triggered the synthesizer from the Linn on two or three tracks. It's a nice way to lock in a riff. You've got that ability with the synthesizers and you don't with the piano, but there are still a lot of songs that I write on the piano.

How do you go about working out a tune like "Second Home by the Sea"?

That's one we did by working off an improvisation. Again, we were trying to keep some of this spontaneous feel. Phil started playing this drum riff that Mike and I found attractive, and we jammed on it for about two hours one day and an hour or two the next. Then Mike and I listened to what we had done, and we organized the bits that we liked. And then we learned exactly what we played down to the last detail. Of course, we worked on a few bits, extended some, changed others, just trying to get it into some cohesive form. Some of those things happen on really weird beats. We found ourselves sitting there counting things out trying to get used to playing them. It all sounds very natural on tape, so we knew it was a natural thing to go for. But it took us quite a while. Phil obviously adapted some of the things he was playing to suit what changes we'd made. It's amazing to hear the original stuff that it came from. There's a lot of good stuff there, but we had to keep it down to about six minutes. It could easily have gone on for a lot longer.

Did "Abacab" happen the same way?

We didn't actually organize the improvisation the same way. We had lots of bits—phrases and things—that we used in the original version, which was 15 minutes long. We edited out two ten-second phrases and then faded it out. We were quite keen to put the whole 15-minute version out because it all sounded good, but you never know. Like "Mama," which we had to shorten down to six and a half minutes. There is an eight-and-a-half minute version on the single, and on the B side there's a long version of "It's Going to Get Better," which we edited down for the album. You've got to do that for the dreaded "album can't be too long" question.

Does it ever feel like pulling teeth to edit a song down?

We don't like doing it, but I know that the shorter you can get a thing and still have it work, the stronger it's going to be. Most things can be edited down. You know instinctively if you've gone too far in one direction or another. I can often listen to other people's music and say if it's too long and could have been edited down. I think what really matters is that you still get the tune across. When you hear singles on the radio, you'll hear Culture Club one minute and the next you'll get something new. You've got to make things happen quickly. You don't have a minute and a half to get into a song, whereas onstage you can take as long as you like.

What kind of chord progression really grabs your ear?

I have no idea. I never quite know what makes one chord progression feel better than another. I think a lot of it is done by how it feels on the keyboard. Some things just feel lovely to play. One example is the main chord sequence in "Mad Man Moon" [from *Trick of the Tail*]. It fit on the hands so well. I like there to be something unusual in a chord progression. It doesn't have to be bizarre, just unusual. You can't go on playing *C-Fm-G* forever. That jam we do at the end of our set, the medley of all the old rock and roll and R&B tunes, a number of those songs just go *B-E-B-E*. It's amazing how many songs stick with those kind of changes, which is good. Sometimes we slip into that sort of change in the second section of a song. Like "Afterglow," for example. The basic song is in *G* and the chorus is in *E♭*. The relationship between those two keys gives the whole tune a more wistful feeling. Then when you come back to the big chorus at the end, we change from E♭ to C, which is a very dramatic kind of change. There's a lot you can do with key changes to make a song more interesting.

Do you actually make a point of changing keys within a tune? .

Not particularly. In a lot of earlier songs you'd have one section that would be in E and another would be in B minor and another would be in E♭. And it was down to me to find a way to link them up. I became an expert at working out modulations. The easiest way is to go to a diminished chord. They can get you anywhere. "Afterglow" and "Firth of Fifth" [from *Selling England by the Pound*] are two examples of that. There were so many times when you could create a dramatic effect by using that kind of key change, and that was often the reason why it was done. We didn't fight it.

Then there were times when we found that changing the keys of two bits so they'd fit together didn't work. One wouldn't sound right. There were times when Steve would have written something in D—D has a very special sound to me— and we'd try to put it in B♭. But that didn't work. So we'd try to come up with a modulation that worked. Some people thought that it sounded awkward, while others thought it interesting. That's where you lose some of the crowd. The Beatles were always very good at key changes. They were never outrageous, they did just enough to be interesting. [Songwriters] Holland and Dozier were masters at it. "Reach Out, I'll Be There" is great. I'm not sure of the key, but the change is something like going from a C chord down to B♭ minor, which is an unlikely key change, but it makes the thing that occurs after it—playing a B♭m and Eb—sound so much more exciting. You realize how simple it is, and that had it been in the same key it wouldn't have been half as exciting.

A lot of your chord voicings involve playing unusual bass notes under fairly straightforward chords.

Those things have been developing over the years. When we first started doing it, there were certain things people were doing where you'd have one root note suspended through a bunch of chords. "Downtown" is an example of that, where you have a C in the bass being held through the F and G chords as well as the C chord. That was done quite a bit. But the idea of going straight to that G with the C in the bass wasn't done at all in the early days. And that adds an amazing character to the chord. It's really no longer a G chord anymore. The idea is that you come up with interesting changes when you change chords simply by changing the bass notes. It's difficult to explain, but when I'm at the piano it's almost like I'm creating music by making mistakes. When you come up with something nice, you stick to it, and you come up with some really unlikely things that sound good. Like in the introductory bit to "The Eleventh Earl of Mar" [from *Wind & Wuthering*]. One of the chords in that is basically a Gm chord with an Ab in the bass. That sounds unlikely, but it sounds great in context. A lot of this comes out of improvising—doing things that you originally didn't intend to do and finding that it sounds nice.

Do you still find yourself gravitating to those kinds of chords?

Well, I try to use them a lot less now. You can overdo it, because there is a certain character that comes from chords like that. And each time you use it, you find yourself relating to it. It reminds you of the previous song you used it in. So I try to think less in terms of chords now. Which is probably why the music sounds a little simpler now. Tunes like "Mama" have chords in them, but they aren't as important an aspect of the song. It's more the mood.

Do you feel you had fallen into a rut with chord voicings?

I think it's always possible to. I don't feel we've actually done it yet. There are still times when you run across totally new ways of doing things. "From the Undertow," from *Curious Feeling*, has a whole new way, for me, of bridging chords. I used a lot of combination chords on that album. You find a lot of those kinds of chords in Ravel and people like that. But probably because of the lack of enthusiasm shown for that album, I've stopped experimenting in that direction. Had it been a monster hit, I'm sure I would have gone a lot further in that direction.

How much Genesis material includes the original basic tracks?

It's difficult to say. We put down so much of the last album using the drum machine. I played along with it most of the time, and we did keep a lot of my original tracks. "That's All" has my original piano part on it. But in a lot of other things, we didn't keep any of the original tracks. We just put them down to get the lengths right, and then everybody would replace their parts.

Do you find that working with drum machines makes you work in 4/4 much more than you normally would?

I think that's definitely true. I think their only drawback is that they tend to simplify music a little too much sometimes. It happens with us. There is also the tendency to never vary the rhythm because it's so easy to stay with the one. It's hypnotic. And it traps you a little. Some of the things we did with them involved Phil playing a straight rhythm against the drum machine, which was playing a weird rhythm. We did that on "Silver Rainbow" [from *Genesis*]. But in the end we took out the original drum machine part, which was doing all these funny things in the background. On the original version, the machine was playing in six and Phil was playing in four, and things would happen in strange moments just by chance. There is a tendency to avoid rhythms like seven, because at this point in time they sound a little bit dated. Like the seven we used in "Cinema Show." You can go into the studio, tap out a rhythm in seven, and almost say it's "Cinema Show" because it's so identifiable. Sometimes you get weird rhythms that don't even sound weird; like the main riff in "Turn It on Again" [from *Duke*], which is actually in 13 because that's the way it sounded the most pleasing.

What did you use to get that Mellotron-ish string sound on "It's Going to Get Better"?

That was done on the Emulator. I recorded a four-note string phrase. When you play chords with it, you get all these harmonies happening at different speeds. It's something I just stumbled across with the Emulator. I was attempting to record a string note, and I got the first four notes instead of just the one. I happened to put the looping on after the four notes instead of after the first. And it was an amazing sound. It sounds like a Mellotron because it's a sound from a record.

What sound did you sample for the percussive effect in "Mama"?

That was a koto. It happened to be in the studio so we recorded it into the Emulator. I couldn't get anything else to fit the song so I ended up using it. Because the koto is an instrument that you tend to hear from a distance, it sounds very good because there's distance in the sample of it. It fits well with the Linn drum box, which we put through an AMS digital reverb and ran into a little Fender amp and distorted to hell. We also mixed a little bit of straight sound with it to give it some character. The distortion on that is quite an important part of the sound. Something about the Linn—it's got such a pure, clean, and in many ways horrible sound. It's great because the sound is so good, but it needs character. That's why we like distorting it. That's the trouble with synthesizers. You've got to be careful not to make everything sound too clean.

TONY BANKS:
GENESIS ON THE ROAD—LITERALLY—WITH PHIL COLLINS AND MIKE RUTHERFORD

"Gawd," said Tony Banks. "This is a big car!"

There, docked in front of the HBO offices near Gramercy Park in Manhattan, waiting to sail majestically uptown to the WNEW studios, was the mother of all limos. It didn't have its own pool, like the one in the back of Phil Collins' car in the "Take Me Home" video, but it would do. So, with the *Keyboard* cassette recorder firmly in our grip—an earlier tape machine had been lost a few nights before in Soho, but that's another story—we followed Tony Banks, Phil Collins, and Mike Rutherford into the megamobile, praying all the while for a traffic jam.

Though our interview time had been cut short due to the usual scheduling chaos, we wound up getting nearly everything we needed by the time we reached the radio station. Banks, Collins, and Rutherford—a.k.a. Genesis—are pros in the interview department. After some 20 years in the pop music whirl, the last 13 of them as a trio, they've learned how to speak both very clearly and very quickly when time is short. A nice trick, especially since few comparably huge showbiz phenoms try so hard to really answer the questions they're asked.

With *We Can't Dance* just released and the debut single, "No Son of Mine," already shooting toward the top of the Billboard chart in its first week, Genesis is about as big time as you can get. So, of course, they deserve that big car, especially since there are three of them. In an era when pop icons tend to be singular—Madonna, Paula Abdul, name your Jackson—these guys are a bona fide band. They have the same sense of interplay, the same preference for collective creativity that any other band has. Though each has his own solo career and side interests, when they come together as Genesis, they are just as much an all-for-one kind of outfit as they were back in the '60s, when they founded the group specifically as a "songwriting collective."

The cars were smaller then, but music was in some respects bigger. By the early '70s, working as a fivesome with guitarist Steve Hackett and singer Peter Gabriel, they were honing a style based on extended pieces whose marathon structures were tempered by a disinclination to indulge in the kinds of flashy, wanking-off display some of their colleagues in the progressive rock movement embraced. Where ELP, for example, sometimes created the impression of three guys duking it out in a Battle of the Virtuosos—"This band ain't big enough for the three of us, stranger! Take that drum solo!" "Oh, yeah? Well, watch this arpeggio, hombre!"—Genesis always came across as the product of a unified artistic vision.

Further, their flair for drama, their interest in sound, and their pursuit of simple central ideas even in the most distended arrangements anticipated those qualities that guide pop music in the '80s and '90s. After whittling down to trio size, they pared their sound as well. But even on their new bite-sized singles—"That's All" from 1983, "Invisible Touch" from '88, and the current hit—their old prog sensibilities add a feeling of dimension rarely heard in mainstream radio today. What other band, for instance, risks the kinds of titanic climaxes heard in "Tonight Tonight Tonight" from *Invisible Touch* or, more recently, "Driving the Last Spike" from *We Can't Dance*?

When we met Genesis at HBO, they were just staggering out of several hours' worth of banter with a sequence of interrogators who, in their own remarkable display of inadvertent collectivism, seemed to ask the same questions over and over again. This left us with an obvious opening gambit.

So what haven't you been asked yet today?

Rutherford: Nobody's asked about keyboards.

Okay. So, Tony, what kind of rig did you use on *We Can't Dance*?

Banks: A lot of the stuff has changed in the five years since we did *Invisible Touch*. I was using the [E-mu] Emulator II a lot on that. On this record, I used the Korg Wavestation a lot; that's really the most important one. I also used the Ensoniq VFX, the Roland JD-800, and the EIII.

So you've moved up from your old Emulator.

Banks: Yeah, although in some ways the Emulator II is much easier to handle. The main advantage with the EIII is the fact that it's stereo. It's great to be able to do stereo sampling; you end up with a much better sound. The fact that you can manipulate that sound to a greater degree is good too. But by the same token, I quite like sampled sounds that are very imperfect; sometimes that gives them a strong character. Rather than fiddle around too much with the samples I've taken, I tend to use whatever I end up with. If I can make it sound good in a piece of music, I'm happy.

Would that noisy sample that you play in "No Son of Mine" as a minor third be an example?

Banks: Certainly, although I cheated a bit because on the video it looks like I'm playing a descending minor third, but in fact the sample was [*hums the figure*]. It was a bit of guitar noise from Mike, slowed down. It sounds like this fabulous thing, but it wasn't.

Rutherford: Thank you very much [*laughs*]!

Banks: What I mean was, it was very ambient, very distant. It wasn't set up like, "Okay, Mike, I'm gonna start sampling now." I've often got a mic set up on the Emulator, and every now and then I switch it on without telling anyone what I'm doing. I'll just sample around 18 seconds in the room and see what happens. In this case, that was what I did, and that sound, which is like an elephant trumpeting, is what sets that whole song in motion. Sounds like that don't necessarily end up on the track, but they can set you off on an idea and change the mood.

"No Son of Mine," where you brighten your pad sound as you go into the chorus, is also a good example of how you often use changing texture as a dramatic device.

Banks: In the old days I used to do that a lot on the filter with Polymoogs and stuff like that, but on this song I used a simpler method, which was to play one pad and, through MIDI, fade a second one in. I had "ooo"-ey sort of sound on the Wavestation, then I faded up a brassy VFX sound. It's more controllable than opening up the filter, which I was always desperately trying to do not too fast. Also, it's easier to do in the rehearsal room. The idea came out of the improvisation while we were writing the song. All the sounds on the record are pretty much what I played when we were first working out the ideas.

Collins: On the overdub stage, we all chip in a bit on the sounds . . .

Banks: . . . because every overdub we do is an extra thing that wasn't part of the original song and can therefore change the character of a song. You want to be careful about what you add, so at that stage we do confer.

The electric piano sound on the title cut certainly seems to have been a fundamental ingredient in the concept of the song.

Banks: That song actually went through lots of changes. When we started playing it, we did a much heavier thing. Mike had a basic riff, and I was playing the same part on synth at that stage. Then we extended it and did a few little turns to make it into a 16-bar pattern. We defined the song that way, but it wasn't very exciting.

Rutherford: It was getting to sound a bit old-fashioned, like something from "Squonk" [from *A Trick of the Tail*], with more layers. But the minute Tony hit that pattern on the drum machine, it made it a little bit . . .

Collins: . . . more modern.

Banks: It changed the whole character. One thing about playing the drum part on the JD-800, as I did on that, is that it stopped me from playing any keyboards at the beginning of the song. That's not a bad thing necessarily, but as soon as you put a keyboard on that kind of a song, you change its character. Without the keyboard it sounds a bit Stonesish; with the synth playing the riff, it sounds a bit more slick.

When you do come in on "We Can't Dance," your part is very minimal. In some places, you're just playing two quarter-notes.

Banks: The piano part on that one is one of the most minimal things I've ever done. I was thinking of early Traffic. "Feelin' Alright" was a great song, but very simple.

Was that an electric piano?

Banks: It's the Roland VK-1000, set on a very middle-y kind of sound.

Why did you do the drum part on the JD-800?

Banks: It was just quite fun to use that special drum setting, which I didn't even know was there when I bought the instrument. I got the JD-800 because I like the idea of fiddling with knobs. I hate multi-function buttons. They're the bane of modern keyboard playing. Even here, you've got a degree of multi-functioning; otherwise there would be too many buttons. But I didn't realize it was going to be such a good preset instrument as well. The sounds on the JD-800 are really good. They've got great clarity.

Do you use the onboard effects on the JD-800 and the Wavestation, or do you add your effects in the studio?

Banks: I've started using the effects in these instruments more and more because that makes it easier to change instantly from one sound to another without having to set up everything again in the rack. I've never been very good at doing MIDI control of multieffects manually, so it's nice to be able to go from a radically ambient sound to a very dry one just by flicking a button. The effects in the Wavestation are particularly easy to access. It's got a great variety of fuzz box-type stuff, which I love. The best thing about it, though, is its lovely sustained sounds. I also use a couple of the Wavestation's lead sounds quite extensively.

How do you decide whether to use live drums or a drum machine on any Genesis song?

Collins: If the part is more percussive than usual, and not just a simulation of real drums, we usually end up keeping the drum machine part and overdubbing drums to the percussion part, which is really important to the mood of the song. But when the drum sounds are regular snare and regular bass drum, you usually need real drums. It also depends on how intrinsic the drum sound is to the mood of the song. On something like "Fading Lights," the atmosphere is set up by the drum machine.

You seem to have a trademark drum machine sound—basically the sound of the pattern on "Take Me Home."

Collins: The Roland drum machines definitely have got the edge on anything else when it comes to those kinds of sounds. They're all percussion sounds—not timbales, triangles, and claves, but odd percussion sounds that you can't identify.

There were several cuts on _We Can't Dance_ where those types of sounds played a major role. Are these drum

sequences typically the starting point when you write these songs?

Collins: Quite often. Sometimes there are patterns that have been floating around in the machine from my home use. They can be a good basis to start something, then you can take them out at the end. At other times, I'll just turn the machine on in rehearsal and start mucking about. It's like bait: You wait to see if anybody picks it up [*laughs*].

On "Living Forever," the live drums come in midway through the song to supplement the drum machine pattern.

Collins: The original working title for that song was "Hip-Hop Brushes." I had gotten some new disks for my [E-mu] SP-1200. One of them was a jazz kit, and while the regular drum sounds didn't interest me, the brush concept did seem original. So I wrote a pattern with them that happened to be a hip-hop kind of thing. I tried to make it sound like what a drummer would actually play. Then we started playing off of that.

Do you play brushes yourself?

Collins: Not for quite a while. On a Clapton tour I played with brushes on "Can't Find My Way Home."

It would seem harder to get the subtleties of brushwork into a drum machine pattern than to do a convincing stick pattern.

Collins: That's true, but to be honest, the brush pattern on "Living Forever" took me ten minutes to write. Normally at a writing session, in the moments of silence between one idea and the next idea, I'll very quickly program something at random. That's how this pattern happened. All our drum machine parts happen quickly. You have to get something going before everybody puts his instrument down and goes for a cup of tea [*laughs*].

Your drum sounds are a hot item on the sample market. How do you feel about that?

Collins: Well, I do think that the sound is only 50 percent of it. It's how you use the sound that really matters. You can sample Eric Clapton's guitar and get that sound, but you still need the personality to really get his sound.

Banks: And the sound is never the same twice, in actual fact. This is the illusion: A sound can seem the same on two different records, but in fact a different sound was used to produce the same effect on the second song. So if you take what may be a Phil Collins snare and put it in another song, it doesn't always sound right at all.

Collins: People are always saying that I have a big ambient sound. But with [previous Genesis producer] Hugh Padgham, and even with [*We Can't Dance* producer] Nick Davis, even if we kept the mics up between songs, we always stripped everything down in the sound and started with a clean sketch each time.

Banks: Sometimes people think there's more magic in it than there actually is. It's quite easy to produce these sounds yourself. Whether it's drum sounds, keyboard sounds, or anything else, you don't have to think, "If I steal this, I'll have something really great." You can recreate those sounds yourself.

Collins: The other thing is, of course, that the two most widely sampled [drum] sounds are "Sussudio" and "Don't Lose My Number," and both of those are drum machines. I actually bought an [E-mu] SP-12 with those sounds on it. But "Don't Lose My Number" is a Linn, although tom-tom fills occasionally crop up. And the backbeat and bass drum on "Sussudio" is a Roland, with a mixture of Oberheim DMX. I didn't even do that one; David Frank did.

Still, when you're actually playing, is there a consistent approach that you follow in order to attain some sort of continuity in sound?

Collins: I always mic my drums in a regular fashion, pretty much the way everybody mics drums. But the environment is interesting. The room at the Farm, where we do our stuff, is loosely based on the room where we did Peter Gabriel's third album and my first three solo albums. When you clap your hands in it, it seems dead, but it's incredibly live. Even with the carpet on the floor and padding on the walls, it's surprising how live it is. That's why my drums always sound so ambient. We put mics in the left and right top corners of the room to get that ambience, and they're compressed as hell, squeezed almost to the point of distortion. If I'm not using cymbals, we often put gates on the drums to make them sound more interesting. Of course, if I'm using cymbals, we can't use gates, because that would screw up the decay.

Is it a problem to reproduce that effect live?

Collins: Yes, it is. That's why on my tours and on the last Genesis tour we ended up triggering sounds. When you're onstage, you've got no confined space to work with. If you put compressors on overheads above the kit, all you get is the audience noise coming up when you're not playing. Unless you put the drummer in a soundproof box, which obviously alienates him from the audience, you can't do it. I wish we had more sophisticated triggering at this stage. There's always the problem with double triggering when you're dealing with an acoustic instrument like drums.

What role did the drum machine play in composing "Driving the Last Spike"?

Collins: That was basically written on the 1200. The same drum machine pattern worked at various stages of loudness throughout the whole song. Bit by bit, we took each section as it came once we put real drums on it, then started working on what to keep from the original drum machine. We replaced the machine cabasa with two live cabasas. It's nice to have certain elements of the drum machine in there but at the same time to make it human.

Banks: There's an old drum machine pattern of Mike's, actually, that all the bits were originally written on. We had three or four different jam sessions on it, and different ideas emerged on different days. All the bits worked, so we thought it would be nice to find some way to stick them all together. So Phil wrote a rather more subtle part than what we originally had . . .

Rutherford: Guys! Guys! [*Laughs.*]

TRANSFORMING PROG INTO POP

Phil's entrance on snare marks the peak of a crescendo that seems to rise throughout the entire song up to that point, and it seems that you have to rearrange everything to accommodate that sound.

Banks: It's the other way around. The arrangement was almost there when the drums were put on. The real basis of the end section is the guitar riff. I just did this chord sequence that took it somewhere slightly different. All we try to do is to make the drums fit with what's already there. Let's be honest: Sometimes you know that you're going to have to add more to bits, to build up to the chorus and all that.

That brings to mind the big rise in level on "Dreaming While You Sleep." Why did you decide to have such a huge change in dynamics there?

Banks: That's what came out of the improvisation.

Collins: It's all based on the drum machine.

Banks: We had one drum machine pattern going all the way through. There were no drums added when we did it. Really, we had two very different feels going on the one rhythm. We were all improvising things. I was playing on one sort of keyboard sound, then I started playing a few chords. At that point, Phil started singing a melody line. We had this chorus bit that sounded great; it was just a question of trying to organize the improvisations that ended up being the verse and all the other parts of the song to fit with that chorus. So the whole thing was there; it was never a decision to make the dramatic transition between the two.

Collins: The real drums didn't sound good on the verse. They weren't necessary, because the drum machine pattern held its own. It was one of those patterns that set up half the atmosphere of the song. Then, where the big change came in with the smooth chords at the chorus, I started playing along on drums. You then say, "Okay, that part sounds right. Now let's get a sound for it that makes it sound good." Of course, it all has to get past quality control [*laughs*].

Several cuts on the album have keyboard solos, a relative rarity for Genesis.

Banks: In more recent years, yes. The last one I did on a Genesis album was "Home by the Sea" [from *Genesis*], which wasn't really a bona fide keyboard solo.

Your solos have a very composed quality.

Banks: Yes. I think of them more as instrumentals. We have a good groove going, and I just play around on top. On "Living Forever," there were two feels in my solo. On the first bit, where there was a bit of menace, I was playing all kinds of diminished notes, and then suddenly it goes happy.

Collins: This is your idea of heaven, isn't it? No questions about lyrics [*laughs*].

Banks: We always get questions about lyrics. Anyway, when you first get into this solo, it sounds very dramatic. But the natural feel of the bit was more light. At some point I knew I'd have to change, so I thought I'd make the change quite suddenly—a change in tone, from the VFX to the Wavestation, and a change in notes—and immediately bring in a different feel. I just wanted to keep this a lightweight solo, a breezy sort of thing, without being too intense, because I knew I had a more intense solo later on the album.

That would be on "Fading Lights," on which your solo line has a rough, almost vocoder-ish quality.

Banks: That's a modification of a Wavestation sound. I liked it because I could play very aggressively on it. Those sounds are great for leads; they automatically attract attention to themselves. Two or three different sounds are actually used on that lead at different times.

How often do you rely on third-party vendors for sounds?

Banks: Not much. I either use presets or some easily available sounds, or else I make them myself. I nearly always edit whatever sound I've got to some extent. On the early instruments, I used to do all the programming myself. I like programming. That's half the fun of it. I would hate to have someone else trying to get sounds for me. But with the Wavestation, the VFX, and the JD-800, so many of the sounds that you get are so great that you can sometimes use them as they stand. You just sit down and improvise on sounds that you find when you're fiddling with the machine, and that's often all you need to do. "Hold on My Heart," for example, was just a question of finding nice sounds to do the job for me. I didn't have to struggle to find a totally new sound. In fact, I wrote the chord sequence on the instrument I ended up using to record it, which was the Wavestation.

What was that light harmonica-like line that you played in that song?

Banks: That's another preset sound, this one on the JD-800. It sounds almost like rubbing the tops of wine glasses. The thing about that song was that at one point it looked like it wasn't going to end up on the album. Then we did a series of overdubs. We added a few vocal harmonies, and that gave the song a focus that it didn't have before. It doesn't sound like that would make all the difference in the world, but it did. Suddenly, having been something like number 13 in the rankings, it came up to number three or four. It's funny how these little things can affect the way you listen to the rest of the song.

The chord voicings are so meticulously constructed that it would completely alter the character of most of your songs if you change them even slightly.

Banks: That's true. Chords are my specialty. The thing that I understand best is the way chords fit together. You can't just add or subtract notes. Inversions are very important too; a particular inversion of a triad can make a lot of difference. On a lot of songs, the bass note comes from me, since Mike is often stuck to playing guitar. Not that I end up playing the bass, but the natural tendency of any keyboard player is to put a left-hand part in. Often that will define the shape of the chord.

Do you try to stay as close to Mike's bass sound as you can when covering the bass notes?

Banks: When I'm doing it, I'm just playing the bottom parts. Since most bass guitar parts are put on afterwards, it's very important that Mike doesn't disturb the chord emphasis, because it's so easy to change that with a bass. We have one chord in the song "Dreaming While You Sleep" where there was no bass note, so he doesn't play one. Any bass note would give the wrong impression to the chord. This is why the bottom note of a chord is often just part of the keyboard part.

Rutherford: During the chorus of "Dreaming While You Sleep," I tried playing a bass guitar because we wanted a low, powerful sound from the bass end where the drums are a very big part of the song.

Phil, do you mainly compose on piano?

Collins: I use the Yamaha CP-70, same as Tony. The Korg Wavestation has also been a big boon to me, along with the Roland D-50.

Banks: One of my favorite ways of writing at home is to play on the CP-70 and have everything MIDIed to it, each with its own volume pedal. That way, I can fade in any sound that I want at any point. If I want a nice stringy background, there it is.

Phil, is there ever call for you to do a keyboard part with Genesis?

Collins: [*Makes gagging noise.*] No! And I'm happy with that. If I brought things into the band, I'd want them played the way I had written them. But I didn't write the keyboard parts on this album. Tony did. So it's fine if he plays them. It's a question of interpretation. There are certain tuned percussion bits that are my sounds. Even the [Yamaha] DX7 had some interesting marimba, woodblock, and kalimba sounds; I'd like to get involved with playing those. But I can wait and do that on my own, no problem.

Both Mike and Phil have worked with a variety of keyboard players, so you must have some interesting observations on working with Tony as part of a rhythm section.

Collins: "Rhythm section"? Isn't that a contradiction in terms? [*Laughs.*]

Are there aspects to his approach to rhythm that affect you in a different way than the other keyboardists with whom you've played?

Collins: Tony tends to be more original and less technique oriented. That's true of all of us, but since we're talking about Tony, let's say he's not that interested in technique for technique's sake, which means that he gives you some very original results. A lot of keyboard players want to make their statements mainly with technique, so that people will say, "Hey, that guy's a great player!" But that doesn't seem that important to me. Obviously, you want to take technique into consideration, but it isn't the main reason for doing things.

Given Tony's restraint and his emphasis on long chorded textures, does that give you more than the usual amount of freedom for your drum parts?

Collins: It helps. The less busy Tony has gotten over the years, the more enjoyable it has been to play with him. But we all went through that. If you listen to our earlier efforts, we're always going hell-for-leather behind the vocalist.

Mike, would you tend to play a more active rhythmic role in Genesis than you would in Mike + the Mechanics?

Rutherford: Yeah, probably. Having worked with the Mechanics, I can say that the great thing with Genesis is that when you're using other keyboard players who you haven't been with for so long, you'll say, "Try something in this song," and they'll head off in a direction with all kinds of chord inversions. If you tell them that one note is wrong, they'll change the whole thing and not see the difference. Then, when you point that out to them, they get cross. I had a big row with one guy who came to play with the Mechanics. He had to play a very simple part. I don't remember what it was—two chords four times, for example, while the bass ran down. He was running the whole thing down with the bass, and he couldn't see why that was a problem. It annoys you when some keyboard players don't realize that one note makes all the difference.

Banks: Well, guys, that's the problem with keyboard players: They have too many fingers.

Portions of this article originally were published in the November 1984 and February 1992 issues of Keyboard *magazine.*

FOR MORE ON GENESIS

Apart from a reunion tour in 2007, Genesis hasn't done a whole lot since the release of *We Can't Dance*. You can keep up with any news and rereleases at their official website, www.genesis-music.com.

A SELECTED GENESIS DISCOGRAPHY

The story of Genesis is really quite remarkable; the story of the band, that is. From their precocious teenaged beginnings as avant-folkies with Peter Gabriel, through their extraordinarily creative prog rock period culminating in *The Lamb Lies Down on Broadway*, to their reinvention as a pop powerhouse, they've left a trail of excellent music. Tony Banks branched out for a few solo albums and film scores, too.

2007 *Live Over Europe 2007*
1991 *We Can't Dance*
1986 *Invisible Touch*
1983 *Genesis*
1982 *Three Sides Live*
1981 *Abacab*
1980 *Duke*
1978 *And Then There Were Three*
1976 *Wind & Wuthering*
1976 *Trick of the Tail*

1974 *The Lamb Lies Down on Broadway*
1973 *Selling England by the Pound*
1973 *Live*
1972 *Foxtrot*
1971 *Nursery Cryme*

TONY BANKS SOLO ALBUMS
1979 *A Curious Feeling*
1983 *The Fugitive*
1984 *The Wicked Lady (soundtrack)*

ROCKIN'
THROUGH
THE AGES

Chuck Leavell on the road with the Allman Brothers in the mid-'70s, with his touring Steinway and Rhodes.
Photo by Jon Sievert

CHUCK
LEAVELL

BY ERNIE RIDEOUT

ROLLIN' WITH THE STONES

MICK JAGGER COVERS the 200-foot-wide stage seemingly in a few strides. He reaches out, bent on touching each of the 50,000-plus screaming Rolling Stones fans, pulling them to their feet, every move he makes amplified by a factor of 20 on the overhead video wall. Keith Richards leans into his Telecaster, chunking out the hooks that shook the world, while Ron Wood looks on, his smoke bent at an insolent angle as he grins. Bassist Darryl Jones and the horn section cover stage right, backup singers stage left, flanking Charlie Watts, swinging behind his kit. The band's energy fills D.C.'s FedEx Arena.

As if on cue, every member of the Stones turns to look at the guy behind the B-3 at the back of the stage. Chuck Leavell beams a smile and gives a hand signal, and the guitar solo transitions into a final chorus. Later in the set, a few anxious eyes seek out Chuck as things seem to get a bit hairy; he reassures them with a nod on a downbeat. One hit follows another, but in place of the expected rock cliché, guitar-headstock cue endings, the band focuses on the keyboardist as though he were Toscanini. Even Mick keeps an eye on the keyboard chair at nearly every transition.

It's clear that Chuck wields considerable influence over the World's Greatest Rock 'n' Roll Band, and many observers give him the unofficial title of "Musical Director." "Well, to me Keith is really the MD," he demurs, "but I don't mind helping out when it's needed." Being one of the finest rock keyboardists of all time himself, it's no surprise that his 20 years with the band have led him to some sort of integral position. But Chuck is anything but in the spotlight with the Stones; even the trombone player gets more solos that he does (Michael Davis is the Bobby Keys of the 'bone).

The Stones rely on Chuck to carry on another important aspect of their 40-year tradition, one far from center stage yet of prime importance when the highly touted *40 Licks* tour was in rehearsal. It fell to him to catalog and arrange the nearly 150 songs the Rolling Stones wanted to dust off to celebrate their anniversary. Even the earliest songs were resurrected for inclusion in the constantly changing set list; some had never been performed in public at all. Even many of the lyrics had to be transcribed so Mick could relearn them. All of these lead sheets, lyrics, and charts are kept in two enormous binders—the Holy Tablets of Rock—that travel with Chuck's backstage racks. But the information also resides in Chuck's head, and it's this that the Stones depend on to guide them through long-forgotten arrangements onstage.

"This tour is reaching farther back than any other tour," says Chuck, relaxing backstage in the mojo-bedecked X-Ray Lounge. "We've done tunes that haven't been heard in a long time, such as 'Parachute Woman,' 'Love in Vain,' 'Mannish Boy,' 'She Smiled Sweetly,' and 'Rip This Joint,' which has got to be the fastest tune they've ever done. We'll do three, four, or five songs off of a single record in a row. *Exile on Main Street* has been a big favorite, *Some Girls* has been another, and *Let it Bleed*, too. I've always been a fan, so to get to play those tunes is really something."

TIME IS STILL ON THEIR SIDE

Though the current emphasis would seem to be on music history—an impression underscored by the "greatest hits" approach of the new double CD set *40 Licks*—Chuck reveals that the band is working on new material as much now as they ever have.

"Before we began rehearsals for the tour," he says, "we had a month of sessions in Paris. The main objective was to get four new songs for the retrospective *40 Licks*. We went in knowing that was the goal, but in the end, we'd recorded about 25 pieces. They weren't all finished, but 60 percent of them could easily be finished, and the rest could be explored at a later date, too. And there were more songs coming as we were recording.

"The point is that this is a band with an extraordinary work ethic. All you have to do is look at the body of material; it's insane how broad, deep, and great it is. And we're poised for more. One reason is the passion. They love writing songs, recording them, and performing them. And because of the work ethic, they've just become better and better at their craft."

Even at the songwriting stage, Chuck is much more than a sideman to Mick and Keith. "Sometimes I'll have input into a song arrangement right from the beginning," he says. "Sometimes they already have things worked out and I can just add the glue to a track, or add some sparkles here and there. I believe they have me on board because of who I am and what I do, so they expect me to bring something to the table. They'll always ask me what I think: Should it be acoustic piano, Wurlitzer, Hammond, synth, or should it have no keyboard at all. One of the new songs that stands out for me is Keith's ballad called 'Losing My Touch.' It's a nice piano feature, and it shows a side of the band that you've never seen. We recorded it all together, for the most part in one take."

HE KNOWS IT'S ONLY ROCK 'N' ROLL

Chuck's own contributions to rock history quite apart from the Stones put him at the top of every player's list of favorites. From the unforgettable piano solo on the Allman Brothers' "Jessica" in the early '70s, to his stunning work on Eric Clapton's *Unplugged* in the '90s, Chuck's mastery of the keyboard has always allowed him to get more music out of an eight-bar rock solo than most mortals can squeeze out of a four-hour gig. And recent recording successes on songs like Train's huge hit last year, "Drops of Jupiter," keep him on the airwaves and on lots of CD players.

With the Stones, Chuck proudly carries the flame of rock piano as it has been passed to him by his revered predecessors in the band. "It's an honor to work with these guys, and boy is it fun," he says. "I may not get to go out front with a lot of solos with this band, but that's okay. The role is much broader than that. Through these 20 years, I'd like to think that I've left a mark on the band, that I've graduated from my original role as sort of second keyboardist to Ian Stewart, to a player who has put his own style into the mix—as well as navigating the band through this massive number of songs and arrangements, keeping track of the ongoing changes, and providing a certain balance to the music.

"A lot of other great players have left their mark on the band. Nicky Hopkins stands out—he was such an inventive piano player. He always came up with something that was memorable for those songs. Like on 'Angie,' his piano part is more than just fills, it's full of beautiful melodies. His parts helped make the songs what they are. I try to be careful; if we're doing a song that he worked on, I certainly don't want to alter it too much, but I have to play it my way at the same time.

"Ian Stewart left his own mark on the band. His motto to me was, 'You

Chuck Leavell's mid-'70s touring Steinway featured an above-keyboard hot-water sprinkler system to keep his hands warm during outdoor concerts. Photo by Jon Sievert

always want to have them hear the diamond tiaras up top, Chuck.' He'd play all this boogie-woogie stuff, but he'd put these little things on top, and they make you feel good; they're just right for the song. Then, of course, you've got Billy Preston's contributions, especially on organ, like on 'Don't Wanna Be Your Slave,' 'Melody,' or 'I Got the Blues.' Ian McLagan's playing was incredible, too."

All too often, the assumption is that playing keys on a Stones tune involves nothing more than a straight-eighth, "Great Balls of Fire" approach. Nothing could be farther from the truth, as Chuck himself learned when he first started rocking alongside Ian Stewart. "At the start, I'd play straight, but Stu would say, 'No, you're missing out,' and he'd show me how to fill out the left hand. There's a lot more room for swing in the Rolling Stones than people realize—Charlie Watts is a huge part of that. Here's a guy playing in the world's greatest rock band, and really, all he wants to be is a jazz drummer. He can tell you who played what on everything Charlie Parker ever recorded. The point is, he brings that swing factor into the band. That's one of the things that make the Stones so unique. And I totally lock into that."

Even when the pyrotechnics blow sky-high on "Sympathy for the Devil," Chuck doesn't let the excitement override his sense of good technique. "There's an art to playing rock and roll piano," he says. "Playing hard all the time can be a problem. You have to learn to relax. You have to play with finesse and find the right groove. Sometimes you need to restrain yourself in order to do those really wacky figures. Really good rock and roll piano playing is so much more than just banging it out. It's more about listening to the whole and complementing the other players—and it's not as easy as it looks!"

STONE TOOLS

"For my gig with the Stones," says Chuck, "my primary concern is to have great piano, organ, and Wurlitzer sounds. It's a meat and potatoes deal." For the *40 Licks* tour, Chuck gets a double helping of meat and potatoes: The tour features two stages whenever they play an arena-sized venue. The "A" stage is the large stage with all the lights, towering video display, and fireworks—where Mick can really strut. Stage "B" is about the size of a small nightclub platform 100 yards from the main stage, which the band reaches by sauntering along a walkway that parts the teeming masses at a certain point in each show. On Stage "A," Chuck has his beloved MIDI B-3, a B-3 supercharged by Paul Homb of Keyboard Specialties in St. Petersburg, Florida. "This is my baby," says Chuck. "We recently had it refinished and tightened up. It's a great weapon. I can play piano from the lower manual and B-3 from the top, and I can combine sounds. It gives me a lot of flexibility. I have multiple ways to slow or speed up the Leslie, and I can brake it, too. The Leslie is enclosed completely in a combination road case and isolation booth. The mics are mounted inside, and we just plug the cables into the outside of the case. It eliminates bleedthrough, which is a big problem. Because you can't see whether the Leslie's spinning or not, I have a two-LED system on the lower part of the manual of the B-3 that lets me know if it's going fast or slow. And we have a heat sensor with a temperature gauge on the case, for all those hot days."

Sitting on top of the MIDI B is Chuck's Wurlitzer 200A, whose outputs and sustain pedal have been modified to accommodate its Hammond-top situation. A Yamaha P200 furnishes Chuck with his trademark piano sound. Way out on Stage "B," Chuck has another P200, this one topped with a Korg CX-3.

For all the apparent simplicity of the gig, Chuck has a few racks up his sleeve, too. "There are a few percussion loops that I trigger," he says. "On 'Sympathy for the Devil,' I trigger the intro. Since it's so important, I've got a few backups. The original is on an Apple iBook running Pro Tools LE. That's backed up by a TASCAM MX-2424 with the same loop. Then we have a backup on audio CD, too. When it's time to recreate some of the sounds such as strings on a ballad or some other percussion part, I'll use my Korg Triton." Chuck has a Triton on Stage "A," plus a couple of Triton racks underneath the stage. A pair of Kurzweil K2600s provide the sitar sound on the chorus of "Street Fighting Man," among other sounds.

NOT LOSING HIS TOUCH

For every tour the Stones have mounted in the past 20 years, there has been a chorus of critics who chide the band for being simply too old to rock. Chuck's always ready for that one. "They've gotten hit in the press for some of the recent records," he says. "But I tell ya, those tunes have stood the test of time. We've only gained ground. It's getting better, like a bottle of fine wine. The guys are still writing great songs. And yes, the total combined age may be 235-1/2, or whatever crap someone came up with, but the average weight is 145 pounds, and that's fightin' weight. This band is in shape, and it loves to play."

Portions of this article appeared in the January 2003 issue of Keyboard *magazine.*

FOR MORE ON CHUCK LEAVELL

Since this article was published, Chuck toured the world with the Rolling Stones on their *Bigger Bang* tour, and recorded a great new live set. You can keep up with his news and activities at his official website, www.chuckleavell.com.

A SELECTED CHUCK LEAVELL DISCOGRAPHY

Chuck Leavell is one of the most-recorded keyboard artists in rock and roll. In addition to the work below, you can hear him on the best recordings of the Allman Brothers, the Black Crowes, Eric Clapton, Government Mule, and scores of others.

WITH THE ROLLING STONES
2005 *A Bigger Bang*
2004 *Licks Live*
2002 *Forty Licks*
1998 *No Security*
1995 *Stripped*
1994 *Voodoo Lounge*
1991 *Flashpoint*
1989 *Steel Wheels*
1986 *Dirty Work*
1983 *Undercover*

AS A SOLO ARTIST
2008 *Live in Germany: Green Leaves and Blue Notes*
2005 *Southscape*
2001 *Forever Blue*
1998 *What's in That Bag?*
2005 *Chuck Leavell: Piano Instruction Vol. 1. (Educational DVD)*

Bill Payne with Little Feat in 1978, playing his Keyboard Products-modified Hammond B-3, on top of which are his Wurlitzer Model 1040 electric piano and Oberheim Six Voice. Not shown: Yamaha CP-70 electric piano.

Photo by Jon Sievert

BILL
PAYNE

BY ERNIE RIDEOUT

ROCKIN' UNDER THE RADAR, ROLLIN' OVER THE TOP

"MY CAREER," SAYS Bill Payne from the business end of his Yamaha C7 grand, "much like that of Little Feat, has been all about flying under the radar. I'm flying, but not in anyone's view."

It's an apt metaphor. A bit too eclectic for mainstream rock, yet nowhere near resembling a progressive outfit, Little Feat has chugged along for nearly 40 years on the strength of its loyal fan base, occasional chart-busters, and the extraordinary musicianship of its members. Little Feat formed in 1969 with the encouragement of Frank Zappa, who recognized a certain twisted talent in founding guitarist Lowell George's songwriting. Zappa had no direct influence over the band's sound; their unorthodox approach was bred in the bone.

"We've always had some interesting music," Bill explains wryly. "One song was called 'Dance of the Nubile Virgin Slaves,' which was a 15-minute instrumental. This was in 1969. We had a lot of other material like that, and we played it for Ahmet Ertegun from Atlantic Records. His comment was that it was too diverse. So you can imagine that if the first Little Feat record—which is a collage of material like 'Gunboat Willie,' 'Brides of Jesus,' and 'Taking My Time'—was less diverse than we actually were, it boggles the mind [*laughs*]."

Bill's personal musical menu is not exactly meat and potatoes, either. A propensity for improvisation at a very early age coupled with uncommon facility and an adventurous mind let him absorb music rapidly and rabidly. Classical literature, jazz, psychedelia, blues, Cajun, Tex-Mex, the Mothers of Invention, 20th-century composers, and the music of the Marx Brothers' films are but some of the broader categories in his repertoire.

"I've been known to throw Charles Ives into solos," he admits, flatly. "Even when I played with James Taylor, we'd be coming into the climax of

Bill Payne: "I play a lot of different things—I salute a lot of different genres—but I don't play any of them to the letter. It has nothing to do with a lack of respect, but rather something to do with my attention span." Photo by Debbie Leavitt

'Steamroller,' and I'd start playing *Clair de Lune* by Debussy. Then boom! Right back into the blues. I like things that turn your head slightly, then set you back down gently."

Not everyone has appreciated Bill's willingness to be a tour guide into the bizarre, however. He leans forward and confides: "We had some gig with Charlie Daniels in Nashville. There was supposed to be a big finale at the end of the show. It took our crew an ungodly amount of time to get the stage set up, so by the time we got on, people were leaving. I thought that since I'd done a lot of sessions there, I'd do something for the players that were still there to hear us. I went up to [saxophonist] Lenny Pickett in the middle of a song and said, 'Hey, in 18 beats, I'm going to take it left.' He said, 'What?!' 'In 14 beats, I'm going left. Follow me.' I walked back to the keys and launched into a very bizarre atonal duet with Pickett. [*Mimics squeaks, squawks, and poots.*] I learned later that members of the other band actually rushed out to their cars to get their guns [*laughs*]. They were all supposed to come in for this finale, but it fell flat on its ass after that. I was actually proud to get that kind of reaction out of people, musically."

Such incidents obviously had little impact on Bill's stellar reputation as a studio player. Bob Seger's "Hollywood Nights," the Doobie Brothers' "China

Grove," Bryan Adams' "Everything I Do for You," and countless other chart-bound recordings bear his piano, B-3, and synth work. Such success doesn't come without its drawbacks, however. "My career has been like the elephant and the blind men," he explains. "Some people hire me because they think, 'Billy? He's the one who plays the hell out of the B-3.' Others would say, 'No, no, he's a rock and roll piano player.' Then others think I'm a middle-of-the-road player because of all these hits.

"I play a lot of different things, I salute a lot of different genres, but I don't play any of them to the letter. It has nothing to do with a lack of respect, but rather something to do with my attention span. It's helped me in the long run, because there are guys that have such respect for the jazz tradition that they'd never attempt 'Day at the Dog Races.' Or they might have an intimate knowledge of classical music, but they'd never think of throwing Charles Ives into the middle of a solo. I love that music, but I have just enough knowledge to get me into trouble."

On the other hand, producers who are familiar with Bill's reputation but not his abilities will call him in to "put a little rock and roll edge on it."

"I'll go out and do just that," he says. "But I'll just be waiting for the button to go down at the end. They'll invariably say, 'Umm. . . .'" And I'll say, 'Not that much edge, huh?' They'll say, 'Yeah.' Then I play it the way I knew they wanted it in the first place, and they say, 'Perfect.' In Nashville, for example, they won't let me go for the throat."

One aspect of what takes Bill's playing over the top (taking the rest of Little Feat with him) is his sensitivity to many different gradations of swing. He'll routinely move from a stiff New Orleans style to a jazz swing within a song, or emphasize a 3-against-2 feeling at the quarter-note or the eighth-note level. The New Orleans feel that he uses on tunes like "Dixie Chicken" and others is a perfect example, where he maintains the same basic half-time groove, but he plays quarter-note triplets on top. He'll shift abruptly, not into double-time but into quadruple-time, the pulse changing from half-notes to eighth-notes. He'll shift from eighth-notes to quarter-note triplets to eighth-note triplets and then to various combinations. He'll shift the apparent feel by thickening voicings and playing lines to create accents.

"I'm always moving in and out of straight time and triplets," Bill explains. "You've got this pulse, then you've got the triplets against it. I don't know how I'm doing it; I've just got two hands doing two different things. The internal pulse I'm feeling is straight quarters, but I'm doing lots of syncopation against it. It's like dancing, when your body wants to move one way and your head wants to move another, and it pulls you apart. You're anchored normally in a straight swing feel, then when you start adding things, that has as much to do with the syncopation of the bass as anything."

Swinging of a different sort occurs in Little Feat's hit from 1988 that almost didn't happen. "Whether you know Little Feat or not, you've heard us," Bill says. "If you've been to a sporting event or to a movie theater in the last ten years, or turned on a radio or TV. You've probably heard 'Let it Roll.' I feel pretty good about it because at the time I told the guys, 'You watch, this song'll be picked up by every sport in the world.' It happened even though we didn't push it.

"It all came out of this boogie-woogie bass thing. But at one rehearsal Richie said, 'You know, I really don't like that song.' We had a fight about it, and I pulled it out of rotation for two weeks. I was sitting at home agonizing about it. Finally I went up to him and asked if he could hear what I was playing. He said, 'Not really.' So we turned my part up in his monitors, and I said, 'We're going to do this song.' And thank God we did. Sometimes when you think you've got something, all it takes is one person, close to you or not, to go boo and most people will go, 'By God, they're right. Why would I ever come up with such a foolish thing?'"

"Let it Roll" has a relentless drive as a result of the offbeats in the right-hand part of the basic groove. The horn line resembles a jump blues big band number with its syncopated stabs and ornaments.

"The swing comes from the horns," says Bill. "That's what I heard, and that's what Richie couldn't hear when he didn't like it. That's what Little Feat does pretty well—those syncopations that flow in and out of each other. It sounded straight to him, and I've got to admit that it wouldn't have been fun for anybody to play. It allows him to address his hi-hat, where the tension is in that kind of music between it and everything else, not the snare. If we're all doing the triplet feel, it gets too bouncy. It's more of a tug and pull kind of thing, and very effective. It's taken me years to figure out that that's what we do."

Little Feat is apt to break into this type of groove in other songs as well. In the version of "Dixie Chicken" on *Live From Neon Park*, a tune with a flat-out "Sing Sing Sing" feel pops up here and there; it turns out to be from the score to the Marx Brothers' *Duck Soup*.

Swing and syncopation are one thing, but Bill manages even to put fast tunes into overdrive with his blazing right hand. "To understand this, you have to understand how I hear rhythm," he explains. "The piano is a rhythm instrument. When I hear [guitarist] Fred Tackett play something, I react to that signal and respond right back. I've just got good facility."

"Oh Atlanta" is enjoying a resurgence of popularity with the recent summer Olympics, and it's another one of those vehicles for Bill's gonzo approach to rock and roll piano. One of his classic licks from this tune begins with a percussive technique, to say the least. "[Drummer] Richie [Hayward] lays down a very straight beat, and then I do this independent thing on top of it. That's what's so fun about our band. Where else can you play this stuff?"

Where else indeed? Yet Bill doesn't see such a tremendous gulf between the essence of what Little Feat is about and what's at the core of some of the more popular music he gets hired to play. "I think that the two things that Bob Seger and Little Feat have in common is that the writing comes from a real heartfelt place," he opines. "It's a real American roots kind of music. That's not to say whether or not it'll go out of fashion; it just never has for us as players and songwriters. We don't write hit songs, we write tunes like 'Oh Atlanta' that people like and use for the Olympics. But Seger's, James Taylor's, and our music is real. You don't get the sense that you're listening to some machine pop out another hit. What people like about us, or love about Seger, is the fact that it's the real thing. That's not to say that they're not going to dig Michael Jackson, or Madonna, or Bryan Adams.

"People have at their fingertips a library of great music. My library is chock-full of Gershwin, Glenn Gould, Stravinsky, Howlin' Wolf, Muddy Waters, Pygmy music, Cajun music, a lot of stuff. I like it all for the same reason: It's real."

On the other hand, he continues, "Musicians are always going to have to acquiesce in certain ventures. You gotta go to a record company, there will always be conventions, and you'll either do it or you won't. Little Feat never did. Fine, we've flown under the radar. We've had a long career, but we also are still this enigmatic thing. It's great in one sense, certainly to our fans; I think they'd just as soon keep it to themselves. In one way I like it, but I also would like more people to know that we're there."

Little Feat's move to Zoo records in 1995 has given the band a chance to do just that. "I've taken a more active role in the business side of it," explains Bill, "to spur people on, to keep them honest, and to hold them to the same standard they hold me to, which is to play it the right way. I've noticed that in the business end of things there are some people who play it like this [*plays random atonal clunks*]. There's no one taking responsibility for it. But there's a way to make people feel like they're part of it."

Zoo's management seems to welcome this type of participation from Bill. "They're very smart," he says. "With artists like us who have been around the block a few times, we've got enough knowledge that we could sit in an office and do that job, but we're not so knowledgeable as to think that we know it all."

Bill feels that knowledge, experience, and information are critical elements in artistic and business growth for musicians. "Those who are armed with information and can utilize it," he insists, "are the ones who are going to be doing something with it. It's like taking a piece by Bach [*plays an excerpt from one of the French suites*]. How does that affect how I play [*plays a "Dixie Chicken"-esque riff*]? What does one mean to the other? It's all finger memory, it's how you get around. To me, I use classical music to give me the chops, so when I sit down and play, I can go anywhere. It's all information.

"We have a tendency to not want information," he continues. "'Synthesizers? I don't want synthesizers. They're going to ruin my sound.' If Randy Newman or I or Professor Longhair sat down at this piano, it'd sound like three different pianos. Put that together with all the varied sounds of synthesizers, and now you've got a world open to you. That's why I stopped thinking, 'I'm not going to play a synthesizer because it's going to take away my character and I'll sound like everybody else.' You're only going to sound like everybody else if you play [*plays octaves and fifths in straight rock eighths, not changing notes*].

"It's time and place," he goes on. "That's what your voice is as a player. We all have this unusual thing, like with Little Feat, to provide that voice. That's the good news. The by-product is that it's such an original voice that you may not ever be a household word."

With *Live From Neon Park*, Little Feat has taken some of the devices that are prevalent in jazz, such as recording the same piece more than a couple of times. "This album is another snapshot," says Bill. "This is where we are at this time and place. Most artists, unless they're actually doing a retrospective, will rarely record something twice in a career. It's that way because we're all performance-oriented individuals. With us, you're getting these musical snapshots. Over this long peri-od, you get some interesting growth."

And speaking of growth, he continues, "I'm hopefully going to have an impact on people with a solo album, just as a player, as a guy who sits and lets things fall off the fingers. Hopefully that'll get me into some people's lives. You never know until you do it. That's the thing. I've waited a ridiculously long time to do it.

"I'm just a slow bloomer. I'm 47 years old, and the last record that Little Feat did, *Ain't Had Enough Fun*, I sang more on that record than I'd ever done before. I did it because Bill Wray, who helped produce the record, said, 'Look, we need you to sing on this album, and I like your voice.' I pointed out that I had only a five-note range, and he said, 'Fine, we'll bring it up to seven.' With Shaun Murphy in the band, the keys have gotten higher, more into my range. So you take songs like 'Cadillac Hotel,' 'Drivin' Blind,' 'Borderline Blues,' and all of a sudden, I'm singing really intricate background parts.

"It's the same with songwriting. We had a six-year hiatus. I didn't write more than eight or ten songs. But since I've been back with Little Feat, I'm one of the majority writers. Part of it may have to do with the curse of being a pretty good player, and just saying, 'Well, I'm just gonna play.' And leave it at that. I didn't have a lot of confidence in my writing ability.

"At one point, I didn't even have confidence in what I could play. I listened to Randy Kerber, he's fabulous. He can play circles around what I do. I've talked to Ralph Grierson, who is another killer, and both guys sat me down and said, 'Look, Billy, we're good players, we can read, we can do this and that. But we don't do what you do, either. You sit down and you go *brrm*, and do that stuff you do. That isn't the type of thing that we do.'

"So I took it to heart; they had no reason to bullshit me. Then I began to realize that maybe I had something to offer. Maybe the phone wasn't ringing as much as it used to, but I just got back into the idea of playing. I set up some stuff back at the house, and got into it again. Slowly but surely the phone started ringing again. It was a real good lesson for me. That was in the early '80s, right after Little Feat split up and Lowell George died. After a year or two of James Taylor and Linda Ronstadt, I was feeling better about my playing.

"Basically, with anybody I play with, James Taylor, Little Feat, or Bob Seger, I try to up the ante a little bit. Not out of boredom, but because of what's happening at that moment, you can always get away with a little bit more."

Portions of this article appeared in the October 1996 issue of Keyboard *magazine.*

FOR MORE ON BILL PAYNE

Little Feat continues to tour and record, and Bill Payne continues to broaden his creative endeavors. You can keep up with his news and activities at his official website, www.billpaynecreative.com, and at www.littlefeat.net.

A SELECTED BILL PAYNE DISCOGRAPHY

With his incendiary chops and boundless imagination, Bill Payne defined the sound of rock piano and B-3. In addition to the recordings listed here, you can hear his work on recordings by the Doobie Brothers, Bob Seger, Bonnie Raitt, Emmylou Harris, Robert Palmer, Linda Ronstadt, and scores of others.

WITH LITTLE FEAT
2008 *Join the Band*
2004 *Highwire Act Live in St. Louis*
2005 *Barnstormin' Live, Vol. 1*
2003 *Down Upon the Suwannee River*
2003 *Kickin' It at the Barn*
2002 *Live at the Rams Head*
2000 *Chinese Work Songs*
1998 *Under the Radar*
1996 *Live from Neon Park*
1995 *Ain't Had Enough Fun*
1991 *Shake Me Up*
1989 *Representing the Mambo*

1988 *Let It Roll*
1981 *Hoy Hoy*
1979 *Down on the Farm*
1978 *Waiting for Columbus*
1977 *Time Loves a Hero*
1975 *The Last Record Album*
1974 *Feats Don't Fail Me Now*
1973 *Dixie Chicken*
1972 *Sailin' Shoes*
1971 *Little Feat*

AS A SOLO ARTIST
2005 *Cielo Norte*

PUTTING
THE CLASSICAL IN
CLASSIC
ROCK

JON

Jon Lord tweaking his off-white ARP Odyssey. Photo by Fin Costello/Redferns/Getty Images

LORD

BY ROBERT L. DOERSCHUK

THE ORGAN THAT ROARED

EVEN AS WE SPEAK, somewhere in England, the man who soldered classical themes to brain-frying rock and roll several years before Emerson, Lake & Palmer had even learned one another's first names, who squeezed anguished squeals and roars from his Hammond organ while pre-synthesizer keyboardists were still picking out tidy melodies, who dared to show rock fans that long unaccompanied keyboard improvisations could be at least as interesting as Ginger Baker drum solos, is sequestered with his current band, getting ready to spring a new album on an American public when they least expect it—and perhaps when they most need it.

Just for a moment, put aside your electropop records, you sons and daughters of disco and the synthesized new wave, and put on the organ solo in your hoary old recording of Deep Purple's "Hush." The rhythms don't metronomically click; they punch behind Ian Paice's restless drumming. And the keyboard lines don't cycle by in hypnotic repetitions; they follow the emotional tides, falling and rising in lower-manual smears like animal growls, and erupting in escalating staccato chords until a Leslie speaker springs to life and splatters sound across your walls in a climactic finale.

Just another day's work for Jon Lord, arguably the godfather of progressive rock and now the keyboard maestro with Whitesnake. As we go to press, Whitesnake is disappearing into the English studios to prepare a new album release. Their last recording sold respectably in America, but there have been changes in the lineup and in the group's focus that may make for a bigger impact next time around. If Jon Lord speaks true, we may be hearing more keyboards, something closer to the instrumental balance that made him and guitarist Ritchie Blackmore rock and roll's hottest solo combination years ago with Deep Purple. In those days, rock was flexing its young virtuoso muscles, something that Lord feels it needs to do again in order to revitalize itself. And he may be the man to do it.

Lord, who was born in Leicester, England, on June 9, 1941, put Deep Purple together with Paice and Blackmore in February 1968 while all three musicians were in Hamburg, Germany. Lord brought a solid musical grounding into the band, with years of classical piano, drama school study, and jazz and rock playing already behind him. They recruited bassist Nick Simper and singer Rod Evans, then recorded an arrangement of the Joe South song "Hush," which popped into the American top five by the summer. Their first three albums quickly followed its footsteps into the U.S. charts, pushed by Stateside tours in late '68 and early '69.

These successes gave Lord time and money to explore a longtime interest in blending elements of rock and classical music into a single style. He had tried transplanting familiar orchestral themes into extended introductions and chamber quartet interludes in various Deep Purple tunes, but, fueled by the heady experiments being undertaken in English rock during the late '60s, he went a step further and composed a concerto for rock band and symphony orchestra, presenting it in London's Royal Albert Hall with Malcolm Arnold conducting the Royal Philharmonic Orchestra on September 24, 1969, and again at the Hollywood Bowl a year later. Similarly grand projects, like *The Gemini Suite* and a film score for *The Last Rebel*, flowed from Lord's pen during this same period.

But it was Deep Purple, and his groundbreaking organ work with them, that remained at the center of Lord's attention. They continued to fill concert halls and sell prodigious numbers of albums around the world despite personnel changes, including Blackmore's departure in 1975. Eventually, though, the band elected to split up. Following its demise in July 1976, Lord and Paice put together an ill-fated group with singer/pianist Tony Ashton, then organized Whitesnake with the last Purple singer, David Coverdale.

Jon has remained active with that band up to the present. They enjoy steady successes particularly in Europe, and Lord has expanded his arsenal to incorporate a collection of synthesizers and other sundry keyboards. But because of Whitesnake's particular style and structure, he has been playing more of a background role than was customary with Deep Purple, so it is his early work that remains most indelibly etched on the minds and ears of his fans.

Rumors of a new contract with Geffen Records and of his re-emergence as a powerful solo voice prompted *Keyboard* to track him down in England. There

JON LORD

we found an amiable and highly articulate Jon Lord, elated at the Geffen deal and anxious to come forward once again. Musically he will do so on the next Whitesnake LP this summer. And in terms of his ideas and opinions for matters past, present, and future, he takes the opportunity to speak out here and now.

Before Deep Purple came together, you had already done a lot of recording and club work in London, much of it with some very good players. Why do you think it was Deep Purple, rather than any of these other groups, that attained success?

I think it was the first hard rock band to use keyboards in another way than just as a cosmetic background effect, particularly in the earlier parts of the '70s, when Ritchie and I were trading licks and swapping solos and doing things like that that were taken from jazz but were unusual in rock. My style evolved through my playing with Ritchie, who is a very forceful personality. His guitar playing is very full; it fills most of the spaces. So I had to evolve a style that was kind of a rhythm organ, rather than a rhythm guitar. Through having to fight like that I think I might have come up with a rather unique way of playing. It wasn't until I got into Deep Purple that this began to happen. What I was doing before was pretty derivative. I was a Jimmy Smith freak.

So in the beginning as an organist, were you more concerned with duplicating Jimmy Smith sounds than finding your own style?

At the very beginning, it was difficult not to play a Hammond like Jimmy Smith or Jimmy McGriff or all those '60s organ stars. But if you've got any kind of searching mind at all, copying somebody else gradually becomes very unsatisfactory. After a while I wasn't doing anything fulfilling. I desperately wanted to sound like Jimmy Smith, but then I thought, "What's the point? I'm not going to achieve that on my L-100 anyway."

That's when I started to search around the organ and find other ways of using it. It was really a process of learning by example. There was a marvelous man, Graham Bond, who at that time had a band with [bassist] Jack Bruce, [drummer] Ginger Baker, and [saxophonist] Dick Heckstall-Smith—a marvelous man who, unfortunately, is no longer with us. He played Hammond slightly like Jimmy Smith, but with a kind of individuality that was really quite stunning. The band I was in used to open a lot for his band in clubs, so after several months of this I kind of sucked his brain dry. I was always asking him questions and getting him to show me bits and pieces—tricks of the trade, if you like. He was invaluable. Just watching him was a lesson. It's very important that he should be credited with a great deal of what I've managed to achieve at the organ.

Were you also exploring alternative modes at that time? Some of your later Deep Purple solos seem to indicate that you were interested in moving beyond bluesy accidentals.

I really tried—and I still do try—to say to myself that I don't see why there should be any barriers, so that if I want to use an influence, I will use it, if it works. Just because it's hard rock doesn't mean that I can't use an Eastern scale, or a whole-tone scale, or try a classical allusion, because all those things are part of what I've always been. I'm quite catholic in my approach to music. Obviously the song is important. When you do a solo, you're interpreting the words and the feel of a song in a different way, and there's no point in stitching something on that has nothing to do with it. I have done that occasionally. There are a few solos in the Deep Purple catalog that make me cringe with embarrassment. There's one on *Who Do We Think We Are?* in a song called "Rat Bat Blue." I remember putting a bit of Bach at double speed into the solo and thinking, "This will be wonderful," but it comes and goes right by on the record, and you think, "What the hell was that there for?"

Did you play organ from the beginning, or did you start on piano?

I started with piano at the age of seven. We'd been given an old piano by an aunt of ours who was better off than we were. She had bought a new piano, and dumped this old one on us when I was about five. I used to plunk around on it to the point where I think my father got enraged enough by the untutored noise I was making to insist that I take piano lessons, for which many thanks to him. I'm very grateful for that. So I studied for ten years in the normal classical mode. The first couple of years were fairly unfruitful, but when I was about nine or ten I got hold of a really brilliant teacher in my home town. His name was Frederick Alt, and he was a concert pianist. A fantastic man, and a really superb pianist. He died a couple of years back. You know how a really good teacher can impart the joy of knowledge and make you feel the joy of what you're learning, rather than making it a chore that you have to do? That was really when I began to take off.

Did you have ambitions of becoming a concert pianist yourself?

Yes, for a while, until I realized it meant eight to twelve hours a day practicing. I like to call myself essentially laid-back, but sometimes my wife calls me lazy [*laughs*]. In any event, the amount of effort involved in getting to that standard was greater than my need to do it, so I just decided to become a gifted amateur.

Do you still play classical pieces?

Yes, I do. Funnily enough, my father came down to see me about a year ago with a great pile of the music I used to play, and some of it I can't play now, which is most disturbing! When I was about 15 or 16, this teacher had me playing Liszt and some of Brahms' really hard, heavy piano music. What I really most preferred playing, though, were the French composers: Debussy, Fauré.

That's so different from the music you're associated with.

Absolutely, but it's delightful to play at home in a kind of introspective way. I also had quite an early flirtation with jazz, and I found out that a lot of the jazz pianists—Bill Evans, and later on Chick Corea—were influenced by that same Impressionistic style of piano writing. I still play it at home. It's a cleansing kind of music to me.

Jon Lord in his Deep Purple prime, with his trusted Hammond B-3 topped by an ARP String Ensemble. In the rear are two off-white ARP Odysseys; to the right is his Fender Rhodes. Photo courtesy of Keyboard magazine

Why are you unable to play other pieces from your student days, though? Has rock and roll had a negative effect on your technique?

I would say so, yeah. It's awfully difficult, especially if you're a busy rock and roll musician, to keep up the kind of practice that is required to play these pieces successfully. I can still stumble through them, but I remember that I used to play them a lot better. I'm working on them again and trying to get them back, because I'm a great believer in the necessity of technique, which allows a musician to be able to translate his ideas into sound. If I hear a marvelous solo in my head and my fingers won't play it, then something worthwhile to me has been lost. To that end I try to keep my technique up, but during the busy years with Purple, '70 to '75, when I got home all I really wanted to do was to kick off my shoes and lie back in my chair. Pounding away at the piano for a few more hours was not high on my list of priorities.

Did rock make any technical demands that classical lessons might not have prepared you for?

Not in terms of being able to move your fingers along the keys, but certainly in terms of endurance and strength. I found very quickly that large concerts were a completely different environment to sitting in the front room at home and playing the piano. Stamina became a factor, so more than ever I was pleased that I had gotten a technique. At that point, it only became a question of hardening that technique up.

Was hand tension the real problem?

You've hit the nail on the head. It is hand tension. I tend to find that the hands start to tense up rather than staying nice and loose. For me, it's just a question of thinking through it, but I know some keyboard players, friends of mine, who find it quite difficult to keep playing by the end of the evening.

Part of the problem may lie in playing different keyboards at different heights with different actions. Your arm angle would be constantly changing.

That is unnatural. I was taught to play "properly," with the wrist held high and the back of the hand over the keyboard rather than hanging down in front of it, and sometimes it is impossible to assume that position. And I also play standing up now, which is a different ball game again. But on the whole I didn't find a great deal of difficulty in transferring from one keyboard to the other.

When did you get interested in playing rock?

When I first heard Jerry Lee Lewis play that intro to "Whole Lotta Shakin' Goin' On." Beethoven and Mozart just went out the window for a while. I just couldn't work out how he got that effect. It was quite a shock to hear.

Was your wrist action strong enough to play that way?

No, that's what I couldn't get. I could do it from a technique point of view, but it sounded wimpy. It sounded awful, in fact. So that proves one thing: Rock and roll may be simplistic, especially in some of the early stuff, but if there's no feel behind it, it won't work. Rock is feel music as much as anything else. Technique is still a very important factor, certainly in my way of wanting to play, but I had to realize that I hadn't yet developed the feeling I needed to play it right. I had to work at my craft.

So what did you do?

I came to London and went to a drama school—anything to get out of Leicester, you know? I had three good years there, but during that time I was playing all kinds of piano. I was doing sing-along stuff at a pub in the evenings to earn a few pounds, I played in a small modern jazz outfit, and I occasionally got to play a bit of rhythm and blues, which was the up-and-coming music in the early to mid-'60s. There was a very thriving club scene in England then. I learned by example. Nobody had written a book saying how to do it, and unfortunately, because my mind had been tutored and classically trained, it needed a book at that time to tell it what to do—I had to get out of that way of thinking and just go with the flow.

Can you recall the first time you realized that you had gotten the right feeling for playing this music?

Oh, I remember it very well. It was at a place near Portsmouth in south England, and one of Manfred Mann's early bands was playing. I sat in with them on a terrible old piano that was stuck in the corner; they miked it up, and the next hour went by in what seemed to me like 20 seconds. It was great. I enjoyed myself immensely. They came up after and said, "Hey, that was fabulous. Come sit in again." I knew I'd gotten somewhere. I recall it very strongly, actually. I recall drinking too much beer afterwards as well [*laughs*].

Did you begin phasing jazz out of your style around then?

Yeah, around when we had gotten the Artwoods together, because of certain things that had happened to me while I was playing with them. The band was very much based on R&B improvisation. There'd be two or three choruses, then off you'd go. By this time the guys were saying that Hammond organs were going to be the big thing, so we bought one of them on a hire/purchase plan.

In other words, you rented it, and the money you spent on rent could be used toward buying it.

That's right. So I was using piano and organ onstage, and as I did solos, a bit of classical music would creep in. The audience seemed to like it, so I started to get a bit of a name in the clubs as a different kind of player. I was trying to pull the band away from being a straight 12-bar blues R&B band into something a little more adventurous, for want of a better word. I don't want to disparage the other guys in the band, they were lovely musicians, but in the end I began to outgrow them. What I wanted to do began to stick out in the band like a spare groom at a wedding. It didn't fit properly anymore, so I needed to start working with musicians who would allow me to grow in that direction. That's when I met Ritchie; he was talking my kind of language. I'd heard Hendrix by this time, and I'd heard Vanilla Fudge, so I knew there was more for me out there than I could see in an R&B band.

And yet there were very few keyboard players around at the forefront of that scene. Most of the creative energy was still coming from guitarists.

Absolutely, and I was determined to change that, along with a couple of friends of mine like Emerson and Wakeman. Back in the late '60s the three of us were really grouped together in England, although obviously our differences came out later on.

What was your first encounter with Keith Emerson's music like?

I went to see Keith play one night because I'd heard that his band, the Nice, was good. To my amazement I found that he was doing the same sort of thing that I was doing, although I'd never met or heard him before, and he, similarly, had never met me or heard me play. It was possibly understandable that we should have such similar ideas, because we had both been classically trained before going into rock and roll situations, and we were arriving at roughly the same conclusion. But then Keith took it a good deal further into a totally keyboard-oriented band, which was not what I wanted. I wanted to play with a guitarist.

Emerson never really did work with a guitarist.

No, and I hope he'll forgive me if he reads this, but I think it showed. There was an occasional overindulgence. I feel that I can say this because I have also stated publicly that I happen to consider him one of the finest modern keyboard players in our kind of music. But I'm afraid that, for me, he lacks a little soul.

Was the Hammond the first non-piano keyboard you had ever played?

I had played a pipe organ in church while I was at school. My school had a big pipe organ in the school hall, and I'd gone in for a couple of organ competitions.

So you played the foot pedals too?

Yeah. In fact, in the first Deep Purple back in '68, I used to play the pedals, but I soon got rid of them because it was actually rather pointless. With the sound quality in those days, you could never hear them, and it looked like I was trying to stamp out a cigarette [*laughs*]. There was just this great amount of thrashing going on.

What model was your first Hammond?

My first one was a small L-100, but when I got my first C-3 in '68, I was hooked. I've still got that same organ. It's a beauty; I love it. It's been around the world so many times, but it's never let me down—he said, touching wood. I've had a lot of modifications done to it, of course.

Like what?

One of the most startling ones is that there's an RMI electric piano built into it.

Triggered by the organ keyboard?

Using the same contact system, yes, as the keyboard of the Hammond, so on the top manual I can play just organ, just RMI piano, or both. That's how I get that really huge dirty sound, which is a bit of a trademark for me.

On the introduction to "She's a Woman" by Whitesnake, from *Ready an' Willing*, it sounds like you have a Clavinet doubling the organ line. Is that the RMI-Hammond interface?

That's the RMI and the organ, yes. Another secret bites the dust. There are other little refinements on the organ too. The bottom two octaves of the lower manual can be hooked up to trigger a synthesizer, so I can have my Minimoog set down on the floor and linked up to the Hammond. I just click a switch and there it is. I can't bend pitch that way, of course; it's just for when I need a straight doubling sound.

Who did your modifications?

A gentleman in England named Bill Hough, who is a positive genius. He did Keith's keyboards, and he went out on tour with McCartney. All I would have to do would be to say to him, "Look, I have an idea. I want a phase box where I can just press a button and phase any of my keyboards." And he'd build it, and all these other little things, which have all become a big integrated system.

What about your amplification? Are you using Leslie speakers now?

I did get rid of the Leslies at one period in the early '70s. I went to straight speakers for a couple of years, which oddly enough really improved my technique, because they made it even more difficult to play smoothly. The Leslie somehow fills out the sound; it gives it life. The straight speakers tend to make the sound more direct; it doesn't breathe as easily. I had to match my technique to that to make it work. That was good for me, but we went back to the Leslies when we found out how to boost them in a way that was useful for me.

How were they modified?

I've got a Crown amp running them, but the Leslies are completely gutted, with 15" Gauss speakers and heavy-duty JBL horns built into them. Each cabinet can take about 1,300 watts before they start to blow up, and I've got four of them. It's a huge amount of power, but I've still got that lovely Leslie effect. Two of the Leslies are miked, top and bottom, and as they rotate at slightly different speeds, you get a nice swirling effect out front. They're also miked into the monitor system, so I can hear myself along with everybody else in the band.

It's funny that you run everything through Leslies now, since with Deep Purple you hardly ever ran the Leslies at full speed. You seemed to prefer that straight overdriven growly Hammond tone. Does that seem like a fair characterization of your sound back then?

Yes, I would say so, but even now I try to save the fast speed on the Leslies for the climaxes. I prefer the slow swirl of the chorale. And yes, I do like the organ to growl. I don't like polite organ sounds too much. They're all right for Holiday Inn lounge jazz. The Hammond organ is not really your archetypal rock and roll instrument, and to try to make it one, to keep it in the context of what I'm doing now with Whitesnake and what I did before with Purple, has been a fight, a battle—a very pleasurable one, and ultimately one in which I think I succeeded. But the piano is a much easier keyboard to play in rock. I love playing rock and roll piano, because it blends much more easily.

Yet it's a more physically demanding instrument than the organ.

The piano? Oh, yes, and I've got the scars to prove it.

Are there any recorded solos you're particularly proud of?

On *Made in Japan*, the live album, there's a solo on "Lazy" that I'm quite happy with. Most of the organ work on *In Rock* and *Machine Head* I'm very proud of. But I always found it hard to solo as well in the studio as I do onstage. Of course the time element is different. In the studio somebody always says, "Right, you've got 24 bars, now, fill 'em!" But, number one, you want the solo to be integrated fully into the song, and number two, you want it to shine. You want people to say, "That's a good solo," when they hear it. The sterility of the studio sometimes defeats that possibility.

Are you more of a fully-integrated multi-keyboardist with Whitesnake than you were with Purple?

I don't know. I still think of myself as "Jon Lord: Organist," not "Jon Lord: Keyboard Player." I am really an organist in the rock and roll sense. I love to play the piano and the synthesizers when they're appropriate, but basically I'm still an organist.

What do you think of *Gemini Suite*, now that you can look back on it?

Ah, bless its little heart, it's very naive. I thoroughly enjoyed doing it, and it was amazing to work with the London Symphony Orchestra. The thing that Deep Purple did before that, the *Concerto for Group and Orchestra*, was great fun, and a great event. To have been there and seen it was enjoyable, but musically it was also very naive. I've come a long way since then.

If it was an attempt to fuse rock with the classics, you'd have to admit that it failed, because the rock and orchestral sections generally alternated, with a minimal amount of blending.

PUTTING THE CLASSICAL IN CLASSIC ROCK

Yes, exactly. That's why I say it was a naive attempt. I did do one album in Germany in '75, which again I don't think was ever released in America, called *Sarabande*, where I think I succeeded. I did it all in the studio, as opposed to in a concert hall, so I was able to have greater control. I had the group actually playing with the orchestra a good deal. But one had to make concessions in the orchestration because of that. I do believe now that never the twain shall meet, at least not with each style having its own terms. One or the other, the rock or the classical side, would have to make concessions. In the end I became disenchanted with the whole idea, although I had a hell of a lot of fun trying to make it work.

Outside of your orchestral experiments, when working with Deep Purple, you have been credited with helping to lay the foundation for the heavy metal sound, although I've never been able to understand why some people categorize Purple purely as a heavy metal band.

I'm very pleased to hear you say that, because I don't understand it either.

Your music seemed much less simplistic than the music we associate with heavy metal, and yet because of Deep Purple's approach you usually had to keep your ensemble parts pretty simple, with open fifth voicings and unison lines with the bass. Did you find your role harmonically restricting in any way?

Again, a good question, and one that will take a lengthy reply, rather than just a simple "Yes," which is in fact the answer. Okay, yes, it was difficult, and perhaps initially harmonically restricting. But one of the great joys about Purple was that this forced me into searching for ways to make it more interesting for myself, and therefore for the listener. That's why we could never be classified as a heavy metal band. It might have spawned a lot of heavy metal bands, and it was loud and raucous, but it was more than that. It could also be soft and tender, it had dynamics, and it had humor. And incidentally, I don't consider Whitesnake a heavy metal band at all. If you like, I consider it a modern R&B band. It has tendencies toward what people might call heavy metal—it's loud, and it tends to be aurally exciting—but playing heavy metal music to me is like giving somebody a strange pill that pins their ears back and produces a kind of numb lethargy. Constant grinding riffs are not my idea of rock and roll.

A lot of bands in that genre play nothing but I-IV-V progressions, but Purple was never that restricted.

No. We really felt we were doing something different. There was a lovely feeling of experimentation and adventure at the beginning, and it lasted a good long time. We were blazing trails in a way. Okay, other people were doing the same in other directions. We weren't alone, but because we had that almost missionary zeal to spread the gospel according to St. Purple, it gave us a kind of freshness that I don't think can be locked in as heavy metal. And part of that freshness was the knowledge that I had to contribute in a way that was fulfilling for me, or I'd be lagging behind the guys who were making the band great. I feel the same with Whitesnake in a slightly different area. I've got to find it interesting. If I don't, I wouldn't be able to give it the shot in the arm it might need.

Are you surprised that you're still doing this for a living after all these years?

Constantly. I wake up some mornings thinking about that: "What the hell are you doing? When are you going to get a real job? Or buy a small farm?" The weird thing about it, though, is that it seems so short. As much as any other reason, I think that's why I haven't changed. I mean, I love it. I really do. I'm reasonably good at it. And I can't really do anything else! I don't actually have that many other talents that I can parlay into a career. So, in a way, I've painted myself into a corner. But it's a corner I'm happy to be in.

Portions of this article appeared in the March 1983 issue of Keyboard *magazine.*

FOR MORE ON JON LORD

Jon Lord has been touring extensively, performing his compositions for piano and orchestra. Rumor has it he's planning a new B-3 based project, too. You can keep up with his news and activities at his official website, www.jonLord.org.

A SELECTED JON LORD DISCOGRAPHY

Jon Lord did things in organ solos that no one had done before, doing it with conviction and facility that rivaled the most flamboyant guitarists. Deep Purple reunites periodically, and though their best releases are listed below, there have been several excellent box sets and reissues. Several of Jon's solo releases are orchestral in nature; no crossover here, these are strictly classical.

WITH DEEP PURPLE

1998 *Abandon*
1996 *Purpendicular*
1987 *The House of Blue Light*
1984 *Perfect Strangers*
1975 *Come Taste the Band*
1974 *Stormbringer*
1973 *Who Do We Think We Are?*
1972 *Made in Japan*
1971 *Fireball*
1970 *Deep Purple in Rock*
1969 *The Book of Taliesyn*
1969 *Deep Purple*
1968 *Shades of Deep Purple*

WITH WHITESNAKE

1982 *Saints & Sinners*
1981 *Come an' Get It*
1980 *Ready an' Willing*
1979 *Lovehunter*
1978 *Trouble*

AS A SOLO ARTIST

2008 *Boom of the Tingling Strings*
2007 *Durham Concerto*
2004 *Beyond the Notes*
1999 *Pictured Within*
1982 *Before I Forget*
1976 *Sarabande*
1970 *Gemini Suite*

Keith Emerson, on the rumor that Jimi Hendrix almost joined ELP: "I thought Hendrix might take the attention away from me—I'm a bit of an egomaniac. If Hendrix had been interested, though, I'd have given it a go."
Photo by Peter Figen

KEITH EMERSON

BY DOMINIC MILANO

KEITH EMERSON. HIS unique use of the Hammond organ; his fusing of classical, jazz, and pop styles; his almost single-handed creation of the popular image of the multi-keyboardist; his pioneering use of the synthesizer; and his all-around technical ability—all these have served to prove that he is indeed one of the most important, if not the most important, innovator in the field of rock keyboards.

Emerson was born in 1945, in Todmorden, Lancashire, England. He began his study of piano at the age of eight. His parents, both being musically inclined, thought that music would be a nice sideline for Keith to make some extra money with in later life. Surprisingly, Keith never had any formal training in music. All of his teachers were local "little old ladies."

Keith took a job as a bank teller after leaving high school, playing in various bands at night. Eventually he left his day job, focusing on music full-time. The bands he played in included Gary Farr and the T-Bones and the VIPs—which later became Spooky Tooth. In 1967, Emerson joined the backup band for American soul singer P. P. Arnold. Most people remember this band as the Nice.

During his stay with the Nice, Emerson developed a stage act that he would be both praised and criticized for. It involved the seeming destruction of a Hammond L-100 (although in fact he did nothing more than pulling the reverb springs, making it feed back, and putting knives into it to hold down certain notes) and playing between the L-100 and a Hammond C-3. This proved to be more visually exciting than sitting behind an organ that, in Keith's words, "looked like a piece of furniture." The praise came from fans who obviously enjoyed the show. The criticism came from people who saw no point in the theatrics and were too quick to assume that that was all Emerson could do. In either case, it was a stage act that brought him widespread attention and helped

PUTTING THE CLASSICAL IN CLASSIC ROCK

to open people's minds to the use of keyboards in rock music.

In late 1969, Keith met bassist/vocalist Greg Lake of King Crimson in San Francisco, where the two were playing on the same bill. Both were dissatisfied with the bands they were in, and each liked the other's playing. The two joined musical forces and began their search for the proper drummer. Carl Palmer of Atomic Rooster was their choice, and so was formed Emerson, Lake & Palmer—ELP for short.

Their most recent recording, *Works, Vol. 1*, has been the subject of much talk among the followers of ELP because of the extensive use of an orchestra throughout the album. Many feel that the band is smothered behind the lavish strings and brass, while others find those elements pleasant additions to the ELP sound. Another radical move on the album was Emerson's forsaking his Hammond organ and modular Moog synthesizer, the latter of which he had been the first to use in a live performance situation. Instead, he chose to use Yamaha's mammoth $50,000 GX-l polyphonic synthesizer and a Steinway grand piano.

In the early spring of 1977, the group mounted a tour that included a 59-piece orchestra, six vocalists, 19 technicians, six roadies, and others, for a total of 115 people. It was the largest touring production ever attempted in a rock context. However, by midsummer the group was forced to drop the orchestra for financial reasons.

Emerson is shy and modest yet very jovial, and seemingly quite unaffected by his superstardom. His I'm-just-a-regular-guy composure is nearly enough to make you forget that his accomplishments include such minutiae as walking away with top honors in *Keyboard*'s annual readers poll.

When did you first start playing organ?

I was about 18, I think. I got fed up with playing pianos with the hammers broken off of them. That seems to be a fairly typical thing that happens to players. I saved up for about two years and bought the L-100.

Did your technique change to fit the organ?

Yes, it did. I realized it was obvious that you couldn't do all of the styles that you could do on the piano, so it was a bit limiting. Unless you're playing in a classical style on the organ, there's really no other use for the left hand. It gets a bit too boggy. You've got to comp with it. It is not as challenging as playing the piano.

When did you add the C-3 to your setup?

It was about 1968, I think. It was always the L-100 before that.

What gave you the idea of using the two organs together?

Well, at that particular time I was into throwing the L-100 around and making it feed back. I had developed this stage act and it seemed to go down quite well. I couldn't do that with the C-3, you see, and it was a necessary part of the act at the time. I liked the C-3 sound. It was far superior and the octave range was greater than on the L's.

How did you get the L-100 to feed back?

It would feed back from being so close to the onstage speakers if you switched the L-100 off, because it had speakers in it. And using a fuzz box exaggerated the effect even more. By altering the direction between the speakers in the L-100 and the onstage speakers, I'd get various howling noises.

Did Jimi Hendrix have any influence on your use of feedback at the organ?

Yeah, very much so. I did a tour with him, actually. He had bought himself a home movie camera, and whenever we were playing I'd see him looking between the amps, filming. He was always there. He loved the act. When he'd gotten his films developed, there was hysterical laughter coming from his dressing room. I poked my head around the corner to see what all the laughter was about, and they were running the film of me doing the bit with the organs. They were speeding up the film and running it backwards—it was all completely stupid. Hendrix was great.

But as far as that early stage act went, there was an organ player in London by the name of Don Shin. I don't know where he is today. He was a weird-looking guy, really strange. A very twittery sort of character. He had a schoolboy's cap on, round spectacles, really stupid. I just happened to be in this club when he was playing. He had an L-100. The audience—you know there were a lot of younger chicks down at the Marquee—were all in hysterics. Giggling and laughing at him. No one was taking him seriously. And I said, "Who is this guy?" He'd been drinking whiskey out of a teaspoon and all kinds of ridiculous things. He'd played an arrangement of a Grieg concerto, and I'd already played things like that with the Nice, the Brandenburg and all [from *Ars Longa Vita Brevis*]. So my ears perked up. Somebody else was doing these things. Playing it really well, and he got a fantastic sound from the L-100. But halfway through he sort of shook the L-100, and the back of it dropped off. Then he got out a screwdriver and started making adjustments while he was playing. Everyone was roaring their heads off laughing.

So I looked and said, "Hang on a minute! That guy has got something." He and Hendrix were the controlling influences over the way I developed the stage act side of things. Nobody really went for the organ in those days. The L-100 looked like a piece of furniture. I think Georgie Fame was the first to use it in England, and Graham Bond came along doing a heavier sort of thing. But most people's reaction to seeing an organ in the band was "Yuk." I mean, people hated the sound of it. What I wanted to do was change people's image of that, make the organ sound more attractive. It didn't look that good, and the player usually sat at the instrument, so it didn't have any visual appeal at all. I guess seeing Don Shin made me realize that I'd like to compile an act from what he did. A lot of people hated it, said it was totally unnecessary. They thought that was all I could do. Some people still think that.

There's a story that Hendrix was going to be a part of ELP. Is that true?

Well, it was one thing, which was suggested by [drummer] Mitch Mitchell when the band was first forming. Unfortunately, the press got hold of it and blew it up. They made all sorts of speculations. Their imaginations ran wild. At the time,

Greg and I were talking with Mitch about joining us. He was happy with the suggestion, and he said, "Well, I'm seeing Hendrix tonight, maybe we could ask him to join too." Mitch said Hendrix thought a lot of my playing, and I told him the feeling was mutual. I thought it would be fantastic, although I was a bit skeptical about it. I thought Hendrix might take the attention away from me—I'm a bit of an egomaniac. If Hendrix had been interested, though, I'd have given it a go.

The L-100 and the C-3 have a slightly different sound. Do you make use of that difference?

No, not really. Occasionally I'll use my left hand on the L-100 and my right on the C-3. There's no percussion on the lower manual of the C, and in things like *Tarkus* it's useful to play the ostinato on the upper manual of the L-100 with the percussion on and also play the upper manual on the C-3 with the percussion on. You get more distinction. If you'd done that on just one organ, the percussion wouldn't happen.

What drawbar and percussion settings do you use on the Hammonds?

It's pretty standard. My favorite is the first three drawbars pulled full out with the percussion on the third harmonic. The vibrato is on chorale 3. Depending on the acoustics of the hall, I'll add a slight touch of the top drawbar. I like a tacky-sounding organ. One that spits a bit, you know. I'm still searching for the ideal organ sound. It's still a bit too hard at the moment.

How much did jazz organists influence your sound?

Well, it was the Jack McDuff organ sound that really turned me on. I didn't really like the Jimmy Smith organ sound, though I liked what he did. But I worked for ages trying to get the sound that Jack McDuff got on "Rock Candy," from *Brother Jack McDuff Live!* It starts off with a very husky voice saying, "Presenting jazz organist Brother Jack McDuff!" with dubbed-in applause and then an amazing sort of tacky, spitty-sounding organ. I think it must have been a freak of the recording; I found the sound by pure accident. You use a Marshall amplifier with the presence and treble turned full up. It exaggerates the contact sound. Lately, I've got a much cleaner sound, but I still like an element of click.

How did you get the screaming chorus effect on the organ on "Jerusalem"?

That was double-tracked and the second organ was put through a flanger. I tried to develop an electronic thing which would produce that effect live. It would accept the direct signal and split it in two. One signal would remain straight and the other would go just a fraction out of tune to give the organ a ringing sound. It worked okay and sounded all right, but there were all kinds of side noises. The people who were making it never perfected it. I wanted to use that on the piano also, so you could go straight from a honky-tonk piano to a normal piano sound. I think there are things on the market that do that now—Eventide Harmonizers.

How do you go about re-arranging tunes by classical composers?

I sit down with the score. As far as Aaron Copland's "Fanfare for the Common Man," on *Works*, goes, it needed transposing, so I did that first. I wanted to improvise in a key that was sort of bluesy. It ended up in *E*. The rest of it was straightforward, really. You know, in order to get the shuffle sound, the timing needed to be changed, but it was common sense.

What about earlier things like "The Barbarian"?

That was taken from Bartok's *Allegro Barbaro*. There were a few timing things that needed to be changed to fit what we were doing there. Ginastera's *First Piano Concerto*, fourth movement, which we called "Toccata" on *Brain Salad Surgery*, was about the most complicated piece we did. I had to go through the whole thing and condense it, to bring out the parts of it that I thought were the most important. Of course, we couldn't do it exactly the way Ginastera had written it because all of it uses the whole keyboard on the piano. So those bits I got the synthesizer to do. Ginastera loved it when I took it along to him. He made some comment that that was exactly how his music should always sound. And the same with Copland. In fact, I've got a tape of what Copland thinks of our version of "Fanfare for the Common Man." This always pleases me, because I don't want to adulterate the music or anything.

How do you orchestrate your keyboard parts?

You mean what music is to be played on what instrument? I don't know. I invariably start with the piano. From there on it'll go out either to the organ or to another instrument. It depends on how it sounds and on what the original intention is for the piece. If I'm pretty convinced it is going to be, say, a piano concerto, or it's going to be for ELP, then that will determine what instruments I'll use. Sometimes I've got that in mind before I start. I swap around for variety. I may have been playing one line on the organ for a long time and just by way of a change I'll play it on the Yamaha.

Where did your interest in arranging other people's music come from?

Simple reason—I like the tunes. I want to play these tunes, but I want to play them in a way that's acceptable to our audience, and that will stimulate new interest in the original. You know I started doing this back in the '60s, and that was my intention. But obviously since that time, audiences have become far more perceptive and intelligent. One doesn't really have to do that now. I think people are going for classical music as much as for any other form. You wouldn't have had your Chick Coreas five years ago. Chick Corea doesn't have to really dress up in blazer gear to get a wide following. It just goes to show you that it's not a question of image these days. It's more a question of the actual music. So I don't mean to be insulting the public's intelligence by saying the reason I'm playing "Fanfare for the Common Man" is because I want them to listen to the original. That may have been the case six years ago, but since then it's become part of what people expect of me. I still occasionally enjoy other people's music. If a piece comes out which lends itself to a particular situation, a particular meter, then I use it. If it doesn't, I don't force the issue. My music has been tagged with the label "classical rock," which I guess is okay. Broadly speaking, I guess that's true, but it's not a term that I want to really like.

Do you write out all of the music for the band to learn?

Now I do in order to get the orchestrations down, but the earlier stuff like

Tarkus wasn't written out. I'm very aware of what Carl and Greg like to do, and in the case of *Tarkus* Carl was very struck by different time signatures. He told me that he'd like to do something in 5/4, so I said I'd keep that in mind and started writing *Tarkus* from there. Greg wasn't too sure about it at the beginning. It was too weird. But he agreed to try it, and afterwards he loved it. Listening back to those things, I think they just scratch the surface. It moves too quickly from one idea to another. One thing I manage to do now is expand more on an idea. I get more out of it than doing just little bits and pieces. I think if I did *Tarkus* again today, I'd orchestrate it and it would sound marvelous.

Do you think you used your keyboard setup like an orchestra before?

Yeah. Listening back to past records, I don't think I really listen to them as they are. I've always thought they were something far bigger. And I found that every time I listened back I'd say, "Well, it could've been this way." So I figured, why not go ahead and do it? So I made the decision to go ahead and start using the orchestra. I had had an amount of experience with the Nice and the Royal Philharmonic. In fact, the Nice were one of the first bands to work with an orchestra live. Jon Lord with Deep Purple did it too. He had a bigger success than I did with his concerto, but I think his came after my *Five Bridges Suite*. I don't know how well *Five Bridges* did, but I liked the record. I found it quite a lot of fun working with orchestras then, and I thought I'd like to do it again.

Have you had to bring the L-100 back into the act?

Yeah. We also thought we were going to drop "Tarkus", but we're doing a somewhat abbreviated version of that, too. We really didn't expect to drop the orchestra at all. So obviously we had rehearsed what we'd be playing with the orchestra. When we stopped using the orchestra we were faced with me working overtime to compensate for what the orchestra used to do. I've really got my hands full. And even so, there were a few numbers we couldn't do without them—"The Enemy God" and so on. There are so many orchestral lines in that that it's impossible for one person to play it. And with ELP alone it's only possible to play the first movement of my concerto. Then I have to play some of the orchestra's lines. Luckily, people have come expecting the orchestra and still haven't been too disappointed. In fact, a lot of people said we sound better without them. I'm inclined to disagree with that. They do get more of a chance to see ELP together as a threesome, though. I think that some of them are under the impression that the orchestra is taking a lot of what we are meant to be doing away from us. It's really untrue. Actually, what the orchestra is enabling us to do is more of the ELP repertoire than we've ever done before. Like the "Bolero" from *Trilogy*, We tried doing that as a trio in all manner of ways. I even taught Greg to play keyboards for it.

Didn't you have him playing Mellotron and Minimoog?

That's right. Then we had the strings on a tape recorder and Carl had head-phones on. He played drums to that. It didn't work for too long. The tape broke down one night and everything fell to pieces. So we never used that again. I think the only number that suffers without the orchestra is "Pirates." It sounds a bit too thin for my ears, but the audience still goes along.

How much influence did Copland have on the orchestration of "Pirates"?

Well, I've always loved Copland. I don't know if there is any conscious influence. There is one part that's vaguely Coplandish, but I think in general it's all pretty integrated with all my musical influences. It's really hard to point out. I guess you might say there's more Stravinsky than Copland there. That was intentional, with those pounding accents coming in. It wasn't exactly the same as *The Rite of Spring*, but I had that in mind.

When did you add the Moog to your setup? Did you consider it an extension of the organ?

It was. In those days I didn't really know what I was looking for. It was all trial and error. A lot of the sounds I was getting from the L-100 were completely accidental. With the Moog, I went into a record shop where they knew me. Walter Carlos' *Switched-On Bach* had just been released. They played it for me in the shop. I didn't honestly like it. The guy played it for me because it had the *Brandenburg* thing in *G*, which I had done with the Nice [on *Ars Longa Vita Brevis*]. The guy asked me if I'd heard this version, played it for me, and asked me what I thought of it. I said it sounded horrible. It was too boggy, too laid down. But there was a picture of the thing it was played on, and I said, "So what's this?" And he said it was like a telephone switchboard. And I said, "Oh, that's interesting." So I bought the album.

I got word through my office that a guy by the name of Mike Vickers had had a Moog shipped over to England, so I asked if I could have a look at it. We got together, and he set it up in his room. He explained to me the functioning of the instrument. I said, "Well, can it be used onstage?" And he said, "No way. You don't realize the complications in this. There's no way you could do that." I thought there must be some way, and asked, "What if you hid down behind this thing and programmed it while I was playing it? You know, set up all these things and keep it in tune?" I was playing at the Festival Hall with the Royal Philharmonic and the Nice. I thought I'd use the synthesizer as an added touch. So Mike Vickers was hunched down backstage, but he'd pop up every now and then and put a plug in somewhere. It worked excellently. So I immediately sent off to Moog and got some literature back. At that time Bob Moog was developing his preset thing, so I said, "I want one."

What happened when you got it?

It arrived in a box, no instructions or anything. It was all in bits and pieces. I couldn't even get a sound out of it. I was at the point of throwing the damn thing out the window. I frantically rang up Mike Vickers and asked him, "How do I get some sound here?" He said, "Oh. You got it! I'd love to see it!" So he came around, and he couldn't figure it out either. He knew how to operate his unit, but it had taken him ages because he hadn't gotten any instructions either. He couldn't work out the presets. But he kept it for about three days and rang me up and said, "I think I've got it." He came over with diagrams to show which switches were the envelope generators, and which were the voltage-controlled amplifiers, and which were the voltage-controlled filters, and which were the mixers, and so on. He worked out a number of presets that were usable. I've been using that unit with the band ever since. But then there's the age-old problem of synthesizers going out of tune. That was very annoying. We finally got around to getting a frequency counter.

So you took it out onstage right from the start.

Yeah. That was the first time it was ever used onstage. Well, I think they had a thing called the Moog Quartet or something that used it live, but that didn't last long. Nobody had ever toured with a big Moog before.

Do you find yourself using synthesizer mainly for effects?

Yeah. I think my use of synthesizer is basically all effects. It's just been a case of trying to get new sounds that you wouldn't hear on any other instrument. It's got to have a definite characteristic that's obviously a synthesizer. I think it's excellent what other people have done with, say, the Minimoog, where sometimes you can't tell whether it's a Minimoog or a guitar. They've found clever uses for the pitch and modulation controls. But I've never used the synthesizer to copy. There's no real point in it if you can't tell if that's a guitar playing or a Moog. With me, you say, "That is definitely a Moog." Otherwise you can get confused. It gets mixed in with the organ sound.

What about on "Abaddon's Bolero" from *Trilogy*? Isn't that contrary to what you're saying?

Yeah. That was an attempt to copy the Walter Carlos thing. That was one occasion where I tried to copy trumpet sounds and the like.

How did you get the string sound at the beginning of "Trilogy"?

That was a Minimoog. I used one oscillator for the audio and the third oscillator for modulation. But I don't know. I'm not that keen on it anymore.

You sound like you want to stop using the synthesizer.

I think I want to, yeah. It's just such a lot of work. And a lot of worry, you know? Something can always go wrong, at least it does for me anyway. Even with having the best people working for us, there's still a great element of risk. Dampness and everything affects its tuning, and I can't devote my head fully to the music. There's always that worry that it's not going to work when I reach for it in the next passage. Is it going to be in tune or isn't it? If it's out of tune, there's nothing I can do about it, because I'm too busy with my other hand. So you have to make snap decisions all the time. I don't think one should be forced into a position like that in playing. To play properly, you need to have a clear, open head.

What would you replace the synthesizer with?

I think I would go back to the organ and the piano.

Would you still keep the Yamaha GX-1 around?

I think I might be tempted to. I do like that instrument. Yet the problems are great. Without Nick's device it would go out of tune. And when I hear that people like Stevie Wonder used it and backed off from using it live, it makes me real-

Keith Emerson: "Ginastera . . . made some comment that that was exactly how his music should always sound. And the same with Copland. In fact, I've got a tape of what Copland thinks of our version of 'Fanfare for the Common Man.' This always pleases me, because I don't want to adulterate the music." Photo by Peter Figen

ize that it's a bit of a gamble. Nevertheless, I'm committed, because I've recorded with it, and things wouldn't sound right on anything else. I've tried playing "Fanfare" on the organ and it really sounds horrible. It doesn't sound good at the piano, either, yet it sounds all right with the Yamaha.

How did you develop your knowledge of what the synthesizer can do?

Just by working with it. Mind you, the patching arrangement I've got now on that big system is stupid. Everything interlocks and there are so many things going into multiples and feeding into different places it's like a jigsaw puzzle. If something goes wrong with it, then it usually fits into about ten different categories. Finding that it's not in one of those means I have to search back from the leads.

While you're playing?

I can't do that. It would take too long. It's totally impossible.

So what do you do when something goes wrong onstage?

Pray [*laughs*]. Well, if it's gone totally crazy, I just switch it off. Sometimes it's been playing on its own, so I've had to find some way of shutting it up completely. I have to yell to the roadie to switch the thing off. It did that at the California Jam. The humidity drove it crazy. Everything on it—fans and all—couldn't keep the humidity from settling on it. The guy looking over it was checking on it as if it were a baby. It was fine. He was listening with headphones. I kept asking if it was still okay. He'd say, "Yeah, just fine." Then five minutes before the show I listened to it and it was stuck playing on its own. So I said, "We can't take it out like that." Then it stopped and we took it out. When I started playing it, on the first synthesizer lines in *Tarkus*, it wouldn't stop with the last note I'd hit. It was as if the VCA was wide open, but it wasn't. So then I thought it might be the ribbon, and I disconnected that. But it didn't stop. You'd play a line and it would go *nnnnnnn* at the end. In order to play it I'd have to switch the audio off and then on when I needed it again.

How is the opening synthesizer part to "Hoedown," from *Trilogy*, done?

The actual rise time is from the envelope generator. It's attenuated. The actual harmony is controlled by the sustain on the envelope generator. That can also be varied by the attenuator. That also alters the pace. The rest is conventional: oscillators into the filter, controlled by the envelopes, into the VCA, and out to the trunk lines. I came up with that just by messing around. All of a sudden this wailing noise came out, and I thought, "Oh, I've got to use that in something. It sounds very nice. Sounds like a hoedown. A pretty far-out sort of hoedown."

How did you get that honky-tonk sound on "Benny the Bouncer," from *Brain Salad Surgery*? And was that the same way you got it on "The Sheriff," from *Trilogy*?

Let's see, how was that done? One of them was done by putting one of the strings out of tune. Detuning it so that it had the right number of beats to get the effect I wanted. The other was done with one piano being straight and another piano being overdubbed that was put through a flanger. I played the same line on both pianos, but one of them was slightly out of tune because of the flanger.

How far in advance do you know you're going to do something like that in the studio?

We usually rehearse quite extensively for about three weeks before we go in to record, and by the time we get in the studio we've got a fair idea of what we're going to do. I won't make many changes, but what can happen is that when I've heard the tape played back a few times, there'll be something in my head that goes on and says to me, "This line should really be in there. I can improve on that. This is how it should sound." And I'll overdub that line. Occasionally I've gotten carried away and put down overdubs that are just impossible to do when I play it live. But I don't get in the habit of doing too many overdubs. Sometimes they're done just to enhance a particular sound, like with the organ being double-tracked on "Jerusalem."

How do you structure an improvised solo, like, for example, on the live recording of "Rondo" from *Everything as Nice as Mother Makes It*?

Well, I fall into a framework, but if I'm feeling particularly adventurous in a gig and the acoustics are good, and everything is in my favor, I sort of break away from any structure I've clung to in the past. A lot of things really depend on it. The lower you start and the more relaxed the approach is at the beginning, the more ground you've got to build on to get to a heavy climax. If you start on a heavy approach, then you've got to work your ass off to climax enough to make it a sensible solo. Sometimes I have what I call landmarks in the structure that I head for. These landmarks help to keep the audience in touch, because you might be getting too far off the subject. It gives some method of association. These landmarks can be various things. One thing that I like to do is to use quotes. I'm not sure, but I think that "Rondo" had some quotes in it. You know, in general, I'd say the Nice were more improvisational than ELP.

Was the solo at the end of "Lucky Man," from your first album, added as an afterthought?

As is usual on Greg's acoustic pieces, Greg goes into the studio while the rest of us aren't around. I just happened to be in the studio with my synthesizer at the same time Greg was doing "Lucky Man." And Greg said, "Why don't you do something on the end?" So I improvised something. I didn't think much of the solo. Honestly, it's a lot of shit. But it was just what he wanted. I just did a rough setting on the synthesizer, went in, and played something off the top of my head.

Portions of this article appeared in the October 1977 issue of Keyboard *magazine.*

FOR MORE ON KEITH EMERSON

Keith continues to tour and record, with his own band and recently with Spinal Tap! You can keep up with his news and activities at his official website, www.keithemerson.com.

A SELECTED KEITH EMERSON DISCOGRAPHY

Blessed with astonishing technical virtuosity and the artistic sensibilities to apply it to a new musical vision, Keith Emerson inspired an entire generation of keyboardists, and helped create the community that *Keyboard* magazine was launched to serve.

WITH EMERSON, LAKE & PALMER

1977 *Works, Vol. 2*
1977 *Works, Vol. 1*
1974 *Welcome Back My Friends to the Show That Never Ends*
1973 *Brain Salad Surgery*
1972 *Trilogy*
1972 *Pictures at an Exhibition*
1971 *Tarkus*
1970 *Emerson, Lake & Palmer*

AS A SOLO ARTIST

2008 *The Keith Emerson Band*
2006 *Off the Shelf*
2003 *About Time*
2002 *Emerson Plays Emerson*
1995 *Changing States*
1987 *Harmageddon/China Free Fall*
1986 *Murderock*
1985 *Honky*
1981 *Nighthawks*

FROM STUDIO CATS TO ROCK LIONS

DAVID PAICH
STEVE PORCARO

Steve Porcaro relaxes at home with Damius, the Polyfusion modular system, the Roland JP-4, the Roland MicroComposer (which Steve is programming), the Oberheim DS-2 sequencer, and the Linn Drum Machine. Photo by Neil Zlozower

INTERVIEW BY
DOMINIC MILANO,
INTRODUCTION BY
ROBERT L. DOERSCHUK

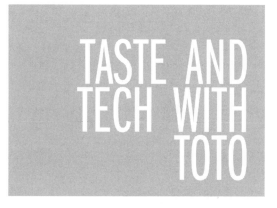

TASTE AND TECH WITH TOTO

WHEN WE LAST SPOKE with David Paich and Steve Porcaro in 1979, they were taking their first steps out from the womblike warmth of the L.A. studios and plunging into the cold blast of the concert stage with their new band, Toto. Both had had live performing experience, of course, though not as a twosome. Both had already carved out formidable reputations as session players, but their faces and skills were still unfamiliar to the public at large.

They were at the beginning of their first tour, fresh from the band's anonymous trial debut in Hawaii, peering down a tunnel of club gigs toward a promising but uncertain future. Little did they know what they were in for.

Today, Toto is one of the biggest draws in rock, and David and Steve are the hottest keyboard combination around. Though they are heavyweight technicians, they've learned through countless hours of studio experience to go for the knockout solo only after setting the stage for it with extraordinary taste and restraint. The solo in their summer hit single,

"Rosanna," proves the point; rather than overwhelm, they unfold a complex delicate line without giving up the spirit of spontaneity. And, as they explain in the following interview, they do it together. Clearly, they are the duo keyboard team to beat.

And they are a major reason for Toto's popularity. True, you can find more hooks in the band's best-selling songs than in a snarl of fishlines off the Santa Monica Pier, but where other groups simply milk their hooks dry through excessive repetition, Paich and Porcaro adorn theirs with subtle synthesizer colorings and shifts in dynamics. Perhaps the kalimba-like patch in "Africa," from *Toto IV*, was an obvious device, but it was applied artfully within the arrangement and not overused. Structurally, "Africa" is a fairly basic tune; what makes it hypnotic, along with drummer Jeff Porcaro's steady beat and the band's pyramiding harmonies, is the variety of keyboard textures in the background. They seem to shift every few bars, dropping to a jungle hush after the chorus where the typical rocker might stampede into a crescendo, or augmenting the nuances of the group's performance. Even when they're not as flashy as their old hero Keith Emerson, Paich and Porcaro are working nonstop, tinkering, adjusting, and discreetly bringing the song to life.

Blend is the crucial word. After backing up scores of singers and players in an array of styles, David and Steve have had no trouble developing an effective approach to mixing keyboards with Steve Lukather's aggressive guitar and Bobby Kimball's soaring vocals. Lukather's style is essentially a polished update on the Jimmy Page power trio tradition, a guitar ethic that frequently obliterated all but the most manic keyboard accompaniment and drove countless young synthesists into keyboards-only new wave bands. But in Toto, the keyboards complement rather than compete, with shifting tone colors and block chords moving restlessly through a succession of inversions before settling on a root position tonic. You can hear this in the chorus to "Rosanna," and as far back as "Child's Anthem," from the first LP, *Toto*; in both cases and on many cuts in between, strings and circuitry meet in a middle ground and produce a sound that is as emotional as it is clean.

Lots of the savvy that goes into all this stems from David and Steve's background. As they explained in their first *Keyboard* interview, their fathers were both fixtures in the L.A. music scene—Marty Paich and Joe Porcaro were revered as arranger and drummer, respectively. David and Steve grew up at the elbows of the best players, engineers, and producers in Southern California, so they're about as well grounded in the art of making hit records as anybody could be.

Now, add to this their love for and mastery of the latest keyboard technology. Though they only take part of their equipment reserve on the road, they have been accused of overindulging themselves in electronic paraphernalia onstage. Most visually riveting among the scattered CS-80s, JP-8s, GS-1s, and assorted other instruments is Porcaro's gigantic Polyfusion modular synthesizer, a brooding wired giant they affectionately call Damius. Not too many people haul those imposing towers around with them, and on the first three Toto albums the material didn't really seem to demand its services.

That changed with the release of *Toto IV*, specifically with regard to the solo we mentioned earlier. There are actually two keyboard solo spots in "Rosanna"; Paich takes one on piano toward the end, but it's the synthesizer break that epitomizes what Porcaro has been trying to do with his modular gear since he first got it a few years ago. It's orchestrated with changing timbres within lines, riffs played on multiple instruments, and polyphonic sequences that sidestep familiar clichés. It is short, but it says a lot.

In 1979, we looked back on David and Steve's development and profiled the gear they were using at that time. Some changes have been made since then, so this time around we zeroed in on the machines in the Toto keyboard and amplification arsenal.

What equipment are you taking out on the road with you?

Paich: We practically take the whole studio. We're leaving some of the Polyfusion gear behind this time because it's being hardwired. Steve and I always have duplicate equipment in our setups. We each have a Yamaha GS1 with a Yamaha CS-80 on top of it. I'm playing a 9' Hamburg Steinway with a Roland JP-8 on it, and in back of me I've got a little Roland VK-9 organ and a Yamaha CS-70M polyphonic.

Porcaro: I'm using a GS1 with a CS-80 on top of it, as David said. That faces the band. On the other side, I've got an E-mu Emulator, a Roland JP-8, and a Minimoog. Then I have the banks of Polyfusion modular gear behind me. I have those configured as four stock Minimoog-type voices and one big bass drone voice that has about six oscillators in it. It's like two Minimoogs put together as far as the hardware goes. I've also got a Roland MC-4 MicroComposer and an LM-1 Linn drum machine.

Paich: I did have a Hammond, an A-100 that I was using on the road. I had some problems with it, so I got this Roland VK-9 that I just put into a 147 Leslie speaker. It does the trick for all the things I used to use the Hammond for. I'm also using a Yamaha CE20.

How do you split up the role of playing keyboards between the two of you?

Paich: Let me preface the answer to that by saying that when we originally formed the band, my background was in piano. I also played a lot of Hammond. I spent a lot of time listening to Booker T. and Procol Harum. Steve had also studied a lot of piano, but he was more into the Keith Emerson type thing where everything is arranged. So when we were putting the band together, instead of getting another keyboard player in the band who had the same kind of background I did, I got Steve because he more complemented than doubled what I was doing.

Porcaro: I was working with Gary Wright when they asked me to join. I had been doing the live Minimoog bass playing so they knew I could handle playing synthesizers live. I was your classic second keyboardist who played all the [ARP Solina] String Ensemble parts. I was in Toto originally to cover David's overdubs live. Since that time, I've grown as a musician and things have changed quite a bit. David has come to realize that I'm not going to be happy sitting there playing String Ensemble lines forever.

And at the same time, I'm very honest with myself. If there's a part going on an album that I've written, I won't play it just for the sake of me playing it. If David will do a better job of it, David plays. it. There are some things he can do quicker than I can. I love the way he plays piano. His playing has always inspired me to practice more. That's one reason I've gotten into synthesizers more. I've found that my place in the band was to be playing the synthesizers.

Paich: It's not the case anymore that one guy does the synthesizers and the other does the piano. We both end up swapping parts of those roles. It's usually the case that the guy who wrote the tune ends up playing the piano on it, but we stay open about it. I've got a 24-track tape recorder in my house, and after we've recorded the basic tracks, we'll take it there and sort of choreograph the keyboards. But the parts go back and forth. There are no set rules.

Porcaro: Most keyboard players are territorial bastards and have trouble getting along with one another. David and I work very well together.

Do you learn a lot from each other, then?

Paich: Steve's the best synthesizer teacher in the world for me, and I turn him on to a lot of orchestration things.

Do the other guys in the band critique the things you two come up with in terms of keyboard orchestration?

Porcaro: Yeah, but they're starting to catch on to what we've been trying to do. The solo in "Rosanna" was the turning point. They've had to put up with me dicking around with the banks for years. I've always had to say, "But wait until you see what I'm gonna be able to do." When we finally did the solo in "Rosanna," I was able to say, "See there. That's what all this does." It was nice to have something to show that was concrete. The guys in the group were wondering why we bothered with the modular stuff at all. Now they're at the point where they don't want to do shows without the modular gear. They've come around to understanding what it is we do with the orchestration and the modular gear.

Do you actually write out your arrangements for the keyboards?

Paich: Yeah. When I demo a tune like "Rosanna," I'll do it on 8-track for the band. Before we go in and record it, Steve and I will make up a work sheet. It's not so much for the band to use since we don't use charts when we're recording—everyone has memorized it by then—it's for our own reference. Steve will know exactly what I'm playing, and I'll know what he's playing. Everything on my bass and piano parts is written down. Then we'll talk about it, and Steve will make a little score. From there we'll work up synthesizer ideas. What's going to play what, what kind of range it's going to be in so we're not doubling up voices, and so on.

Porcaro: It's so hard to adhere to a single notational system for synthesizers. Every time we do something—every time I try to work out a classical piece for synthesizers—I have to devise a new way to notate what I'm doing.

How much of the solo in the middle of "Rosanna" is done with the Roland MicroComposer and how much of it is played by you two?

Paich: It's a combination of both of us playing. It's mainly Steve, but we both start at the beginning. When we were doing that song, we found we had to put a solo in the middle of it. It was a question of what do we do now. Steve has always said we should use our imaginations. So I kind of started out with trying to incorporate everything we have at our home studio. Instead of doing a regular Wurlitzer or Hammond solo, we decided to try different things. We started playing lines and finally sat down and Steve wrote out the initial basis for the solo that you hear now played mostly on the modular system.

Porcaro: It's actually a hilarious story. We thought about how to do that solo for weeks, and it all came together one day at five in the morning.

Paich: When you hear the opening lines, that's Steve playing a modular trumpet sound. Then we knew we wanted a sequence running down, so I programmed a little thing into the MicroComposer that Steve dropped into the solo. Then there's a Minimoog part, and at the end it's a combination of Steve and I both playing CS-80s, Prophets, a Hammond organ, and a GS1.

Porcaro: There's even a line in there that was from an older solo that David did which I forgot to erase. It was a very pieced-together solo. It was a great example of what can happen when two keyboard players get together and start messing around with technology. You get stuff that you don't plan on getting. Everything was written out, and then the written-out stuff was abandoned. It's the right combination of discipline and non-discipline. It's also a good example of what can happen when you're not stuck in a studio with a bunch of people hanging over you saying, "Okay, let's do the keyboard solo now." We did it at home, and I was able to spend a couple of weeks at it. The way it happened wasn't in the norm at all.

More or less the opposite of what the piano solo that follows was like.

Porcaro: Yeah. That's the thing I love about it. The piano thing is pure unadulterated Paich being pure unadulterated Bill Payne.

How does improvisation fit into the way you play?

Porcaro: See, I've never been a very good improviser, but I'm a good composer. I get into writing stuff out. I've always wanted to sit down and write out a solo.

FROM STUDIO CATS TO ROCK LIONS

Are you programming the MicroComposer by punching data in, or are you playing it in from a keyboard?

Paich: We're doing it both ways right now. I think it's according to which piece of music we're working on. If it's a classical thing or something really symmetrical-sounding, Steve will load it in from the computer keyboard. But if it's something with more phrasing and nuance, we'll play it in. But we'll always rewrite the gates on it and some of the steps and the phrasing to make it consistent.

Are you both well versed at programming it?

Paich: Steve's fastest at it. It still takes me a while to get used to it. Steve's been dealing with the MC-8 for a long time. The manual to that is ridiculous, but he stuck with it and learned it. Now the MC-4 is like a blessing, because when you make a mistake, you don't have to erase the whole thing and start over. Steve's gotten to the point where he can load numbers about as fast as you could load in notes. Because of having gone through the technical thing, I think he's becoming less technical. Our whole system has come about in order for us to be musicians. Like Steve says, as soon as he hears the right sound, he won't be messing around with the stuff anymore. It's like with the Yamaha GS1. We don't have to mess with the modular stuff getting bell sounds and celestes, because they're nailed on the GS1. But you go through the technical thing to where it becomes second nature, and you can get back to being a musician. Everybody thinks Steve is a technical genius, but they forget that he spends hours and hours at it. He's mainly just a keyboardist like myself who likes playing Hammond organ and piano.

Porcaro: The thing that drew me to the MicroComposer was that my setup, when I first started, was a Minimoog and an Oberheim DS-2 digital sequencer. I got very good at the DS-2, but I wanted to go beyond that. And I wanted to go beyond what most of the polyphonic sequencers you can get these days do. As great as they all are, they seem like toys compared to the MicroComposer. When it comes down to really trying to record something with them, you run into all kinds of problems. They sound great when you're in a music store. You sort of throw something in and play it back, speed it up, and it's all very impressive, but when it gets down to having to be in sync with other things, it gets to be impossible. But the MC-4 and MC-8 and the Linn drum machine and the Emulator all run on the same sync tone. Even in real time, my MC-4 and MC-8 can follow a conductor.

How do you manage that?

Porcaro: I use my sync box. It's designed to let me sync everything together. It has a momentary switch on it that, if I just tap quarter notes on it, the MC-4 and all that stuff will follow me, the conductor. Ralph Dyck built the sync box for us. He works for Roland. I've heard a lot of people talking about live sync, but I've never seen anyone that had it. I've got it. I've been using it.

Didn't you do a live MicroComposer rendition of a Chopin etude?

Paich: Yeah. Steve did a whole number on the *Etude in C♯ Minor*. When we went to check out the Polyfusion modular stuff, we tested it out using that. So far we've done a Samuel Barber thing and a Bartok concerto. We want to record some of this stuff too. But it's like being able to take a Tomita-type sound on the road. We used to open for Rick Derringer and bands like that, and when it came time for the keyboard spot, Steve and I would hit the MicroComposers and walk off stage. It really sounded like rock and roll, even though it was a Chopin thing.

Rick Derringer audiences got off on it?

Paich: Yeah. Some of them did. Some of them didn't understand it.

Do you feel that playing in large venues is detrimental to your music? Don't you lose a lot of subtlety?

Paich: You do. I'd like to work in the studio and then go out and play 2,000-seaters all the time, but we're caught in the business and so we have to go out and work the larger venues. It means we have to go full out and play stadium gigs. We're going for the Keith Emerson proportions as far as a show goes.

When Steve and I first saw Emerson at the Hollywood Bowl with his Steinway 9' piano and modular synthesizer gear, we knew it was something we had to try to come close to doing ourselves. We're aiming that high. We're saying that we don't want to just go out and gig with our Casios and our Prophets. There's nothing wrong with that approach, but we don't want to do it that way. No one is taking modular gear out these days and using it to play funk tunes.

What decided you on Polyfusion modular gear?

Porcaro: It was just one of those things. I had seen a MicroComposer hooked up to some Roland modular gear at an AES convention, and I wanted it from the moment I saw it. We were on the road and some guys from Polyfusion wanted to take us on a factory tour. In fact, David woke me up at 9:00 in the morning to tell me they wanted to take us on this tour, and he wanted to know if I'd ever heard of Polyfusion. I knew who they were from the ads I'd seen in *Keyboard*, but I'd never seen their equipment. So they gave us a big pitch and sold us on it. I've been very happy with their stuff as far as reliability and stability go.

One time we were in the studio, and a guy came in with some Moog modular stuff. The sound that came out of it made me think, "Oh yeah, that's the way I got into this stuff." My father knew Paul Beaver very well when he was alive, and he used to let me mess with his synthesizers when I was younger. I didn't retain much of it, but I was in awe of it. So I've wanted to have a modular system for years. But there's so much against having any kind of modular stuff. A lot of people still don't understand it.

You're having the Polyfusion hardwired; does that mean no more patch cords?

Porcaro: We're in the process of doing that now, yeah. I'm still pursuing it. I'm not sure if I'm going to go the hardwired route or put a computer on the thing to remember patches or what. There are a lot of companies out there with a lot of interesting equipment that I'm just finding out about. I'm still checking things out before I build my ultimate monster. I'm still nailing down the patches we want in the modular gear, but with my scopes and test equipment I'm at least able to document what it is I'm doing. I'm able to draw block diagrams and measure all my voltages and things like that. But I still haven't learned what I want to have pre-patched.

So you're still trying to figure out what it is you really need and what you can cut out.

Porcaro: That gets back to why I have the modular system. When I had my first DS-2 and Minimoog, I conceptualized my first monster. It was the ultimate super-slick switching system for assigning the sequencer to the Minimoog and having it play an Oberheim Expander Module as well as the Minimoog. It looked great on paper, but it never exactly worked right. It was a valuable lesson. I know a lot of people with equipment who are coming up with bright ideas for modifications, but a lot of equipment isn't meant to be modified. When you do it, you're just asking for problems. My first ultimate monster left me wishing that I'd never gotten rid of all the old wires running all over the place.

Some of your synthesizers have names—Damius, Ramses, Ophelia, and Rudus. What's that all about?

Porcaro: Those are just the names of the different banks of modular stuff. Whenever I'm doing a session I can tell the guys which cabinet to bring. What's in the cabinets changes constantly.

What have you left behind this tour?

Porcaro: I left my Prophet home. I left my MC-8 home. Some of the older keyboards like JP-4s, 2600s, and stuff like that got left behind. We don't take Rhodeses and Clavinets out anymore even though we've got 'em at home. I really take pride in the fact that all the stuff we do bring out, we use. If we aren't using it on the road, it's loaned out to a friend who is using it. I don't get into having equipment lying around. If something is broken, I get really fanatical about it. It's gotta get fixed.

Do you do your own repair work?

Porcaro: No I don't. The only way I've gotten anywhere with the technical thing is through my own ignorance and asking questions. I've gotten to meet a lot of great people like Roger Linn and Ralph Dyck and the guy who did the original design of the MicroComposer. But with synthesizers, the answer to a stupid question brings up ten more stupid questions. When I first got into synths, I'd read *Keyboard*, but Bob Moog's column and Patrick Gleeson's column wouldn't mean anything to me because I didn't have any modular instrument to apply the stuff they were talking about to. But when I got my modular system happening, I finally understood what they were talking about.

What about using an instrument like the Yamaha GS1? You've put some of your own programs into it.

Porcaro: Actually, I mainly just modified existing programs. You load a strip into it, and the programming module shows what the program looks like on four video screens. I would just start dicking with it, isolating different sections and seeing where different parts of the sound were coming from. I've always been attracted to those kinds of instruments because I come from being a piano player. I love the touch-sensitivity, but from a synthesist's standpoint the non-programmability doesn't bother me all that much, because some of the sounds in it are just too kick-ass to ignore.

Paich: From my point of view, I love it because of the immediacy. So many of the sounds that are in it are nailed just perfectly. Like the Rhodes and the marimba sounds. As an 88-note touch-sensitive instrument, it appeals to the piano player in me. I find myself not only playing piano music on it, but writing stuff that's specifically for the GS1. It saves you from having to bring lots and lots of other axes on the road and into the studio.

How do you feel about the CE20?

Paich: I dig it for the same reason I dig the GS1: immediacy. It takes up where the ARP Pro-Soloist left off. The sounds it has in it are really nailed. I don't use it a whole lot live yet, because I have other synths that I use to cover those sounds in different ways. I've been using it on sessions, though. I did a thing with Kenny Loggins where he and James Newton-Howard scored out a piece for synthesizers using nothing but Prophet-10, GS1, and CE20. We put real strings with all that, and you can barely tell the difference between a real orchestra and what we did.

Steve, do you use a CE20?

Porcaro: I use one, but I don't have it in my live setup right now. It changes around a lot. The way manufacturers build things these days, everything has something a little different. That's why it's so tempting to have every keyboard in the world onstage. Any keyboard player could find a valid reason for having everything up there, but it's impractical. That's one of the things I dig about having the Emulator. It lets you use sounds from instruments that you just can't have up onstage with you.

Live, do you change sounds frequently on the Emulator?

Porcaro: Yes. Ed Simeone, my keyboard tech, loads in the disks for me. I'm using the Emulator to play part of the "Rosanna" solo on now, because I've got the MC-4 playing the JP-8—I've had gate and voltage inputs and outputs put into the JP-8—and I use the Emulator to play the JP-8 brass sound.

It sounds like you have to plan each song out in a lot of detail as far as when you're going to play what instruments.

Porcaro: Oh yeah. When I'm trying to devise how I'm going to set up my equipment live, I go through blocking out each song. It's like doing choreography. I have to keep track of what I have to do next after each song. I have to keep track of what sound happens next, what instrument I've got to play with what sound in it, and all that. It's something that I've gotten far better at with time. It's nice having David, because he can be a third hand for me if I need it. When it gets right down to it, and everyone's bashing out their parts, there are times when we realize that his left hand on the piano won't be missed. So he can fill in on one of my parts. I've also started getting used to teaching my left hand to play right-hand parts out of necessity.

FROM STUDIO CATS TO ROCK LIONS

David Paich onstage with Toto and his gear, left to right: Yamaha GS1, Yamaha CS-80, Roland JP-8, and Steinway D. Steve Porcaro is at the other end of the stage. Photo by Neil Zlozower

David, how do you use your JP-8?

Paich: I use it for a number of things. Steve and I both play the horn line in "Rosanna" on them. I really get into the arpeggiator and all the different little tricks on it. I love the fact that with the keyboard split, you essentially have two synthesizers. And I love the fact that you can preset all those different combinations. Another reason Steve and I use it is because we're using the JP-8 as the main interface keyboard with our modular system at the moment.

Instead of the Polyfusion keyboard? Do you miss the touch-sensitivity?

Paich: Yes, I do. But one of the reasons why we're using the JP-8 instead of the Polyfusion keyboard is because when you play the JP-8 and use it to control the Polyfusion modules, you'll hear both sounds simultaneously.

Do you get into blending keyboard sounds a lot?

Paich: Definitely. We always try out lots of different combinations. We use a lot of acoustic instruments along with our synths too. We take orchestral instruments and combine them with synthesizers. Or we make a tape of the acoustic instrument and synthesizer combined and load the sound into our Emulator. On "Africa," you hear a combination of Steve's dad playing marimba combined with GS1.

What else is going on in "Africa"?

Paich: The kalimba is all done with the GS1. It's six tracks of GS1 playing different rhythms. There's a high organ sound that's GS1, and I wrote the song on CS-80, so that plays the main part of the entire tune.

DAVID PAICH AND STEVE PORCARO

How do you feel about the CS-80?

Paich: It's just about the best live axe there is. Steve and I had ours shipped over from Japan before they were out in the States, simply because of the touch-sensitivity and versatility. We use them to this day for getting string sounds.

The fact that you can only put in four of your own programs besides how the panel controls are set doesn't bother you?

Paich: Oh, no. To me, they're still quite immediate. We're having our CS-80s modified by the factory so they'll have all our own presets in them.

How do you like the CS-70M?

Paich: I'm using it mainly for its polyphonic sequencer right now. There are certain things in the show where I'll want to change parts every night and do spontaneous little sequences, so I'll load something in right then and there. I think it's an in-between instrument for Yamaha. It has a ways to go, but it does some very good things. It has a split keyboard mode which, used in conjunction with the sequencer, is pretty interesting. Its main thing is that you can memorize your own presets and play with a touch-sensitive keyboard. I think it's a step in the right direction.

You're not disappointed that it sort of replaced the CS-80?

Paich: Kind of. I love the CS-80. We told Yamaha that. They think it's like trying to compare apples and oranges. I don't know if they were trying to replace the CS-80 so much as come out with something that was on a par with other synthesizers in its category. I think the CS-70 is an in-between instrument because I think that Yamaha is going to come out with some stuff that's going to do it all.

You like the idea of having one instrument that does it all instead of having a battery of different instruments around you?

Paich: Definitely.

You're not bothered by the aspect of giving up being able to combine the sounds of different instruments?

Paich: Well, when I say one keyboard, I really mean one instrument with maybe two or three manuals on it. Maybe it will have bass pedals and touch-sensitive keyboards. Maybe it will have an artificial intelligence that allows each finger to have a totally different sound. That's one of the nice things about our modular system. You can have different sounds on each voice.

But you run into problems when you cross voices.

Paich: Exactly. That's part of the problem. It's one of the things that needs to be worked out right now. A lot of it has to do with the writing; the actual choreography and orchestration of the voicings that we use. But the instruments are going to have to have some kind of intelligence.

Do you have any trouble with the modular stuff live?

Porcaro: No. As a matter of fact, the Polyfusion stuff is a lot like the way the 2600 used to be for me. I could pack that up, bring it to the next gig, and it would still be in tune. The Polyfusion oscillators are very stable. But Ralph Dyck is building me an auto-tune for them. I don't see anybody trying to build something like that into their modular system, which makes me want to get it happening.

But it's no real problem using the system live?

Porcaro: Right now, it's still keyed down to where it doesn't cause me any big problems. I don't make it that vital a part of the show right now. It's more reliable than anything else I've got on the road with me now. It's more of a bitch to have something go wrong with the CS-80.

What kind of amplification and effects are you using?

Paich: Everything goes through two Midas 24-input boards and then out to the P.A. system. As far as effects go, I'm using a Harmonizer, a Roland 555 Chorus Echo, a stereo Lexicon delay line, one of the new Roland digital delays, and a Yamaha graphic equalizer. I use so many delay lines because I love slap echo.

Porcaro: I've got a couple of Roland 555 Chorus Echoes, a new Roland digital delay, a Lexicon, and a great little thing by 360 Systems—their programmable EQ. I have it modified so that with a Prophet or JP-8, it'll change EQ every 3/4 octave. It takes a CV and a gate input and automatically switches programs every 3/4 octave. It's really helpful for string and brass sounds. I use the Polyfusion stuff to process all kinds of things. It's my all-around signal center, a big junction. I use the formant filters and the parametric equalizers in it. I'll have a control voltage input to the JP-8's filter, I'll have envelope generators being triggered by the drum machine, I do this trip with the LM-l where I take one of the outputs from it, say the cowbell or a conga, and I have it going through an envelope follower which in turn triggers an envelope generator which in turn is controlling a filter. That way, I can have my LM-l running in sync with everything else, and have one of its drums triggering an envelope generator which is controlling a filter or a VCA in rhythm. I also get into doing things like using my MicroComposer to trigger the hold on my JP-8. All these control inputs on the back of synths; the hippest things on synthesizers are the things that no one ever uses. I prove this to myself day after day. On the back of my CS-80 is a thing called the external input. Nobody uses that, and it's the hippest thing about a CS-80.

Doesn't doing all that interfacing make for a lot of hassle when it comes to keeping things straight during live gigs?

Porcaro: Yeah, but that's the thing. You get it all together and have snake cables made. It's hard enough making synthesizers sound good on record. Making them sound good live you need everything you can get. I don't know about other keyboard players, but I have a bitch of a time making synthesizers stand repeated listening. Whether it's having a portamento footswitch or a sustain pedal, it all takes practice, so you don't have it hooked up for the sake of having it hooked up. You have to know where and when to use it. Before we go out on the road, I like to orchestrate the show. That's something that's very hard for me to do, because when we record, I set up the configuration of the keyboards in the room differently for each and every song so that I can get to them when I need to.

DAVID PAICH AND STEVE PORCARO

David, what about your piano? Why a Hamburg Steinway?

Paich: I never thought I'd be able to get a Hamburg Steinway on the road. But I went to Pro Piano in Los Angeles and they had one. I also have one at my house. I've got two Steinway O's and a Baldwin SD-10, a nine-footer. One of the Steinways is a Hamburg, and the other is American. I think Hamburg Steinways are the hippest, because they are the meatiest-sounding pianos around.

Do you have any trouble getting them to reproduce through a sound system?

Paich: I've got the hammers slightly doped, a process that hardens them, making the tone of the piano brighter. I'm using Helpinstill pickups and a new thing from England called the Seducer. It has two contact sound strips that go across the bottom of the keyboard. It picks up all the harmonics that Helpinstills don't.

What piano do you use for recording?

Paich: I mainly use the Baldwin SD-10 for recording. I bought it three years ago. I needed a piano to bring into the studio with me.

What kind of action do you prefer on your piano?

Paich: At home 1 prefer heavy for practicing. I love a heavy action because every hour you put in on a heavy action is like putting in three hours on a light action. When I'm on the road 1 love a light action. I almost like the GS1 action better than a piano's action. It's so similar to a piano action, it's ridiculous. But pianos don't have any aftertouch.

That added touch-sensitivity is really nice.

Porcaro: I can't wait until I have that kind of sensitivity in a general synthesizer keyboard. I'll be able to have my Emulator sounds going through VCAs that are controlled by the velocity-sensitive output of the keyboard, so the harder I hit, the more the E-mu is let through. So when I'm doing string sounds I can have more of that real bow sound kick in the harder I hit it. Things like that are the reason you need modular systems.

Is much of the equipment modified beyond what we've spoken of?

Paich: Certain things have been modified. We probably have the most up-to-date Emulator on the market, in that we have it synced up to our Linn drum machine. We will shortly have it hooked up to our JP-8 so that the JP-8's keyboard will play the Emulator. In general, we don't believe in having things modified that much. We don't believe in having this or that put on a Prophet because it wasn't there to begin with. That's why we've got the modular stuff. We do have little things here and there, like unison switches on our CS-80s. We've had CV gates and triggers put in our Prophets—which we've left home. We have a whole bunch of keyboards that we don't use live.

Do you leave them behind with the idea that you're going to cut back on the number of keyboards you take out?

Paich: Yes. As soon as we can do it with one axe or two, we will. We have cut down. I think having the GS1 onstage has eliminated my using a Minimoog and a Prophet. I think you're going to see keyboard setups being cut down with more

Emulators and GS1s coming out. I'm going to add an Emulator just so I can have sounds like that.

Are most of the keyboards recorded at your home studio?

Porcaro: I'd say about 80 percent are. A lot of artists reach a point where they can afford a home studio, and so they start doing everything at home, and it sounds that way. I don't think we want our studio to turn out that way. We use it for doing the things that eat up a lot of time. What we don't try to do is record all the piano parts and the Hammond parts. They're done at a studio because there's a better selection of mics and a better acoustic situation. Also, the Hammond parts are put down on the basic tracks with all the guys playing. The studio we've got at home is more set up as a keyboard player's studio. Everything that you need to record the electric keyboard parts is there. You don't have to monitor what you're playing through headphones, and you don't have to try to communicate with an engineer through a piece of glass. Everything is right there in front of you.

Do you feel that Toto has a Southern California sound?

Paich: I guess it might. I don't think there's a definite Southern California band sound except for the fact that we've played on a lot of records that have come out of Los Angeles, so it may seem like there's a definite sound that comes from down in L.A. I could play you a bunch of records where you wouldn't be able to tell who's on them. We're on a lot of records where you'd swear it was some guys from Chicago or New Orleans. One thing you do get into when you make records is that you get to be radio oriented. Not that you're catering to that, but there are certain variables that make something more radio-worthy than others. I think that may be the way we play. I don't think we have a definite Southern California sound. I was more influenced by English stuff. There aren't that many American bands that have a sound similar to the one we have.

What about in terms of production quality?

Paich: Right. I think there's definitely more production work that goes into our sound than is usual for bands. I think that's one of the ways we separate ourselves from other bands. The ability to do overdubs and certain production things without getting to sound really over-produced. It's funny. When something sounds better to us, like a double on a vocal or an orchestra overdub, we just do it. We don't have any rules about it and say, "Oh, people are going to say this sounds over-produced." We just go with it because it may sound better. Same with the Beatles. They used a lot of doubling and tripling techniques. Everybody's so conscious of the production, of it sounding like it's in the studio. Sometimes things like that sound better. I just know that when you double something, when something's tight, it sounds real good. But I know what you're talking about. I think we're getting better at it. I think we're loosening up. We're getting less slick. There are a lot of albums in the top ten right now. The whole industry is very oriented to slick-sounding records, in my opinion. You listen to a lot of records—

Steely Dan, Supertramp, Foreigner—those records are slicker than ours. So that's kind of the name of the game with radio right now. You can't get away with a whole bunch of loose, raw stuff now because they would be tearing your record contract up.

Do you follow what's being played on the radio a lot?

Paich: Not really. I keep up with what's going on on the radio, but it's not very hard to do because I know what's going on with how they make records. I've done it for a long time. I've produced enough and put enough records together from scratch to know how to do it. I hear things and I really don't hear anything that new. What we are trying to do is be true to our music. If we have a rock song or a song like "Africa" or an R&B song, we try to be true to its essence instead of saying, "Let's not be hokey and use real African instruments," or, "We don't do R&B." We like the combination, the marriage of both things. We never really try to sound like the way we sound. That's just the way it turns out. I think we're just a product of our environment, having grown up in Los Angeles in the record business.

You've been involved in records from an early age, then.

Paich: Very early, because I grew up in it. The Porcaros' father was doing session work and so was my father, so I was in the studio watching sessions since I was five years old. I started doing sessions myself when I was 13 or 14.

Can you give us an idea of who you've done sessions with?

Paich: I started my first sessions with Seals and Croft. "Diamond Girl" was one of the first records I was on. I think the things I'm most proud of are the things I've done with Steely Dan. I've played with Quincy Jones and Boz Scaggs. I've worked with Loggins and Messina, Paul McCartney, Michael Jackson, and Elton John. The list could go on and on. I'm not doing a whole bunch of sessions right now because I've taken on Toto full time. Now I find that I have to practice piano and synthesizer every day, so I don't get the time to do sessions.

What do you do when you practice synthesizer?

Paich: Well, when I say practice synthesizer I mean work at it every day. That means either just play it to get used to the touch-sensitivity, or find sounds, or learn to articulate sounds using the way certain envelopes are set.

Do you bring anything into your hotel rooms to practice with while you're on the road?

Porcaro: Yeah. You have to dig what I have in my room. At every hotel suite, I have a drum machine, a new TEAC Portastudio, a Yamaha analog delay, a Roland JP-4, an MC-4, an Oberheim Expander Module, an ARP 2600, and a Wurlitzer electric piano.

That's bigger than most people's stage setup.

Porcaro: I know. It's disgusting. But we've got the stuff and we use it. All the guys use it and we write our butts off. When I get in there by myself, I practice using the MC-4. I'm still working out getting dynamics with it.

Do you do many sessions, Steve?

Porcaro: Last time I was home, I did some work with Quincy Jones and Paul McCartney. As a matter of fact, the first time I ever used an MC-4 in a studio situation was on the new Donna Summer album. I love doing studio work. I love to program. It's great, because you normally have some great keyboard player banging away while you come up with the sound. That's how I've come up with a lot of sounds for myself.

When you're programming, do you find yourself showing guys how to pitch-bend and things like that?

Porcaro: Not a whole lot. When it gets down to it, most studio work is just them asking you for certain sounds. I really could make a list of them. There's a Moog bass sound, a string sound, a single-line string sound, a brass sound. That's what it comes down to.

How do you know what equipment to bring with you to each session?

Porcaro: It's knowing who you're going to be working for. I did some work with Kenny Loggins at the house. He wanted a string sound, and we were using the JP-8 a lot. I said it's hard to get a good string sound on a JP-8. And he said, "Well, can't you get it on that," pointing to the banks. They waited around while I did exactly what they wanted, using the modular system. It was great because they were willing to wait. Kenny was into it and didn't mind, whereas most sessions you'll take a JP-8 to for starters. Then I'll use maybe a CS-80 and a Minimoog. You have to do things real quickly. I keep a facsimile sheet for all my sounds. That's one thing about me. I'm into sharing that sort of information. I'm against all this territorial bullshit that goes on between keyboard players. Because the way I've learned everything is by looking over other people's shoulders. If somebody has a JP-8, I always give them all my sounds on a cassette in the hope that they'll maybe do the same for me. That kind of give-and-take is the best thing for everybody.

Portions of this article appeared in the October 1982 issue of Keyboard *magazine.*

FOR MORE ON TOTO

Though Steve Porcaro left the band in 1986 to pursue other musical activities, Toto still reunites for tours and recordings, with David Paich holding down the main keyboard chair, and sharing duties with guests such as Jeff Babko and Greg Phillinganes. You can keep up with news and activities at the band's official website, www.toto99.com.

A SELECTED TOTO DISCOGRAPHY

Toto achieved huge success on the basis of an unusual attribute: astonishingly high levels of musicianship. David Paich and Steve Porcaro brought their

DAVID PAICH AND STEVE PORCARO

session-stud playing and programming chops to bear on creating some of the most interesting and musical keyboard parts ever heard on the airwaves.

2006 *Falling in Between*

2002 *Through the Looking Glass*

1999 *Mindfields*

1995 *Tambu*

1993 *Kingdom of Desire*

1988 *The Seventh One*

1986 *Fahrenheit*

1984 *Isolation*

1982 *Toto IV*

1981 *Turn Back*

1979 *Hydra*

1978 *Toto*